JAVA UNDER THE CULTIVATION SYSTEM

VERHANDELINGEN
VAN HET KONINKLIJK INSTITUUT
VOOR TAAL-, LAND- EN VOLKENKUNDE

150

ROBERT VAN NIEL

JAVA UNDER THE CULTIVATION SYSTEM

COLLECTED WRITINGS

1992

KITLV Press

Leiden

Published by:

KITLV Press
Koninklijk Instituut voor Taal-, Land- en Volkenkunde
(Royal Institute of Linguistics and Anthropology)
P.O. Box 9515
2300 RA Leiden
The Netherlands

CIP-GEGEVENS KONINKLIJKE BIBLIOTHEEK, DEN HAAG

Van Niel, Robert

Java under the Cultivation System : collected writings / Robert Van Niel. - Leiden :
KITLV Press. - (Verhandelingen van het Koninklijk Instituut voor Taal-, Land- en
Volkenkunde ; 150)
Met bibliogr., index.
ISBN 90 6718 042 4
Trefw.: Java ; geschiedenis.

ISBN 90 6718 042 4

Printed in the Netherlands

Contents

Introduction

When I had completed the preparation for publication of my book on *The Emergence of the Modern Indonesian Elite* (The Hague/Bandung: W. van Hoeve, 1960), my attention was drawn to the backgrounds of the period covered by the book, i.e., 1900-1927. The nineteenth-century history of Indonesia held strong attractions for me because I felt that it might reveal some of the forces behind the events I had recently written about. A few friends asked me to carry my elite study forward to the present day, but it seemed to me that many well-trained scholars were already applying their talents to contemporary events. The nineteenth century, on the other hand, was not being heavily researched during the 1950s. John Bastin had produced his excellent volumes on Raffles and his time, W.F. Wertheim's sociological studies had been based on nineteenth-century events, and the last of the dissertations of C. Gerretson's students at Utrecht which used nineteenth-century materials had appeared. Compared to what had appeared or was about to appear in the way of twentieth-century Indonesian studies, this was not much.

The situation was almost the reverse, however, if one looked at the scholarly productions of the first forty years of the twentieth century and the last half of the nineteenth century. Here there was a vast body of material that dealt with all manner of subjects of which only a small part was strictly history but all of which was grist for the historian's mill. I had a feeling, right or wrong, that a sort of final judgment had been rendered on the events of the nineteenth century: the works of D.H. Burger, F.W. Stapel, and A.D.A. de Kat Angelino even today produce in me somewhat the same feeling. I think it fair to say that I felt challenged by this general complacency, I simply could not believe that it was all so cut and dried.

In these circumstances, the first order of business was to read and analyze these earlier writings and to discover what ideas or views might be challenged. Consequently the reader will find that several of the papers in this volume are quite historiographic in their approach, questioning earlier perceptions before advancing new ones. In this process of looking at nineteenth-century Indonesian history, I was drawn to the time of what was then usually called in English the Culture System, Cultuurstelsel in Dutch. The English term is applicable if you understand that the word 'Culture' was meant in the sense of agriculture or horticulture, whereas the more commonly accepted anthropological use of the word 'Culture' seemed to me to obscure the sense of Cultuurstelsel. I felt that the term Cultivation System would be a more appropriate term since it would clearly indicate what the whole thing was about. I have, therefore, consistently used the term Cultivation System from the beginnings of my writings on the subject. My terminology has been taken over by many, but by no means all historians.

Why was I drawn to the Cultivation System period (roughly 1830-1870) instead of an earlier or a later time in the nineteenth century? I find this a difficult question to answer today. As I recall it, the following influences had some bearing on this decision. The orientation of my graduate studies in both European and Asian history had been largely socio-economic, so I was by training drawn to problems of this sort. Since the late 1940s I had been reading extensively in economic history, especially the revisionist European economic history of the time, and was attracted by many of the views that were being posited. Of the entire history of nineteenth-century Java, nothing seemed to me to be more in need of rethinking than the time of the Cultivation System, which historical scholarship over a century had pictured as very bleak and grim. I remember being particularly struck by G.J. van Soest's statement to the effect that everything was known that there was to be known about the System and that therefore nothing new could be said about it. From my studies under P. Geyl in 1948-1949, I came strongly to the opinion that history was a debate without end: no one said or knew everything about anything in history, not now or ever. These factors, I believe, determined my choice to research the history of the Cultivation System.

The ten essays collected in this volume were written over more than two decades. They represent my thinking on the Cultivation System. The ten pieces are placed in the order in which I conceived and began work on them. This is not necessarily the sequence in which they appeared in print. It will not be difficult to trace an evolution in my thinking or my approach to each topic, but to clarify my intent – and set the stage – I have provided a brief introduction to each essay. Each essay is essentially reproduced as it was originally published or delivered. Where I have made more than syntactical changes I have given an explanation in the introductory statement or have supplied the emendations in notes.

Frankly, I have ambivalent feelings about bundling together a set of papers into a book – even though they clearly focus on a single subject – instead of actually writing a book. For some years I thought that I would write a book but I never seemed able to resolve enough of the doubts and problems about various aspects of the Cultivation System to do this. Every time I started I would encounter another problem that I had to resolve by writing an article. I suppose that this says more about the state of my mind than it does about the nature of the subject, for however many unresolved dilemmas one faces in undertaking a project one should push ahead. Yet, I was unable to do this, for I wanted both clarity and certainty in the perception that I had of the past. Alas, that never arrived and still has not arrived, but the ten essays in this volume show my efforts to approach it.

Since these essays appeared in various publications, a number of fellow scholars who have made use of them in their teaching and research asked if I would bring them together in a single source. I agreed to do this, for I knew that I would not write a book on this subject and that I had in one way or another said about everything I was going to say on it since my interests had moved into now an earlier period. Several of these friends offered to honor me by writing an introductory statement, but I felt that whatever had to be said about this enterprise I had better say myself with utmost candor. Whatever contributions these essays may make to the understanding of the Cultivation System in Java, I do not feel that they answer all questions satisfactorily. Other scholars have been researching and writing about the System since the mid 1970s and have not always come to the same conclusions that I have. It strikes me that this is as it should be. Along with them I have worked to shed light on an aspect of Indonesian history that may seem remote from present events but is really very basic to gaining an understanding of what Indonesia is today and what it will become in the future.

Throughout the years as these essays have appeared, I have enjoyed the friendship of colleagues who have commented on my work and who have stimulated me to consider other problems or other aspects of the System. In this regard my discussions with Prof. C. Fasseur of the University of Leiden and with Dr. R.E. Elson of Griffith University have been the most critically pertinent to my own work; I have been enlarged by their comments. My most constant helper in my work, however, has been my wife, Eloise, to whom I dedicate this volume.

CHAPTER I

The Function of Landrent under the Cultivation System in Java

In 1964 my first article dealing with the Cultivation System in
Java appeared in *The Journal of Asian Studies*, Volume XXIII, No.
3, under the above title. I had received a grant from the American
Council of Learned Societies for the academic year 1960-1961 to
collect materials in The Netherlands. I worked at the Netherlands
State Archives (Algemeen Rijksarchief) and the Royal Institute
for Geography, Linguistics, and Ethnography (Koninklijk
Instituut voor Taal-, Land- en Volkenkunde, KITLV) both of
which were then in The Hague. The archive of J. van den Bosch
had recently been opened for public use with a temporary
inventory, which was later altered without any concordance. The
archive of the Ministry of Colonies and the archive of J.C. Baud
were also heavily consulted in those years. The book and journal
collections of the KITLV were also invaluable sources of
information.

I soon learned that the amount of primary materials on and
about the Cultivation System was very large; in the years that
followed it became even larger. It appeared to me that the
materials did not present enormous problems of bias, for
although they were almost entirely records produced by
Europeans, there was a vast amount of critical commentary both
in the archives and in books and journals. Even the diversity of
views, however, did not compensate for the lack of materials
written by Javanese and/or expressing a Javanese point of view.
There was little I could do to alter this situation at this time and I
resolved to proceed with what I had which gave me sufficient
evidence for revising many of the standard historical interpretations. However, as the years went on and as I continued my
research into the Cultivation System, I continually sought sources
that would illuminate the Javanese vision on events.

In the face of vast quantities of source materials touching upon
many aspects of a complicated System that functioned for more
than thirty years, I had to organize my writing around themes. A
theme that seemed most immediately obvious to me was that of
landrent and the way it functioned within the Cultivation
System. The prevailing literature argued that the continued
collection of landrent under the System was an abuse, for the

System should have supplanted landrent. This was obviously a misinterpretation, and in this article I set out to show why. To re-evaluate this one aspect of the Cultivation System I had to analyze a number of texts, both in English and in Dutch, and show how and why this interpretation had gone astray.

The article was written in Troy, New York, where my family and I were living at the time and where I taught history at Russell Sage College. The article is reproduced here with the kind permission of the Association for Asian Studies, Inc. and is exactly as it appeared in 1964 with two minor alterations. First, I have changed the dossier numbers in the footnote references to the Van den Bosch archive to reflect the new inventory arrangement. Second, I have added a clarifying note at one point which will appear in italics.

The introduction and operation of the Cultivation (culture) System in Java were closely tied to the collection of landrent. Reinsma has noted this clearly and succinctly in his contention that 'the landrent served as the lever for making use of an important part of the labor and land of the people.'[1] Yet the closeness of this relationship has frequently been overlooked. An all-too-frequent impression today is that landrent was superseded by a requirement to cultivate ground. The fact that landrent continued to be collected is regarded as an abuse of the system, a sort of double taxation. As a result, a certain confusion about how landrent functioned within the Cultivation System now pervades the thinking on the subject. This confusion is especially apparent in the English-language histories dealing with the system, but is by no means limited to these. The fundamental source of confusion can be traced back to the writings and pronouncements of Johannes van den Bosch, the man who conceived and breathed life into the Cultivation System during his years in Java from 1830 to 1834.

Landrent had been introduced into Java during the English interregnum (1811-1816) by Sir Thomas Stamford Raffles, who gleaned many of his ideas on the subject from the land revenue systems of British India. Even before the English arrived in 1811, there had been proposals and experiments by the Dutch to alter the existing system in Java, but the system of landrent is attributable chiefly to Raffles.[2] Landrent was premised upon the rights of the sovereign to ownership of all the land. The land was rented to village chiefs throughout Java, who were in turn responsible for subdividing the land and collecting rent on it. This rent could originally be paid either in money or in kind, but in time the emphasis came to be upon money payment; by 1827

---

[1]   R. Reinsma, *Het verval van het Cultuurstelsel* ('s-Gravenhage, 1955), p. 81.
[2]   J. Bastin, *Raffles' ideas on the land rent system in Java and the work of the Mackenzie land tenure commission* ('s-Gravenhage, 1954), Ch. I.

the Dutch government was to decree that a major part of the landrent had to be paid in gold or silver and the remaining part in copper coin.[3] The amount of rent was to be based upon the type of land (i.e., either wet or dry fields) and its estimated productivity in rice. The assessment ranged from one-half the produce for the best wet lands to one-fourth on the thinner dry fields; in general two-fifths of the produce was regarded as the average assessment. Shortly after introducing the system, Raffles had changed his mind about the village form of assessment and collection and had sought to deal directly with the individual cultivator.[4] This had not proved practicable, however, and upon the return of Java to the Dutch in 1816, the decision was made to retain the landrent system, but to return to the village basis of collection and assessment.[5] This decision was necessitated by the total lack of accurate surveys or soil analyses. From its inception, the landrent lacked accurate data upon which to build an equitable system; this shortcoming was not rectified during the entire time that the Cultivation System was in operation. Not until the 1870s was a cadastral survey inaugurated. In the absence of a definite criterion for assessing the landrent, the annual assessment was arrived at by estimating and dickering, in which the village head would seek to lower the levy and the Dutch officials would seek to raise it. The resulting arrangements were without uniformity and, since the village head was usually successful in disguising the extent of the village lands and the productivity of preceding years, the resulting assessment was appreciably below the two-fifths average which was supposed to prevail. An investigation into the incidence of landrent in 1836 in the Residencies of Cheribon, Tagal, and Pekalongan shows an actual relationship varying from 9 to 27 per cent to the total monetary value of the product.[6] This is clearly below the two-fifths standard, but it was widely felt that the two-fifths figure would be oppressive if rigorously applied. For our purposes, it is sufficient to note the arbitrary and inexact nature of the assessment, and the fact that it occurred on a village basis.

During the 1820s, Dutch policy toward Java was subject to review. Governor-General Van der Capellen had applied a policy characterized by granting the Javanese free use of their land and its produce. In return, the Javanese were to pay landrent as described above. The policy at this time sought to reduce the influence and role of Europeans in Java; it was hoped that the Javanese would be motivated by liberal economic concepts to

---

[3]   *Staatsbladen van Nederlandsch-Indië* 1827, No. 48. (Henceforth N.I. Stbl.)
[4]   Bastin, Ch. 8.
[5]   N.I. Stbl. 1819, No. 5.
[6]   S. van Deventer Jsz., *Bijdragen tot de kennis van het landelijk stelsel op Java*, III (Zalt-Bommel, 1866), 45-64.

produce salable products which would more easily enable them to pay the landrent. This policy broke down after 1825 for a number of reasons, chief among which were the extra expenses engendered by the Java War and the declining world prices of tropical agricultural commodities. King William I sent Viscount Du Bus de Gisignies to Java in 1826 as Commissioner General with extensive powers to cut expenses and make the colony pay. In the famous 'Colonization Report' of May 1, 1827, Du Bus outlined his major plans for making Java a remunerative asset.[7] In essence, he proposed that the unused lands of Java be sold or leased to Europeans who would cultivate them with the use of Javanese labor, which would be attracted through a free wage arrangement. This scheme had liberal economic concepts at its root also, but looked to the Europeans rather than the Javanese as the font of entrepreneurial activity. Du Bus argued that the granting of free disposition over land and labor to the Javanese had not produced salable products which could compete on the world market; the Javanese were to be led into productive activity through contractual arrangements with Europeans. The pressure toward this end was, of course, to be applied through the landrent, which would enhance the need for money.

In response to this colonization proposal of Du Bus, Johannes van den Bosch submitted an 'advice' on March 6, 1829,[8] clearly in opposition to both the free disposition over land and products by the Javanese and the sale of unused lands to Europeans. This is the first statement on what later came to be called the system for cultivating products suited for the European market, or simply the Cultivation System (Cultuurstelsel). It is not my intention to describe the Cultivation System here in all its ramifications. Suffice it to say that Van den Bosch wished to make Java an asset to the motherland in the shortest possible time by having it produce tropical agricultural products, chiefly coffee, sugar, and indigo, at such low prices that they could compete with similar products from other parts of the world, especially America (i.e., the West Indies), where slaves had been or were being used. To achieve this end, Van den Bosch suggested a system which he claimed was more in keeping with the traditions of the Javanese, based upon forced cultivation and the delivery of products to the government. In many respects, this was a reversion to the system of the former Dutch East India Company, but to carry this comparison too far would be misleading and would divert us from our central theme of landrent. Van den Bosch was given a mandate by the King to institute his system, and to this end he arrived in Java

---

[7]   This report is printed in D.C. Steijn Parvé, *Het koloniaal monopoliestelsel [...], nader toegelicht* (Zalt-Bommel, 1851), pp. 1-125, second part.
[8]   Printed in Steijn Parvé, pp. 294-328.

in January 1830. Its major points have been set forth in various reports, most importantly: (1) the 'advice' of March 6, 1829; (2) the report to the Minister of Colonies dated October 10, 1830, Kabinet letter No. 628/26;[9] and (3) the account of the fundamentals and first results of the Cultivation System prepared by Van den Bosch in 1834 for his successor in Java, J.C. Baud.[10] Pertinent sections from one or more of these documents have been used by all historians in describing the theory and practice of the Cultivation System. Earlier accounts which described the function of the landrent within the total system also referred either directly or indirectly to these documents.

In approaching the problem of the role and function of landrent within the Cultivation System, I would like to move from the outside inward as one would in unraveling a tangled skein: first, the English-language sources concerned with the Cultivation System and the dilemma in which these sources leave us; second, the major Dutch writings used by English-language authors; and third, the above-mentioned three documents written by Van den Bosch setting forth his ideas and practical results. The final step will be to weigh the totality of these theories and written accounts against the evidence of the internal correspondence and orders in Java during the period from 1830 to 1834; on the basis of this latter evidence, I shall posit a view of the function of landrent within the Cultivation System which varies in certain essentials from many views commonly held today. It is only fair to say that much of this latter evidence was not available to earlier writers on the subject, but on the other hand much of their misconception was exacerbated by preconceived ideas and by a lack of disciplined analysis.[11]

[9]   This report is printed in J.P. Cornets de Groot van Kraaijenburg, *Over het beheer onzer koloniën* ('s-Gravenhage, 1862), pp. 339-70.
[10]   The parts of this account describing the cultivation system were incorporated into the State Record in 1834, see N.I. Stbl. 1834, No. 22; the complete account was published in the *BKI* 11 and separately printed in 1864 under the title *Mijne verrigtingen in Indië; Verslag van Z. Excellentie den Commissaris-Generaal J. van den Bosch, over de jaren 1830, 1831, 1832, en 1833, door Z. Excell. Zelv' opgesteld en overhandigd aan zijnen opvolger den Gouverneur-Generaal ad interim J.C. Baud, waarin de grondslagen en eerste uitkomsten van het Kultuurstelsel vergeleken worden met de vroeger gevolgde regeringsbeginselen en de daaruit verkregen resultaten; en beschouwd in verband met de politieke en finantiële belangen van Indië en Nederland* (Amsterdam, 1864).
[11]   Correspondence and communication in Dutch colonial affairs was generally at three levels: (1) Reports and letters between the Ministry of Colonies and the Governor-General (and vice versa) are in the Colonial Archive, which is housed in the State Archives in The Hague; these records were available to earlier writers on this subject; (2) The directives and letters from the Governor-General to and from the leading Dutch civil servants in Java are generally not in the Colonial Archive unless they relate to a special problem; these records for this period I found in the personal archives of J. van den Bosch and J.C. Baud which are also in the Dutch State Archives, but have only recently been opened to the public so that earlier writers did not have all of them at their disposal; (3) The directives and letters from the Dutch civil servants to their subordinates and to the Indonesian Regents and others were

In analyzing the English-language impression of the landrent problem in the Cultivation System, I shall use the accounts of Clive Day, whose book appeared early in the twentieth century,[12] J.S. Furnivall, who published during the 1930s,[13] and D.G.E. Hall, whose account appeared after Indonesian independence.[14]

Clive Day's account of the system is the most detailed and in some respects the most satisfactory, for he makes some distinction between the theoretical statement of Van den Bosch that 'by giving up land and services to the government cultures the people were supposed to be freed from the land-tax,' and the practice of the system whereby 'in many cases they had to bear the cultures and pay the land tax in addition.'[15] He touches upon the truth somewhat later when he notes that despite the legislation of 1834 (N. I. Stbl. No. 22), 'the land-tax was still retained for natives under the culture system, at least in being taken as the standard for their payments.' Quite correctly, he notes that Javanese were not quits with the government by giving land and labor; they were expected to 'produce enough at the tasks the government set them to equal at any rate what they had given before in taxes on their rice lands.'[16] Day raises further questions about landrent, but one cannot argue with the impression created by his account, although one can lament the innuendoes he attaches to his interpretations of the system in practice.

Turning to the statements of Furnivall on the subject of landrent under the Cultivation System, we are struck by a more moderate tone about the system in general as well as by more equivocal and contradictory concepts on the subject of landrent in particular. It is evident from the muddled nature of Furnivall's original statement on the subject[17] that he is hewing too closely to the theoretical fulminations of Van den Bosch. He tells his readers that in lieu of taking two-fifths of the produce in cash, government took only one-fifth in kind, and that a village which set apart one-fifth of its rice-land for the cultivation of export crops was excused from the payment of land-revenue, but that any surplus above the prescribed land-revenue from the sale of produce was credited to the village, and finally that the village was held to have discharged its liabilities and was exempt from land-

---

not available to me or to any other writers on this subject; if they still exist, they are in archives in Indonesia and would undoubtedly shed additional light on the question of landrent, along with many other historical problems.

[12]   Clive Day, *The policy and administration of the Dutch in Java* (New York, 1904).
[13]   J.S. Furnivall, *Netherlands India, a study of plural economy* (Cambridge, 1939). (My citations will be drawn from the 1944 edition.)
[14]   D.G.E. Hall, *A history of South-East Asia* (London, 1955).
[15]   Day, p. 258.
[16]   Day, pp. 280-1.
[17]   Furnivall, p. 118.

revenue when the crop was ripe. The contradictions within the preceding sentence are too obvious to require elaboration. Furnivall is clearly unhappy with the landrent problem, for he soon[18] questions the increase in landrent which occurred and quotes the Dutch economist Gonggrijp to the effect that Van den Bosch's statement of 1834 was 'almost ridiculously insincere' since if one were excused from landrent it would obviously preclude any growth of landrent. Furnivall tries to explain this by two wrong guesses, namely that either the landrent was remitted only on the area surrendered for the cultivation of export crops, or that the Javanese was cultivating sugar for his own profit and was therefore still liable to landrent. The latter guess has at least some truth, in that this did occur in some areas of eastern Java.

Because Hall's account covers more time and area than Day's or Furnivall's, his account of the Cultivation System is much briefer, but he lists nine points that characterize the system as set forth by Van den Bosch[19] and indicates that one-fifth of the cultivated land of each village was to be set apart, free of landrent; whenever the assessed value of the delivered product was greater than the landrent remitted, the difference was to be credited to the people. Hall further indicates[20] that according to Stapel the worst abuse of the system was in the continued collection of landrent despite the above stated freedom.

These three English-language accounts given in sequence cover half a century of historical scholarship on the Cultivation System. They clearly show a worsening rather than an improvement in understanding the system in its practical operation, although this is accompanied by a more balanced effort to assess the impact of the system upon the Javanese. A judicious approach to history is to be highly recommended, but factual accuracy must be a first consideration. Actually, since each of these three writers draws upon diverse Dutch authors, changes in accuracy and attitude contained in the English sources are a reflection of changes in the related Dutch literature.

Hall's account of the Cultivation System takes its message from two large twentieth-century Dutch histories: Colenbrander's *Colonial History*[21] and Stapel's *History of Netherlands India*.[22] The nine-point schema which Hall presents is a translation from Colenbrander,[23] who claims he is quoting Van den Bosch's statement of 1834 which was incorporated in the State Record.

---

[18] Furnivall, p. 133.
[19] Hall, p. 469.
[20] Hall, p. 470.
[21] H.T. Colenbrander, *Koloniale geschiedenis*, 3 vols. ('s-Gravenhage, 1925-26).
[22] F.W. Stapel, ed., *Geschiedenis van Nederlandsch-Indië*, 5 vols. (Amsterdam, 1938-40).
[23] Colenbrander, III, p. 37.

Unfortunately for Hall, Colenbrander is highly inaccurate; the State Record does not say that the one-fifth of the land set apart is free from landrent, but instead states that

> 'a desa (village) which sets aside one-fifth of its rice fields for the cultivation of export crops should be excused from payment of landrent. That furthermore this desa shall receive the additional advantages of the amount which the assessed value of the product should bring in above the amount of landrent due'.[24]

Colenbrander is incorrect; the crops grown on one-fifth of the village's lands should have excused the village from payment of all its landrent, according to Van den Bosch. Stapel, on the other hand, is merely reflecting a prevailing liberal confusion in seeing an abuse in the continued collection of landrent; moreover, he also becomes involved in intricacies between individual and village assessments of landrent which Van den Bosch admittedly did nothing to clarify.[25] Neither Colenbrander nor Stapel was especially keen on the Cultivation System; they reflect a twentieth-century liberal preference to look upon the system as an unfortunate aspect of Dutch rule for which amends were being made in the twentieth century, they elected to look beyond it rather than to probe its function and operation.

It is to the everlasting credit of Furnivall that his account of the Cultivation System has done more than any other work in either Dutch or English to introduce a sense of balance into our understanding of its results and impact. It is true that during the 1930s, Professor Gerretson, the most eloquent spokesman of the Utrecht School, was spiritedly calling for a new view of the system which sought to glorify it.[26] But Furnivall took no part in this unbounded form of praise, nor does he use the writings of Gerretson or his students in speaking of the Cultivation System. Furnivall's sources of information are the official documents of the State Record. His description of the Cultivation System as cited above is drawn from Van den Bosch's statement of 1834 which, as we have seen, was incorporated in the official statutes. Perhaps his more moderate stand on the system was induced by a faith in the printed statute and a belief in Van den Bosch's sincerity. This we cannot know with certainty, but this predilection to adhere to the official text and to attribute sincerity to Van den Bosch's pronouncements was

---

[24] J. Boudewijnse and G.H. van Soest, *De Indo-Nederlandsche Wetgeving*, II (Haarlem-Amsterdam, 1876-1924), p. 71. I have left the translation in a rather literal form to indicate more clearly that *all* the village lands should be excused from the payment of landrent, not just one-fifth part.
[25] Stapel, V, p. 237.
[26] C. Gerretson, 'Historische inleiding,' in: *De sociaal-economische invloed van Neder-landsch-Indië op Nederland* (Wageningen, 1938), pp. 18-9.

reinforced by the Dutch sources which Furnivall used in supporting his view of the system, and especially the function of landrent within it. In general, Furnivall uses Dutch accounts which in their approach to the subject present a guise of scholarly objectivity in preference to personal invective. This is not to say that all these accounts favor the system or show the balance that Furnivall distills from them; quite to the contrary, they are all in varying degrees and forms opposed to the system and show a certain lack of balance. From Van den Bosch's antagonist Merkus, whose anonymous attack appeared in 1835,[27] to Steijn Parvé,[28] Van Hoëvell,[29] Cornets de

---

[27] [P. Merkus], *Kort overzigt der financiele resultaten van het stelsel van kultures onder den Gouverneur-Generaal J. van den Bosch* (Kampen, 1835); and *Blik op het bestuur van Nederlandsch-Indië onder den Gouverneur-Generaal Js. van den Bosch, voor zoo ver het door denzelven ingevoerde stelsel van cultures op Java betreft* (Kampen, 1835). Both works appeared anonymously. Their impact in the Netherlands and in Java is discussed in Van Deventer, III, 5ff. Furnivall attributes both pieces to Mr. P. Merkus, who had been a member of the Council of the Indies during Van den Bosch's years in Java. In this position, Merkus made the most principled objections to Van den Bosch's proposals, for he was a strong follower of the liberal ideas of ex-Governor-General Van der Capellen and of ex-Minister Elout. His disagreements with Van den Bosch produced an exchange of Notes which are for the most part printed in Van Deventer, II. These Notes disagree with the methods rather than the ultimate goals of Van den Bosch, and it is interesting to note that at one point Merkus actually suggested tying the landrent into the cultivation system much as Van den Bosch had done (Note of 30 March 1831). This and other remarkable agreements have led J.J. Westendorp Boerma, *Een geestdriftig Nederlander; Johannes van den Bosch* (Amsterdam, 1950), pp. 89-90, to ask if perhaps the differences between the liberal system before 1830 and the reactionary system after 1830 are less sharp than is generally imagined. I would agree with this proposition. For our current argument, these pieces are of interest chiefly in showing early discrepancies and abuses which crept into the system while also pointing out that the profits reported by the system were largely illusory; they do not cast much light on the problem of landrent.
As regards the authorship of the two brochures, there is little doubt that Merkus wrote the *Kort overzigt*. By his own admission (Letter of Merkus to Baud, dd. Wiesbaden, 24 August 1836, Archive Baud, Folio 550; and Letter of Merkus to the King, dd. 15 July 1836, Archive Van den Bosch, Folio 32), he confesses that he wrote the piece for the information of Elout, and that his friend Van der Capellen had published it without his knowledge. There is, on the other hand, little doubt that Merkus did *not* write the other brochure, *Blik op het bestuur*. Van Deventer, III, 15, interprets Merkus's letter of 15 July 1836, incorrectly and consequently attributes the second brochure to him also. Doorninck's reference work on Anonyms and Pseudonyms leans toward attributing it to Joh. Olivier, Jz., who edited the magazine *De Oosterling* which had sponsored the publication of both brochures. Van der Capellen had the copies of both brochures in The Royal Library in The Hague inscribed with Olivier's name. Westendorp Boerma, p. 139, suggests that ex-Resident Mac Gillavry authored the piece. Whatever the truth of the matter, the style and general tone of the piece would make it highly doubtful that Merkus wrote it.
[28] D.C. Steijn Parvé, *Het koloniaal monopoliestelsel getoetst aan geschiedenis en staatshuishoudkunde* ('s-Gravenhage, 1850), and *Het koloniaal monopoliestelsel [...], nader toegelicht* (Zalt-Bommel, 1851). These books are an extension of the arguments in the above-mentioned brochures. Steijn Parvé's argument runs that the system is immoral because it is not based on liberal principles, and that it is not financially sound because it is built on false grounds. His arguments are quite sound in relation to the external aspects of the system, for there is little doubt that the initial financial gains registered in the Netherlands were

Groot,[30] and Pierson,[31] it is clear that Furnivall made extensive use of the nineteenth-century accounts that argued chiefly from a comparison of the official texts with the reported shortcomings and abuses of the system. Everything thus pointed to accepting the written word of Van den Bosch as a reliable statement of fact. Credibility was further given to Van den Bosch's sincerity through Furnivall's use of the best available biography of the early career of Van den Bosh.[32] This latter work is in no sense responsible for specific statements on the Cultivation System, but it did provide (quite correctly, I feel) an impression that Van den Bosch was a well-intentioned person and not an ogre. Furnivall cites Westendorp Boerma in his rejection of Van Soest's history of the Cultivation System as a 'tissue of insinuations.'[33] Van Soest will be discussed below, but at this point it is not inappropriate to note Furnivall's complete avoidance of this work despite the fact that it is the most comprehensive treatment of the Cultivation

---

highly padded. His line of reasoning is based upon a liberal economic analysis of the official pronouncements. I would contend, particularly with regard to the internal workings of the system in Java, that such an approach will never lead to an adequate understanding of how the system actually functioned. This argument is extraneous to our present concern with landrent, however, and on this topic Steijn Parvé had little new to say. It should be noted that Furnivall quite wisely used these books with great caution.

29   Of the many writings of W.R. van Hoëvell, Furnivall cites the *Reis over Java, Madura en Bali, in het midden van 1847*, 3 vols. (Amsterdam, 1849-54), which gives some indication of Van Hoëvell's concern with forced cultivations, government salt monopoly, and lack of governmental interest in indigenous agriculture. This work is not as critical of the cultivation system as Van Hoëvell's later writings and speeches. Regarding landrent, Van Hoëvell correctly observed in a little known article, 'Vlugtige aanteekeningen op de "Beschouwingen over N. I." door [...] Nahuijs van Burgst [...] door W.L. de Sturler [...],' *Gruno* 1 (1849), pp. 239-47, that the belief that a village was excused from landrent merely by planting one-fifth of its lands with an exportable crop was a wrong interpretation of several phrases appearing in N.I. Stbl. 1834, No. 22.

30   J.P. Cornets de Groot van Kraaijenburg, *Over het beheer onzer koloniën* ('s-Gravenhage, 1862). Cornets de Groot had risen through the Dutch bureaucracy to high government position in Java. The emphasis of his account is upon bringing changes into the system as he had seen it in operation during the 1850s. His account leans heavily on government publications, and is quite moderate in tone. Furnivall seems to have made rather extensive use of this book.

31   N.G. Pierson, *Koloniale politiek* (Amsterdam, 1877). Considered one of the outstanding liberals writing on the subject of colonial policy, Pierson is highly regarded for his calm opposition to the cultivation system based upon examination of the official documents. Clive Day, p. 293, refers to this work as 'the most concise and suggestive.' Pierson's influence upon later writers is generally felt to be great, and it seems highly probable that Furnivall's general viewpoint and his willingness to give credence to Van den Bosch's official statements was largely due to a strong reliance upon Pierson. Pierson's approach to the landrent will be analyzed below.

32   J.J. Westendorp Boerma, *Johannes van den Bosch als sociaal hervormer; De Maatschappij van Weldadigheid* (Amsterdam, 1927). This book deals with Van den Bosch's career only in the years prior to the cultivation system. Westendorp Boerma later wrote a complete biography, *Een geestdriftig Nederlander; Johannes van den Bosch* (Amsterdam, 1950), but obviously this was not available to Furnivall.

33   Furnivall, p. 150.

System. Nor does he refer to Clive Day, who is as impassioned as Van Soest on the subject. Only minimal and indirect use is made of the major source work on the system by Van Deventer, which also contains innuendoes against Van den Bosch and the Cultivation System. These omissions will be discussed presently, but it becomes clear that Furnivall was avoiding accounts that descended to invective or which seemed tendentious in their approach to the subject. Let us turn now to the image created – especially of the problem of landrent – by the more judicious accounts which Furnivall did use.

If we look to the writing of N.G. Pierson cited above as an outstanding example of a moderate liberal approach in the late nineteenth century, and if we analyze his statements concerning the function of landrent within the Cultivation System, we are brought directly to the vortex of the confusion and misconception reflected in Furnivall's account. Pierson believed that Van den Bosch was a man with a heart, who was sincerely convinced that the Javanese would be better served by a tax which demanded his time rather than his money. Such taxation in work had to be imposed by force, but it was less oppressive for the population than taxation in money and more advantageous to all parties. 'Does not the landrent system also rest on force? Instead of being forced to pay money, the Javan will henceforth be forced to deliver products; this is the only difference.' But, continued Pierson, Van den Bosch's plan was never implemented in accordance with his intentions: *his idea to replace landrent by the forced cultivation of products never was realized.* In some areas where the cultivation services were too oppressive, exemption from landrent was given, but this did not occur everywhere: *the landrent remained, and the forced cultivations were in addition to it.* The government needed the millions which the landrent raised and therefore maintained this tax, but this occurred, according to Pierson, against the personal wish of Van den Bosch.[34] The impression given by Pierson concerning landrent is based upon the official statements of Van den Bosch cited on other occasions, and upon earlier writings on the subject such as those of Steijn Parvé. The image created by Pierson is that landrent was to have been replaced by the work and produce of the Javanese, who would henceforth have delivered products and been exempted from landrent, but things went awry in practice and the Javanese was often forced to cultivate and deliver particular crops, *and* pay landrent. This description of landrent seems to fit both the official pronouncements and the apparent divergencies between them and the actual operation of the system. It shows great patience and understanding with Van den Bosch, whose plans were never realized. Small wonder that Pierson has been

[34] Pierson, pp. 92-4. My italics.

recognized as a reasonable and moderate writer on the subject, whose views have influenced many later writers, including Furnivall. There is only one thing wrong with Pierson's description of the function of landrent under the Cultivation System: it is not correct.

Clive Day based his account of the Cultivation System upon Dutch sources which were either not used or were little used by Furnivall and Hall. He was indebted to the writings of S. van Deventer and G.H. van Soest for both his facts and his interpretations.[35] Because of their bulk of information, factual detail, and original documentation, there is little doubt that these two works, particularly that of Van Deventer, are the most comprehensive studies of the Cultivation System. Both used government archives and had access to records not previously available. Van Deventer's study remains the most extensive compendium of source materials on the subject; records are excerpted and reproduced with great accuracy, and are interspersed with a narrative that swells with Wagnerian force toward the crescendos of brutalities, injustices, and inequities which were either inherent in or were worked into the system. The work served the purposes of its liberal sponsors well; the documentation of abuses of the Cultivation System proved overwhelming. Van Soest's *History* is an extension of the same condemnation. Building upon the documentation of Van Deventer and in some instances adding new source material, Van Soest carries the point of view of the earlier work to its previously unstated extreme. The Cultivation System is condemned in both theory and practice, and, as one might logically assume, the founder of the system, Van den Bosch, becomes evil incarnate. No opprobrium is too dark to heap upon him. Compared to this, Pierson's account exudes moderation and human understanding. While lamenting Van Soest's interpretation of the facts, and while wishing that Van Deventer had selected his documents with less tendentious criteria, one cannot quibble over the accuracy of their documentation. If one reads these two works carefully, as Clive Day must have done, one will emerge with a fairly accurate picture of the theory and practice of the Cultivation System and the role of landrent; but one will also absorb the fiery liberal persuasion and harsh vindictiveness of their authors, as Clive Day so clearly proves.[36]

What are the actual facts about the role of landrent within the Cultivation System? Very simply, they are these. Despite Van den Bosch's protestations against landrent, this form of taxation remained at the basis of

[35] S. van Deventer, Jsz., *Bijdragen tot de kennis van het landelijk stelsel op Java, op last van Zijne Excellentie den Minister van Kolonien, J.D. Fransen van de Putte, bijeenverzameld*, 3 vols. (Zalt-Bommel, 1865-66); G.H. van Soest, *Geschiedenis van het kultuurstelsel*, 3 vols. (Rotterdam, 1869-71).
[36] Day, p. 269, calls Van Soest 'one of the best historians of the culture system.'

the Cultivation System throughout most of Java.[37] Either through contract, in which as Merkus pointed out the Javanese was not a free agent, or through pressure from higher authority, the Javanese village planted part of its lands with a crop suitable for sale on the European market. Sugar and indigo were the most common crops grown upon the village lands; coffee was regulated somewhat differently, as I shall presently indicate. The amount of village land set aside for this purpose should have been one-fifth, but soon Van den Bosch was speaking of one-third. Now comes the confusion. As late as 1834, Van den Bosch was speaking of the Javanese as being excused from landrent if he cultivated part of his lands with crops suitable for the European market and delivered these crops to the government (in lieu of landrent). This would leave one with the same impression found in Furnivall and Hall and the various Dutch writers they used as sources, namely that cultivating some land and delivering the produce therefrom to the government relieved or excused the village from paying landrent. Actually this is a wrong impression. If Van den Bosch had been more precise in his description, he would have said something to the effect that if the Javanese cultivated one-fifth of the village lands in a given crop which he delivered to the government after it was harvested, the value of that crop (calculated at a price that would allow processing and distribution of the product at a cost that would be competitive on the world market) *should* have been sufficient to pay the landrent of the lands of the village as this landrent would normally have been assessed on the value of a single rice crop. From a careful analysis of the detailed instructions which Van den Bosch issued in Java, it becomes evident that from the very beginning of 1830, when Van den Bosch was newly arrived in Java, the system operated in practice as I have just sketched it. The assessed landrent remained the measure against which export crops were to be delivered; if a village grew export crops valued at more than the landrent which it owed, it would receive payment from the government for that amount in excess of the landrent; but conversely, if the value of the crop grown on the portion of the village lands did not equal the amount of the landrent, the village was expected to make up the shortage in cash or kind. The landrent remained the *quid pro quo* for all goods and services which the village delivered, and it was consequently never the aim of the Cultivation System to indicate that a Javanese village would be excused from landrent merely by being willing to grow a particular crop on part of its lands; the value of the crop was what counted, and this was weighed against an assessment that continued to be known as landrent and continued to be entered in the

---

[37] Van Soest, II, p. 96. Van den Bosch would retain the landrent because his main aim, increased revenue, did not permit its abolition.

record books under that heading.*

Later writers who lamented the abuse of the system by which both crops and landrent were collected were not really discovering an abuse, but were instead observing the normal working; this becomes a divergence from the accepted standard only if one tries to reconcile it with the pronouncements of Van den Bosch as these appeared in his general accounts of the system which were sent to higher authorities.

Before launching into a detailed account of the above contentions about the early years of the system, it is necessary to insert a few restrictions and limitations to what has been said above about landrent. In the Preanger Regencies, the landrent did not operate as in the rest of Java; the fact that Van den Bosch so frequently based his estimates and comparisons upon the situation in the Preanger served only to augment the confusion about the workings of his system. In the districts of Madiun, Kediri, Bagelen, and Banjumas, which had recently been taken over from the Kingdom of Mataram, the landrent system had never been introduced. Consequently it was necessary to institute a head tax system which could be used as the basis for crop deliveries; this was eventually replaced by a landrent assessment in many of these districts.[38] Finally, the matter of coffee growing raised special problems, since this crop was under forced cultivation before 1830. Generally, however, outside the Preanger, the coffee crop, which after 1832 had to be delivered and sold to the government, was equated against landrent and any surpluses paid to the producer. Since coffee was generally not grown on lands otherwise used for rice production, it was subject to many special considerations within the entire schema of the Cultivation System.

As early as May 1830, Van den Bosch confided to the Resident of Tagal that in making arrangements with villages for growing indigo, an initial remission of landrent might be possible 'on condition that they fulfill this by the planting of indigo'.[39] The next month all residents were encouraged to stimulate the growth of materials for the manufacturing of gunny sacks in selected villages which would be 'dismissed from paying landrent, but

---

*NOTE 1989. This paragraph has been interpreted by later scholars to mean that the assessed landrent determined the value and/or the amount of the crop to be delivered to the Government. That is not what I meant to imply, and I blame these misinterpretations on a lack of precision in word choice. Villages could and did deliver crops of a value above the amount of assessed landrent and received monetary payment for the crop value above the amount of landrent owed. On other occasions villages fell short of the assessed landrent with their crops; then, unless excused because of natural disasters, they would pay the shortfall.

[38] Early in 1833, for instance, Van den Bosch wrote the Resident of Banjumas a scathing letter for not yet introducing the landrent system into his district and consequently pursuing the cultivation system on grounds other than those prescribed. Kabinet letter No. 1553a, dd. 28 January 1833, Archive Van den Bosch, Folio 46. See also, Van Deventer, III, p. 82-5.

[39] Kabinet letter No. 228, dd. 7 June 1830, Archive Van den Bosch, Folio 46A.

instead [would] deliver a certain amount of raw material equal to the worth of the remitted landrent.'[40] This same method was also to be used for other crops, and he suggested closing contracts with villages for the delivery of sugar cane or for workers in the sugar mills; the entrepreneur (or mill operator) would then pay a certain rent for the mill or a particular price for the delivery of sugar which would take the place of the excused landrent.[41] This brought a new consideration into the problem, for it seems that Van den Bosch's initial concept also involved the entrepreneur in the payment of landrent. This emerges most clearly in a letter written to A.M.T. de Salis, acting Resident of Surabaya and soon-to-be member of the Council of the Indies. Lamenting the lack of understanding accorded his plans, Van den Bosch stated that he favored contracts between the villages and the planter (entrepreneur) in which 'it is stipulated that the planter shall pay the landrent, and the village, for its part, shall deliver a set amount of raw materials such as sugar cane, indigo plant, etc. to the manufacturer.' The planter would have to pay the landrent to the government not in specie but in products at a certain price.[42] This explanation, premised upon Van den Bosch's 'advice' of 1829, would seem to confirm the statement of Nahuijs van Burgst, who claimed that the system of European landownership which he encouraged in Surakarta and Jogjakarta many years before was the model for Van den Bosch's initial proposals by which the European entrepreneur would play an active role in the contractual arrangements with the village.[43] Nahuijs admitted that this procedure was soon replaced by a more efficient system in practice – i.e., the more active role of government officials who from the very first and with the encouragement of Van den Bosch arranged the contracts with the villages; the entrepreneur, who was often not a European since there was some reluctance to enter into the processing contracts with the government, was merely to process the products and was carefully excluded from any control or authority within the Javanese socio-political order of things.[44]

Under these circumstances, it is difficult to disagree with Merkus's often stated charge that contracts negotiated between the Resident on the one

[40]   Kabinet letter No. 137, dd. 7 May 1830, Archive Van den Bosch, Folio 46A.
[41]   Ibid.
[42]   Kabinet letter No. 233a, dd. 10 June 1830, Archive Van den Bosch, Folio 220.
[43]   H.G. Nahuijs van Burgst, *Beschouwingen over Nederlandsch-Indië* ('s-Gravenhage, 1848), pp. 14-5.
[44]   This order of business was clearly set forth in many letters and circulars. For instance in Kabinet letter No. 233a cited above, Van den Bosch writes, 'I have in mind making the contracting [...] easy by using the authority of the Residents [...]'. Also his report of 10 October 1830 contains similar sentiments. This point was understood clearly by officials in the Netherlands; Baud's letter of May 1831, No. 132, to the Minister of Colonies is very explicit on this – Van Deventer, II, p. 194. There was never the confusion on this issue that has beclouded a clear understanding of the landrent problem.

hand and the village head on the other were, in the light of the realities of
Javanese life, anything but free.[45] Van den Bosch's insistence upon the
freedom of these arrangements was at best only halfhearted, for he was
convinced that all labor is forced,[46] but his initial statements do seem to
contend that villages would be free to enter or reject the contractual
arrangement – a matter that was questionable from the start and
increasingly doubtful as time went on.[47] Interesting as this point may be, it is
only tangential to our discussion of the role of landrent, though it does
serve as another example of divergence between high-level pronouncements and practice.

In July 1830 the first major step in the widespread extension of cultivation
for the European market was taken with the circulation of a memorandum
on this subject to all Residents in Java,[48] urging each Resident to arrange
contracts with the villages in his district. Details concerning the landrent
arrangements were adjusted in subsequent correspondence. Throughout
this correspondence is the constant prompting to vary regulations according
to local circumstance; only the broad principles need be followed. The
governor-general suggested that (1) villages should be relieved from
payment of landrent for the first year as a sort of advance which would be
deducted from eventual deliveries, and (2) in future years they would also
be relieved of paying the landrent, which would be figured against the price
of the sugar cane (or other product) which they were to deliver.[49] Van den
Bosch was not equally clear and explicit in each letter he wrote, though it is
evident he meant to enunciate the same general principles. His mind was
not set to precise details, however, for he was completely absorbed by his
chief aim, getting the crops planted so that remittances could begin flowing

---

[45]   See the Note of Mr. P. Merkus, dd. 15 February 1831, Van Deventer, II, p. 219-27.

[46]   See 'Advice' of Van den Bosch, dd. 6 March 1829, in Steijn Parvé, p. 316, and Memorandum
of July 1830 in Cornets de Groot, p. 108.

[47]   In Van den Bosch's report of 1834, *Mijne verrigtingen in Indie*, there is no further mention
of freedom; instead the emphasis is laid upon the compatibility of these arrangement with
the traditional patterns of Javanese life.

[48]   I have not been able to find a complete copy of this memorandum, but I have found
extracts in Van Deventer, II, pp. 157ff., Cornets de Groot, pp. 107ff., and *Blik op het bestuur*,
pp. 36ff. Reference to it is also made in numerous Kabinet letters. This memorandum again
advances the active role of the entrepreneur in paying landrent and having free disposition
over the produce – it is clear even here, however, that the landrent is to be paid. This
memorandum seems to say very little in a specific and detailed way about landrent; this
materialized in the subsequent correspondence. This memorandum does devote much attention
to the use and regulation of corvée services, an aspect of the cultivation system that also calls
for reconsideration.

[49]   Kabinet letters No. 312, dd. 5 July 1830, to Resident of Pekalongan; No. 314, dd. 5 July
1830, to Resident of Bezukie & Banjuwangie; No. 315, dd. 5 July 1830, to Resident of Tagal;
No. 318, dd. 7 July 1830, to Resident of Surabaya; No. 320, dd. 7 July 1830, to Resident of
Cheribon; and especially No. 326, dd. 11 July 1830, to Residents of Bantam and Cheribon.
Archive Van den Bosch, Folio 221.

to the motherland. Writing the Residents of Surabaya and Bezukie in the same month, he expressed indifference whether the contracts were for money or toward landrent, just as long as they were in the spirit of his instructions.[50] Writing the Residents of Rembang and Semarang, he clearly indicated that the landrent on rice fields could be met by sugar plantings to the extent that these plantings and harvests met the regular landrent assessment.[51] But in writing the Residents of Cheribon and Pasuruan on the same day, he slipped into the phraseology which was later to appear in his official statements and to lead to eventual confusion, that 'a village which cultivates one-fifth of its land is freed of landrent for all its lands and enjoys (an additional) one-fourth of the amount thereof in money.'[52] From earlier letters to these same Residents, it is clear that he expected them to meet the landrent with the cane which was produced, but in his mind he was already slurring over this detail in the more concise and felicitous phrasing later incorporated in his official statements of October 1830 and January 1834, which became the chief sources for many subsequent writers.[53] The ambiguity of the phraseology concerning landrent is clearly shown in a letter to the Resident of Kedu ordering and explaining the expansion of indigo cultivation. After stating that the Javanese village which cultivated indigo on half the land area which it would otherwise need to pay its landrent would be excused of landrent – thus creating the impression found in Furnivall and Pierson – Van den Bosch went on to say that

> 'The preceding calculation is based on the assumption that a bouw of indigo plants will produce a value equal to the average landrent of a jonk (4 bouws) of rice field. But if the landrent in Kedu is higher than the average, or if less productive land is used, more land will have to be set aside for indigo plants so that the product may serve for the remission of landrent.'[54]

That these landrent arrangements were not easily reconciled with his theoretical pronouncements is evidenced by the remarkable omission of any mention of landrent in his Kabinet letter of August 9 to Messrs. Goldman and Bousquet, who as members of the Council of the Indies were in closest contact with the higher authorities at home. This letter announces a

[50] Kabinet letter No. 348, dd. 19 July 1830, Archive Van den Bosch, Folio 221.
[51] Kabinet Letter No. 347, dd. 19 July 1830, Archive Van den Bosch, Folio 221.
[52] Kabinet letters Nos. 346, 352.
[53] Actually the Resident of Pasuruan, H.J. Domis, provided Van den Bosch with many of the details and most of the calculations which were incorporated in the July memorandum. Pasuruan was one of the districts in which European contractors had arranged sugar production without government intervention, but these arrangements were modified after 1830. In the memorandum, Van den Bosch also drew heavily upon the experience in Pekalongan, as provided by the Resident M.H. Halewijn. This contrasts with the often-made contention that Van den Bosch drew all his information from the Preanger district and sought to impose this Preanger pattern on all Java.
[54] Kabinet letter No. 950, dd. 26 December 1830, Archive Van den Bosch, Folio 226.

readiness to proceed with the contract system – which was already launched – and speaks in some detail of individual labor quotas in the various aspects of sugar production – calculations which reappear in later official pronouncements and which leave the impression that he was contracting with individuals instead of with villages.[55] But not a word about landrent.

It became undoubtedly clear in January 1831 that Van den Bosch intended to evaluate crop production against landrent. Detailing the indigo expansion, he indicated that the price of indigo in areas where it was not previously grown would have to be determined by the government, but that the adjusted price would be able to cover the payment of landrent as far as needed, and the remainder paid in cash.[56] A few weeks later Van den Bosch was again fulminating against the landrent system, but it is clear from the context that he meant the payment of rent in money, for he saw a boon for the Javanese, not in being excused from landrent, but instead in being given the freedom to pay his landrent 'through other means,' i.e., through the delivery of an equivalent in specific crops.[57] Similar statements occurred throughout the four years Van den Bosch was controlling the system from Buitenzorg; it seems unnecessary to belabor the point further that the assessed landrent was to be paid by crop deliveries, and that the Javanese was relieved or excused from landrent only when the value of the delivered crops equalled the landrent assessment. Under a system that placed a premium on adaptation to local circumstances, it would be vainglorious to proclaim the discovery of general principles. So with the above concept of landrent, I would not wish to rule out or overlook exceptions – in eastern Java and Bantam, for example, landrent continued in many instances to be collected in money[58] – but I feel certain that the assessed landrent remained a base line for compensation of deliveries in most parts of Java as I have indicated. That Van den Bosch did not reject landrent is evident from his instructions to the Director of Cultivations as late as June 1832 to the effect that he should gain as much knowledge as possible about the functioning of the landrent system so that it could better be brought into line with the expansion of the cultivations.[59]

On the question of meeting shortages in the produce which was delivered

---

[55] Kabinet letter No. 453, dd. 9 August 1830, Archive Van den Bosch, Folio 222. Parts of this letter, which, as Van den Bosch probably suspected, made their way back to the Netherlands. Van Deventer, II, pp. 162ff. & footnote p. 157, quotes from it, but his major concern is to show that Van den Bosch had increased the amounts of village land used for government cultivations from one-fifth to one-third.
[56] Note of 29 January 1831, Van Deventer, II, p. 216. Van Soest, II, p. 85, makes one of his few factual errors when he refers to 'wage' instead of 'price' in discussing this Note.
[57] Note of 8 March 1831, Van Soest, II, p. 97, and Van Deventer, II, pp. 249, 267.
[58] Kabinet letter No. 77, dd. 14 January 1832, Archive Van den Bosch, Folio 239.
[59] Besluit No. I, dd. 8 June 1832, Van Deventer, II, pp. 405-7.

to meet the assessed landrent, one further item of evidence is contained in Van den Bosch's note to the Director of Cultivations of January 14, 1832. Writing in this instance about the introduction of tobacco cultivation into the Surabaya district, but broadening his compass to include sugar and indigo as well, Van den Bosch came out unequivocally for a production equivalent to the landrent when he wrote,

> '[...] the regulation about working one-fifth of the land for the payment of landrent must not be understood in such a general sense that it would be enough to cultivate one-fifth of the land to be exempted from the landrent. In that case there is a danger of seeing the cultivation neglected and poor grounds selected for it, by which the Government would be subject to great losses. [...] As a result the product often does not come close to fulfilling the landrent. Thus the Residents must be left a certain latitude to have more than one-fifth of the ground cultivated, if they can reach agreements with the natives to this effect'.[60]

In the light of the above-cited evidence, it is impossible to adhere any longer to the prevailing misconceptions of Furnivall and Hall, or to the incorrect statements and conclusions contained in their Dutch sources. Pierson's generous appraisal of Van den Bosch to the effect that he did not wish to retain the landrent seems especially misplaced and misleading. Before considering the central question in this problem, namely, why Van den Bosch's official pronouncements to higher authorities and for public consumption diverged so far on the matter of landrent from practices in Java which he encouraged, I wish to shed some light on Furnivall's dilemma about the increased landrent assessment during the first two decades of the Cultivation System's operation.

Projecting the function of landrent forward from 1830, it is incontestable that the total landrent assessment for Java increased over the years. Furnivall was quite correct in noting this, but was not correct in surmising the reasons for it. It will be recalled that landrent assessments were highly inaccurate and arbitrary; one reason for the increase in assessment is to be found in the gradually more favorable circumstances of bargaining over the levy in which the government was placed, for the Cultivation System gave local officials a closer supervision over the village lands and it became more difficult for the village headmen to understate the size of holdings and the production of the village. Second, new lands were brought into cultivation, in part encouraged by the system after 1830, and these lands were frequently free of landrent for about five years; thereafter, however, they entered the calculation and consequently increased the assessment. Third, there was a growing tendency among the administrators in Java to raise the quality valuation of lands as the production of exportable crops grew, so that lands

---

[60] Kabinet letter No. 77, dd. 14 January 1832.

once assessed at two-fifths of their rice production might have their assessment raised to one-half as it became evident that the value of the export crops exceeded the earlier assessment – this type of re-evaluation was stimulated by the percentages which administrators received and which undoubtedly had the effect of increasing the burden on the cultivator.[61] And finally the increasing market price of rice after 1830, caused partly by curtailed production as lands were forced to the use of export crops and partly by an inflationary spiral resulting from larger quantities of copper coin introduced by the government for payment of crops, resulted in an increased landrent assessment since this had always been and continued to be based upon a given portion of the rice crop which was or could be produced on village lands.[62]

What I have stated here about the function of landrent within the Cultivation System is in rather close agreement with the factual analysis of Clive Day. Thus it would be quite proper to assume that a careful reading of Van Deventer and Van Soest could provide an adequate understanding of how the system operated, although the lack of more detailed evidence would always leave certain doubts (we find these in Day's account too). These doubts are increased as one reads further in Van Deventer and Van Soest as well as other accounts, for Baud slipped into the phraseology of Van den Bosch in the report of his inspection trip over Java[63] and thus already by 1834 it was not entirely clear whether he understood the actual working of the landrent. It is quite certain, however, that by the 1850s, the Dutch administrators in Java no longer knew what the original workings of the system were, and as a consequence thought that Van den Bosch's official statements of 1829, 1830, and 1834 were accurate appraisals of the practical functionings of the system. What they saw about them clearly diverged from the impression which they or anyone else would get from these documents, and as a consequence their feelings and fears that malpractices

---

[61] See R.W.J.C. Bake, *Kunnen en moeten veranderingen gebragt worden in het kultuurstelsel op Java?* (Utrecht, 1854), p. 22. '[...] landrent on the sugar cane fields is always calculated as the most expensive, i.e., lands of the first quality, although if those fields were planted in rice they would not fall under this classification [...].' As early as November 1830, Van den Bosch indicated to the Resident of Bezukie that he should try to get the sugar cane for less specie 'through a reasonable increase of the landrent which can occur because he [the Javanese] draws so much more from his land [...].' Kabinet letter No. 820, dd. 18 November 1830, Archive Van den Bosch, Folio 225.

[62] The impact of rising rice prices upon landrent was already recognized by Van den Bosch in October 1830, when he wrote in a private letter to Baud that losses of government income from the landrent [which would now have a crop equivalent rather than a monetary payment] would be partly offset by rising rice prices as the quantity of rice grown decreased. J.J. Westendorp Boerma (ed.), *Briefwisseling tussen J. van den Bosch en J.C. Baud*, I (Utrecht, 1956), pp. 65-9. Also see Besluit No. I, dd. 8 June 1832, Van Deventer, II, pp. 405-7.

[63] Van Deventer, II, pp. 620-89.

and corruptions had entered the system were reinforced.

Assuming that the argument which I have been advancing is correct, the central question with regard to landrent as well as other aspects of the Cultivation System is why the discrepancies between the written pronouncements of Van den Bosch and the practical application of the system exist. There is little doubt that discrepancies do exist. One can take the approach of Pierson, Furnivall, and other more moderate writers and contend that these discrepancies crept into the system after the time of Van den Bosch or were due to human shortcomings and imperfections for which he was not entirely responsible. Although there is some vague truth in this interpretation, and despite its concession to human foibles, it does not agree with the facts. My impression is much closer to that of Day, Van Deventer, and Van Soest, who would maintain that the plans for the system were disregarded from the very beginning,[64] and by implication that Van den Bosch knew full well that the practical application of the system was quite different from the statements he was making as late as 1834. I would differ with these writers, however, in the imputations to be read into this. Whereas they sought to make Van den Bosch into a force of evil because he opposed liberal economic principles, and were consequently eager to seize upon every discrepancy between his pronouncements on the system and the actual situation in Java as an indication of malevolence,[65] I would be more inclined to seek an explanation for these discrepancies in the personality of Van den Bosch and in the conditions and circumstances both in the Netherlands and in Java with which he was confronted.

Johannes van den Bosch was a man of great enthusiasms and with a mind full of ideas. Both these character traits had for some years before 1830 been applied to his most heartfelt concern, the eradication of poverty and the advancement of social prosperity. The Society for Benevolence, which he fathered, was kept alive largely through his vitality. In turn it provided him with a forum for grandiose planning in the midst of a society that seemed stultified by the economic and political mischances that had overtaken it. To King William I, whose social welfare plans often outstripped his resources, Van den Bosch appeared as a great asset in the task of stimulating the national economy.[66] Compatibility with the King, however, did not necessarily mean a ready and willing acceptance by leading

---

[64]   Van Soest, II, p. 270.
[65]   I am in complete agreement with Westendorp Boerma and Furnivall that Van Soest's history is a 'tissue of insinuations.' I have seldom encountered a more blatant use of veiled inferences and twisted meanings in order to besmirch someone's character. Where Van Soest uses facts, as he frequently does, however, I cannot quibble with their accuracy, only with the use to which he puts them.
[66]   Westendorp Boerma, *Een geestdriftig Nederlander*, p. 52.

Hollanders of the early nineteenth century; they tended rather to be repelled by Van den Bosch's enthusiasm and to disparage the results of his energies. To them he was too authoritarian, too irreligious, and too illiberal.[67] Van den Bosch would have denied every one of these charges, but the fact remains that his deeds and the general concepts behind them were offensive to many persons of influence even though his forthright personality made him rather likeable. His influence with the King provided the channel through which his plans would have to be implemented.

Behind Van den Bosch's plans and ideas lay a crazy quilt of theories patched from a variety of sources of his day. He believed in the benefits of free trade, hoped to stimulate a liberal entrepreneurial spirit in the King's subjects, and accumulated a sizable personal fortune. Yet he also adhered to socialist concepts, believed that poverty and immorality could be eradicated through an improved environment, and viewed the accumulation of private capital as one of society's greatest disasters.[68] For Van den Bosch, the resolution of these conflicting theories was found in a completely pragmatic approach to specific problems. When confronted with a need for action, as in the case of eradicating the poverty-stricken elements from the Dutch cities after the Napoleonic period, he immediately had ideas and plans for accomplishing this specific end.[69] Theories at such times meant nothing to him. When engaged in such a project, he worked with intense vigor and fierce optimism, and was always ready with a counter proposal when a given approach ran dead.[70] This same adaptability, enthusiasm, and vigor characterized his approach to reforming the West Indies administration (1827-28), and to making Java a paying proposition after 1830.

Van den Bosch's every idea and action was accompanied by an effusive stream of general pronouncements and a veritable flood of specific orders and regulations. In every instance, the practical situation of the moment determined the specifics. Generally his mind dealt only in broad and ill-defined concepts which could be endlessly adjusted to practical matters in order to accomplish the overall objective which contained the nucleus of his general idea.[71] The fact that his actions did not conform to his theoretical pronouncements bothered him not one whit; in fact he frequently said that he did not desire uniformity of application or adherence to theory.[72] Both

---

[67] Ibid., pp. 47-8.
[68] Ibid., pp. 25, 33, 34. The 'advice' of 6 March 1829, Steijn Parvé, pp. 294-328, contains many examples of these diverse views.
[69] Westendorp Boerma, pp. 22-4.
[70] Ibid., p. 49.
[71] An example of this is found in his conflicting concepts about Javanese institutions, especially landholding. This is discussed in E.H. s' Jacob, *Landsdomein en adatrecht* (Utrecht, 1945), pp. 65-6. See also Reinsma, p. 20.
[72] It was completely in keeping with Van den Bosch's methods that he could write the

Van den Bosch's broad political-economic concepts and his specific orders and regulations were premised upon elaborate statistics gained from observation and consultation with others. Statistical evidence seemed to provide him with the final answer in all arguments; he had an inordinate love for charts, graphs, and numerical calculations. As the earliest writers opposed to his system, Merkus and Steijn Parvé, have shown, however, much of the information with which he worked was faulty. Later writers have had no difficulty in proving him wrong on various points, and many of his figures are so contradictory that he proves himself wrong. Wrong statistics bothered Van den Bosch greatly, but they did not materially alter his concepts. Lack of specific knowledge undoubtedly made the early years of the system more difficult. B.J. Elias, Director of Cultivations, writing in 1835, summarizes the sources of major difficulties as 'lack of knowledge and experience by European and native civil servants, unskillfulness of the planters, failure to observe carefully local circumstances in carrying through a general principle, and disinclination of the Javan for all that is new.'[73] It must be recognized that lack of good information was one of Van den Bosch's great problems and to the extent that this is true, there is validity in an interpretation which attributes some of the shortcomings of the system to human shortcomings and imperfections. In actual practice, however, Van den Bosch forged ahead with his enterprises with or without statistical support. Like some economic development projects in our time, he based his proposals and actions more on guess and hope than on solid expectations for success.[74]

By the time he undertook to make Java remunerative for the Netherlands, he had had both experience and success in the political-economic realm. The strong opposition encountered by his ideas for modifying the 'colonization' suggestions of Du Bus in 1829 must have made it abundantly evident that he would have to proceed with caution and tact in his plans for Java. He was willing, according to his initial statements, to employ free enterprise or government pressure to achieve his overall goal of obtaining products for sale on the European markets at a price that could compete with similar products from any other part of the world. On the condition that his system allowed room for free enterprise and did not revert to the arbitrary forced deliveries of the Company's days, he obtained the reluctant consent of the leading Dutch officials. His own pronouncements had been

---

acting Resident of Surabaya to arrange for sugar delivery in any way he saw fit, just so that 20,000 piculs of sugar would be obtained for thirteen guilders copper money per picul. Kabinet letter No. 489, dd. 12 August 1830, Archive Van den Bosch, Folio 222.

[73]   Letter dd. 18 April 1835, accompanying Cultivation Report of 1834, Archive Ministry of Colonies, Kabinet 4405.

[74]   Robert L. Heilbroner, *The great ascent* (New York, 1963), p. 117.

slanted heavily against Raffles and his landrent concepts. Yet it was precisely in these realms that the practical solution to his problem lay, as was soon to become evident after his arrival in Java. Free enterprise was both unwilling and unable to take hold, and landrent proved to be the most practicable device for encouraging crop production and ensuring delivery at minimal prices. The official statements which he drafted for circulation in the Netherlands, and even the Fundamental Regulations for the East Indies drawn up at his behest, were all couched in such vague and contradictory terms that they can be interpreted in several ways. Van den Bosch's belief in the preponderant position of the government as the stimulator of crop production did not become more evident until his return to the Netherlands and his appointment as Minister of Colonies in 1834. And never did he fully clarify the function of landrent – probably in part because he was never aware of a confusion on this point, since the vague phraseology which he used had come to have a very specific meaning for him.

My contention, therefore, is that the official pronouncements of Van den Bosch during his time as governor-general and commissioner-general in Java, 1830-1834, must be read as carefully weighted political pieces which were meant to influence a particular climate of opinion. They were not, except in a most general sense, meant to convey the practical details of how the Cultivation System worked. The preceding discussion on landrent is a case in point; similar arguments could be developed for the matters of corvée and of the application of force. Small wonder therefore that writers from the time of Merkus on were incensed by the discrepancies between official statements and practical application. Actually such discrepancy was not new to East Indian affairs; I would also contend that it existed long before and even after the time of Van den Bosch. What made the invective against the Cultivation System and its practical shortcomings so vituperative was that it threatened from the beginning certain fundamental liberal beliefs which constituted the prevailing climate of opinion in the Western world. After the middle of the nineteenth century, when the impact of more formal education for European civil servants for the East Indies began to be felt, there was a burgeoning bureaucratic mentality among the administrators in Java. Adherence to official statute and pronounce ment became more desirable; deviations from statutes and regulations were regarded as arbitrary arrangements. As the century progressed, the Cultivation System not only continued to be regarded as illiberal, but increasing attention was given to the brutalities and arbitrariness of its practical application. It clearly did not operate in accordance with a single specific set of instructions, nor did it seem to agree with its founder's statements. Actually Van den Bosch never wished it to do so; that was not his way or his chief concern.

CHAPTER II

The Introduction of Government Sugar Cultivation in Pasuruan, Java, 1830

This piece was written in 1963-64 and originally presented at the second meeting of the International Association of Historians of Asia (IAHA) in Hong Kong in 1964. It appeared in print in the *Journal of Oriental Studies*, Volume VII, No. 2 (July 1969).

One of the most consistently recurring topics in the materials that I had assembled on the Cultivation System was the cultivation of sugar cane. The introduction of sugar cultivation in Java had occurred long before 1830, but the new System now brought about changes in how this crop was handled from the planting to the milling to the export. The story is immensely complex, so in this essay I focused on one area of Java, the residency of Pasuruan, where sugar cultivation proved quite successful. While the research on this subject provided some new information and interpretations, this article raised more questions in my mind than I could easily resolve. I did not understand enough about the nature of landholding in Java, or about the impact of these cultivations on the Javanese village, or the way in which labor was aggregated and paid, and how the Javanese administrative elite (priyayi) related to other levels of Javanese society and to the System. All these matters are raised but not resolved in this article. These are matters that will recur in later papers in this volume.

In the years since this paper was written the development of the sugar industry in Java has become a focal point of historical and social science research. More than most other crops, sugar cane growing affected most directly the Javanese village since the cane was grown on fields that would otherwise be used by the village for its basic food needs, namely the growing of rice. Clifford Geertz has used sugar cultivation in Java as the central argument for the alteration of the Javanese village in his book *Agricultural Involution* (Berkeley, California 1963). Pramoedya Ananta Toer has focused strongly on the abuses visited upon Javanese society by the sugar industry in his historical novels, especially in his book *Anak Semua Bangsa* (Jakarta 1981). From the viewpoint of the Cultivation System and especially Pasuruan, however, the work of R.E. Elson, *Javanese Peasants and the Colonial Sugar Industry; Impact and Change in an East Java*

Residency, 1830-1940 (Singapore 1984) is by far the best contribution. The sugar industry in Java will long come to occupy the attention of historians and social scientists.

There is a marked tendency in the historical literature on the Cultivation (Culture) System in Java to attribute a greater conceptual and operational unity to the System than it deserves. Partly this is explainable by the need to generalize and overlook local variations. But this does not account for the widespread assumption that the System was a uniform operation by design, and that divergences from the announced plan of the founder Johannes van den Bosch were either detractions from his sincerity and honesty if they occurred during his years in Java (1830-1833), or reflections upon the independence and courage of his successors if they occurred thereafter. It is far more likely that this tendency reflects a readiness to accept at face value the pronouncements which Van den Bosch made for home consumption which pictured his achievements in Java as guided by and through a rationally ordered plan of government.[1] No doubt Van den Bosch felt that the image of a successfully operating system would reflect favorably upon his abilities, and he was not beyond exaggerating his accomplishments.[2] The accepted practice of his day was to pattern theories of colonial control upon a rationality and homogeneity of concept which was totally divorced from the ability to apply them; he was, therefore, only doing what was expected when he 'systematized' his efforts in Java. Quite properly does Clive Day lament that the System has 'so often been judged by the professions of its founder rather than by its actual workings.'[3]

An argument could be made for regarding the external operations of the System, i.e., the shipping, auctioning, and accounting to and in Europe, as regulated, but it is quite unrealistic to expect to find a uniformly ordered and neatly regulated plan with regard to the cultivations and processing in Java. These 'internal' aspects of the System are as much or even more a part of Javanese history than they are of Dutch colonial history, for they were carried out by the Javanese and affected their patterns of development and change. Here is to be found an element in writing endogenous Javanese history. This history cannot yet be written for all of Java, for local diversities and institutional differences must be carefully examined. This paper,

---

1   Van den Bosch's account of his work in Java, *Mijne verrigtingen in Indië* (Amsterdam, 1864) which he wrote for his successor J.C. Baud in 1834, leaves the reader with the impression that a single body of rules and regulations applied throughout Java.
2   Van den Bosch had made rather far-reaching promises to King William I on what he would accomplish in Java. The best account of his actions and motives at this time is in J.J. Westendorp Boerma, *Een geestdriftig Nederlander; Johannes van den Bosch* (Amsterdam, 1950), Cf. pp. 65-81.
3   Clive Day, *The policy and administration of the Dutch in Java* (New York, 1904), p. 250.

therefore, considers only one small corner of Java and one particular aspect of the diverse patterns of cultivation.

A careful reading of the correspondence and orders of Governor General Van den Bosch in Java indicates that he had no expectation of a uniform method of cultivation or single system of regulation to apply throughout the island.[4] His intent, as clearly expressed on numerous occasions, was that each Resident should make whatever arrangements seemed necessary with Javanese notables and village leaders to bring about the cultivation of crops at competitive prices. Interestingly enough, the Residents most highly lauded by Van den Bosch – men such as B.J. Elias in Tjirebon and J.F.W. van Nes in Pasuruan – frequently implemented the cultivations in their districts in ways that diverged widely from the announced plans of the Governor General. Yet their chances for advancement were not harmed but rather aided by this. Nor did their independent actions deter Van den Bosch from expounding upon the conformity and success of *his* accomplishments. Furnivall attributes an 'executive bias' to both Van den Bosch and his successor J.C. Baud, but praises their work in developing the administrative effectiveness of the Dutch colonial policy.[5] This seems a somewhat misleading characterization unless this is to be understood in the case of Van den Bosch as autocratic arbitrariness with wide-ranging flexibility. Baud was indeed more bureaucratic and sought to establish more clearly understandable managerial relationships, but even here administrative effectiveness in the normal sense of the phrase seems misplaced. No one will deny that the colonial administration in Java received much of its form in the nineteenth century, but much of this occurred after the middle of the century. During the 1830s and 1840s Java was governed by placing major reliance in personal autocracy without reference to clear-cut legal forms, administrative uniformity, and human equality as was already known and rather widely accepted in the Netherlands of this time.[6] To imagine an effective administration at work in Java at this time can only produce a warped picture of events.

One noticeable variation from the expressed intentions of the founder of the Cultivation System was the fashion in which sugar cane cultivation was introduced and expanded in Pasuruan Residency.[7] Mention should be made before all else of the fact that the soil and the climate of Pasuruan is

---

[4]   R. Van Niel, 'The function of landrent under the Cultivation System in Java,' *Journal of Asian Studies* 23:357-82 (1964).

[5]   J.S. Furnivall, *Netherland India; A study of plural economy* (Cambridge, 1944), p. 124.

[6]   J.H.A. Logemann, *Over Indië's staatsorde voor 1854* (Amsterdam, 1934), p. 3.

[7]   The Residency Pasuruan consisted of the Regencies Pasuruan, Bangil, and Malang. Sugar cane cultivation was introduced in the two former Regencies, while Malang became a coffee growing area. The regulation of the coffee production in Malang has no relationship to the sugar cane cultivation in the other areas.

unusually favorable for the growing of sugar cane. Consequently the crop was destined to wax. However, the patterns of control upon which this success was built and the development of the internal arrangements upon which this cultivation was based are in large part the work of two very energetic Residents. H.I. Domis had been Resident in Pasuruan since 1827; he had taken some of the initial steps in the expansion of the sugar cultivation at the time of Commissioner General Du Bus and continued this with such success for Van den Bosch that he was transferred to the neighboring Residency of Surabaya in 1831 to improve the sugar cultivation there. The advice of Domis was especially prized by Van den Bosch, and his published writings about Java show a keen and accurate insight into the life and conditions of the areas he knew well.[8] In 1831, J.F.W. van Nes was appointed Resident in Pasuruan. He had been in Java for a decade and had most recently held the post of Resident at the Court at Jogjakarta since 1828. His letters and reports show him to be strong-willed, self-righteous, hard-working, and staunchly independent.[9] By his own admission he was a novice on sugar cane cultivation when he came to Pasuruan, but he set to work with unusual determination to expand the area under cultivation and to regulate the growing and harvesting of the crop. He was later to be charged with favoring the European and Chinese sugar manufacturers over the Javanese planters – a charge he consistently denied – so that his methods have been subject to question, but there is no question about the increase in sugar production while he was Resident. He remained in Pasuruan until 1839; subsequently he moved to higher government posts and ended his career as a member of the Council of the Indies. Van den Bosch had proposed him for the governor-generalship upon the retirement of Baud (1834-35), but he was passed over because Baud considered his marital infidelity sufficient grounds to make him unsuitable for this high post.[10]

Sugar cane cultivation was brought within the purview of the Cultivation System by the resolution of the governor-general of August 13, 1830.[11] For some parts of Java this meant introducing a new crop, but for Pasuruan it meant expanding and readjusting a known crop. Sugar had for

---

[8]   I have found several letters and reports written by Domis in the Van den Bosch Archive. His books *Reis over het eiland Java* and *De residentie Passoeroeang op het eiland Java* both appeared in 1829; the latter was reprinted in 1836. His work in Surabaya did not please Baud, viz. letter 25 December 1834 to Van den Bosch in J.J. Westendorp Boerma, *Briefwisseling tussen J. van den Bosch en J.C. Baud* (Utrecht, 1956), II, p. 147.

[9]   The papers of J.F.W. van Nes are to be found in the manuscript collection of the Koninklijk Instituut voor Taal-, Land- en Volkenkunde in Leiden. Henceforth KITLV.

[10]   Westendorp Boerma, *Briefwisseling*, II, p. 134.

[11]   S. van Deventer, *Bijdragen tot de kennis van het landelijk stelsel op Java* (Zalt-Bommel, 1866), II, pp. 164-165.

many years been grown by Javanese planters in Pasuruan and sold to Chinese contractors for distribution.[12] Domis, describing the situation before 1830, indicates that the Javanese planters received large profits from these plantings.[13] In the Bangil district he reports of payments to the planters averaging almost 11 guilders per picul of sugar produced from the cane in their fields, or between 600 and 700 guilders for the cane on a large *bouw* of land.[14] If one adds to this cost of unprocessed cane the charges of the middlemen and the costs of processing and transportation, it is readily understandable that Java sugar was not at that time competitive with the West Indian product. The changes brought about after 1830 were to alter things so that Java sugar could compete on the world markets. Prices such as noted above are not heard of again; in fact, the price of 11 guilders per picul comes to approximate the price the government pays the sugar manufacturer for the processed picul of sugar, not the price paid for the cane needed to produce that amount of sugar. Payments per *bouw* drop to less than half of the above figures, but probably become more certain. Lastly, the Chinese contractors and other middlemen are eliminated as the government becomes the coordinating agent in the cultivation and processing and marketing. The implementation of new arrangements after 1830 made Pasuruan one of the most successful sugar producing areas of Java.

Organization of cane cultivation under government regulation after 1830 focused upon contractual arrangements. Contracts were closed at two levels for two quite separate aspects of sugar production. One level of contracting was between the local administration and the villages and had as its purpose arranging for the planting of sugar cane on sections of the villages' lands, for the tending of the cane, and, initially, for the transportation of the cane to the factories. The other level of contracting was between the local administration as represented by the Dutch officials and the sugar mill operator (manufacturer) who, with government loans, was to build a mill, process the cane, and deliver sugar at a stipulated price to the government. This paper will examine only the first contracting level. The contracts with the villages were arranged through the native administration with promptings by the European administrators. In a district such as Pasuruan it was first necessary to gain the support of the head of the indigenous social structure, the Regent, whose power had scarcely diminished since the landrent system had been introduced in 1813.[15] In Pasuruan the Regents had

---

[12]   H.I. Domis, *De residentie Passoeroeang op het eiland Java* ('s-Gravenhage, 1836), p. 62.
[13]   Ibid., p. 56.
[14]   The *bouw* in Pasuruan varied from 1,225 to 1,250 square rods while in most other parts of Java the *bouw* was 500 square rods. The rod used was the Rhineland rod of approximately 16.5 feet.
[15]   Domis to Van den Bosch, Confidential letter, dd. 23 February 1831, Van den Bosch

in the past parceled out lands at will to their retainers, and had taken them back again just as arbitrarily. This did not ordinarily affect the man on the soil since the person for whom he worked (*lurah*) did nothing to change the land dispositions within the village. The village, thus, continued to operate at one level while the Regent with his many retainers exercised rights at another level. The landrent system had on paper removed the Regents from their rights to the soil since the government now claimed sovereignty over the land. In the then current concepts this meant that the government became owner of all the land in Java and that the Javanese rented the land for which he paid landrent. The Regent was changed from a landed aristocrat to a salaried official. Domis indicates that prior to the introduction of the landrent system the Regent of Pasuruan had more than 2,400 *jonk* (a *jonk* is approximately 2,500 square rods) of rice fields at his disposal, part of which he gave to various retainers for their use, and an income of well over 100,000 Spanish dollars per annum.[16] The rice fields obviously came with people on them to do the work. It would not be easy to transform such rights into monetary equivalents; it need not surprise us to learn that in Pasuruan the rights of the Regents were changed more in theory than in practice. There were fewer grants of land to retainers by the Regent after 1813, but the Regents continued to draw goods and services from villages without payment, granting in return release from corvée or paying the landrent to the government for the village. Domis could write in 1831 that, although matters were gradually changing, 'the village continued to feel itself entirely dependent upon the Regent.'[17] Under these circumstances it is inconceivable that the sugar cane contracts were freely entered into by the villages, a conclusion completely in keeping with the comments of P. Merkus, member of the Council of the Indies and most principled opponent of Van den Bosch's methods.[18] The Dutch government strengthened the position and prestige of the supra-village sphere of Javanese society in order to assure their assistance in the introduction of the new cultivations, but if this did not achieve the desired results it did not hesitate to use harsher methods. Van Nes indicates in his General Report for 1832 that he had to replace many native civil servants for failure to carry out orders.[19] New power carried the implication of new service for an autocratic government.

The resolution of August 13, 1830, mentioned above, already dispensed

---

Archive, State Archives, The Hague, Folio 217.
[16]   Ibid, appendices I and II.
[17]   Ibid.
[18]   Note of Mr. P. Merkus, dd. 15 February 1831, Van Deventer, *Bijdragen*, II, p. 221.
[19]   Residency Pasuruan, General Annual Report 1832, Third Section, Part B, sub c., KITLV, MS No. 104.

with the limit on using only one-fifth of the villages' arable land for the government cultivations in Pasuruan; the area used for the cultivation of exportable market crops was expanded to one-third of the available land. In the cane growing areas of Pasuruan the one-third portion became the standard calculation for a village's participation in the cultivation. Many villages devoted less of their land to cane cultivation, but on occasion this limit was also exceeded.[20] The contracts provided that the village would receive payment for the cane based upon assessments made while the cane was standing in the field just prior to the harvest. This method of assessment had been used in Pasuruan prior to 1830 and was now continued as a practice that was acceptable to the peasants. The cane was classified into first, second, or third variety based upon the estimation of its sugar content. A payment of 160, 120, and 80 guilders per *bouw* was made to the village for the three varieties respectively. This payment was premised on the assumption that 40, 30, and 20 piculs of sugar would be produced from the respective varieties of cane; this would amount to the village receiving four guilders for a picul of processed sugar if the manufacturer produced exactly the calculated amount.[21] In comparison with other areas of Java this was a higher than average payment.[22] The work of classifying the fields was done by the lowest Dutch official, the Controleur, in the presence of two district heads and the *petingies* and elders of the villages concerned. Van Nes indicates that the Controleurs had orders to conduct their task without connivance or personal considerations, and constantly to classify to the planter's advantage.[23] Yet, he also admits that no one, regardless of experience, can accurately determine the amount of sugar which can be produced from cane by viewing it in the field.[24] He is writing in this vein at a time (1835) when the method of assessment in Pasuruan was being subjected to increasing criticism as the first quality fields were frequently yielding more than the estimated 40 piculs. Although the payment per *bouw* had been raised to 200 guilders in 1834, the price paid to the village when calculated against the piculs of processed sugar obtained from the cane was falling below four guilders, and on occasion below three and one-half.

[20] E. de Vries, *Landbouw en welvaart in het regentschap Pasoeroean; Bijdrage tot de kennis van de sociale economie van Java* (Wageningen, 1931), p. 99.

[21] These calculations for the original government contracts are clearly set forth in a letter from Van Nes to Baud, No. 337, dd. 28 August 1835, KITLV, MS No. 92a.

[22] Van Deventer, *Bijdragen*, II, p. 168, indicates that in Tjirebon the price paid per government *bouw* (500 square rods) of the first quality cane was 70 guilders for an estimated yield of 20 piculs. This amounted to 3.50 guilders per picul which was a more widely used payment in Java. According to Van den Bosch, *Mijne verrigtingen*, p. 140, payments for cane needed to make a picul of sugar are set at 3.60 guilders. This latter figure includes cutting and transportation which were no longer included in the Pasuruan price after 1834.

[23] Letter No. 337, dd. 28 August 1835.

[24] Ibid.

This increased sugar production was mainly attributable to improved methods of milling and production. The original assessment scale was accurate enough in 1831 and 1832 when the more primitive methods of processing were still used.[25] Later efforts to change the method of payment in Pasuruan to a fixed sum per picul of processed sugar were not successful.[26] The equivocation accompanying these efforts, using arguments that more money would encourage immorality among the Javanese and that the existing assessment system was understood and accepted without wish for change by the Javanese in Pasuruan,[27] is indicative of the type of European rationalization which was becoming more frequent as a sense of greed for gain by individual administrators overwhelmed any sense of principle that might have existed. Yet, it cannot be denied that the planters in Pasuruan seemed quite satisfied, even enthusiastic according to some reports, about their improved payments and work arrangements after 1834.[28] Also it cannot be denied that much of the improved sugar production was due to the manufacturer and better equipment, not to the native planter. Westernized techniques were surging ahead of Oriental labor, and the material profits were to flow increasingly to the Western economic sector.

Initially the contracts with the villages in Pasuruan included the harvesting and transportation of the cane to the mill in the assessed price. But in 1834 this was changed. Subsequent contracts provided only for the land, the planting, and the tending. The harvesting and transportation, as well as the work in the mill and the delivery of firewood, soon came to be regulated by supplementary agreements between the manufacturer and the villages. In Pasuruan the government was involved in such arrangements only indirectly. The manufacturer might give money advances to the village for it to purchase beasts of burden for use in transportation, or a manufacturer might have carts built for a transportation pool. The government protected the Javanese peasant by guaranteeing a minimum wage: fifteen cents per day for a man, thirty cents per day for a drawn cart – not considered inadequate payment at the time. Yet the government, through its hold over the Regents and lesser heads assured the manufacturer an atmosphere conducive to allowing such arrangements to be made. In last analysis the government was under contractual obligation to the manufacturer to provide him with raw materials and labor. Van Nes indicates that the manufacturers feared slow-downs or work stoppages incited by the native administration if the government support were discontinued, but at the same time they preferred to work without direct

---

[25] Ibid.
[26] De Vries, *Landbouw en welvaart*, p. 89.
[27] Letter No. 337, dd. 28 August 1835.
[28] De Vries, *Landbouw en welvaart*, p. 102.

intervention by the government if possible, for any work demanded of the Javanese by the administration was always regarded as corvée and done unwillingly.[29] There was never a misunderstanding on anyone's part that the government stood behind the enforcement of agreements.

It would be wrong, I feel, to assume that pressures applied through the traditional native elite were the only form in which the government achieved its aim of having sugar cane grown: the incentive supplied by money was also of primary importance. Domis, for instance, is very positive in 1830 that the expansion of sugar cane growing is possible 'so long as the price is good, but with lower prices the Javanese will cease to cultivate freely.'[30] The lowering of prices described above would seem to contradict this statement, but it is quite likely that the elimination of the middlemen after 1830 allowed as much or possibly even more money to reach the villages after that date than had been the case with nominally higher prices earlier. A further responsiveness to monetary incentives is cited by Van Nes a few years later when he writes that the people came to work willingly and would not countenance outsiders to join in the work when a payment of 1.5 cents per bundle of twenty-five cane sticks was set for the harvesting.[31] Baud reports in 1835 that when payments for sugar cane for the first quality were raised to 200 guilders per *bouw*, conditions in Pasuruan improved as the population strove to produce the best type of cane.[32] Yet it would be unwise to accept these unanimous professions of sensitivity to monetary incentive without raising the question of who within Javanese society was the most sensitized and stimulated. I suspect that the village heads and the supra-village groups were most concerned, but this is a problem I cannot resolve on the basis of the evidence available to me.

In Pasuruan, more than in many other parts of the north Java littoral, the village in the early nineteenth century was still in transition from a community of mutual social relationships to one based on a territorial concept with designated and fixed land arrangements.[33] Relationships were highly personal, and use of the land was neither clearly defined nor fixed in individual holdings. De Vries's major contention that the impact of the Cultivation System in Pasuruan destroyed the independent class of farmers by forcing communal landholding upon them[34] presumes a more modern socio-economic development than is warranted by the facts. De Vries bases

---

[29]   Letter No. 337, dd. 28 August 1835.
[30]   Letter from Domis to Van den Bosch, Very Confidential, La A, dd. 4 June 1830, Van den Bosch Archive, Folio 216.
[31]   Letter No. 337, dd. 28 August 1835.
[32]   Van Deventer, *Bijdragen*, II, p. 666.
[33]   De Vries, *Landbouw en welvaart*, p. 34.
[34]   Ibid., pp. 96-8.

this assumption upon statements made in the Final Report of the Investigation of Native Rights to the Soil[35] made after 1867, and on portions of the Fokkens Report made after 1888 on the problem of obligatory services.[36] A careful reading of this evidence along with statements made by De Vries in other places[37] fails to support the contention that the pressures of the Cultivation System forced new landholding arrangements on the villages in Pasuruan. This charge against the Cultivation System is one that is frequently made, but it is hardly borne out by the evidence either in Pasuruan or elsewhere in Java. It is premised upon reading into the villages of Pasuruan and elsewhere in 1830 the characteristics of individualized Oriental ownership which one presumed to find there later in the century. I would suggest that the villages of Pasuruan in 1830 were just beginning to become stabilized territorial units in accordance with the desires of the landrent system, that they had until recently been highly mobile, family-like units, that they were still controlled by the whim and order of the Regent in their external relationships, and that, as a result of all this, their entire internal household arrangements were characterized by a flexibility under varying pressures rather than a distinctly formulated plan of ownership or holding of land.

Before the Cultivation System was ever introduced, the villages of Pasuruan fluctuated landholding arrangements as conditions warranted. According to Domis, the original divisions of land within the villages were unequal,[38] though De Vries says that the landmeasure of the *bouw* was

---

[35] W.B. Bergsma, *Eindresumé van het bij Goeevernements besluit van 10 Juni 1867 No. 2 bevolen onderzoek naar de rechten van den Inlander op den grond op Java en Madoera*, 3 vols. (Batavia, 1876-1896).

[36] F. Fokkens, *Eindresumé van het bij besluit van den Gouv.-Generaal van Ned.-Indië van 24 Juli 1888 No. 8 bevolen onderzoek naar de verplichte diensten der Inlandsche bevolking op Java en Madoera (Gouvernementslanden)*, 3 vols. (Batavia, 1901-1903).

[37] Citing the investigation of 1867, II, p. 247, De Vries, p. 103, attempts to indicate support for the view that individual possessions were destroyed. Actually, however, many of the examples used here predate the Cultivation System and would tend to support my view made below. This investigation does claim, however, II, p. 245, that the people would gladly return to the old system, i.e., individual possession. I am rather skeptical of this. I incline to the opinion that the Javanese would answer whatever was expected of him, and that consequently the presumed answer tells more about the predispositions of the interviewer than of the attitude of the Javanese.
The Fokkens Report would, according to De Vries, p. 98, have us believe that the control of enclaves of land within the territories of villages by persons outside the village resulted from the sugar cultivation. Yet De Vries himself indicates, pp. 34-5, that the act of 1899 which put an end to these enclaves had a revolutionary effect upon the structure of the village, while Domis, writing in 1831, gives clear indication that the villages controlled enclaves of land in scattered areas long before 1830.

[38] Domis to Van den Bosch, Confidential letter, dd. 23 February 1831, Van den Bosch Archive, Folio 217. This lengthy and interesting letter was written in response to a request by Van den Bosch for information about the socio-economic structure of native life in Pasuruan. Domis used materials from the Residency Archive in Pasuruan in formulating his description

originally an individual cultivator's share and that Van Nes's policies resulted in an individually smaller share in the landholding as reflected by the shift to government *bouws* of 500 square rods in 1839.[39] His argument here is not supported by verifiable evidence. More to the point is Domis' observation in 1831 that:

> 'The inequity in land still exists although the increasing population in some places has caused the farmers to resort to setting aside several *bouws* for the newcomers. Each relinquishes a proportionate share of his possession which is then divided equally among the newcomers'.[40]

Under these circumstances Van Nes's statement that the farmers of a particular village often constitute a family unit and use their plow animals collectively to plow fields which are used for the benefit of the community,[41] and Domis' observation that the villagers made no claim to land ownership, only to the continued use of the land, despite his efforts to encourage ownership arrangements, would indicate that individual ownership patterns were not established in the villages of Pasuruan in the early 1830s.[42] Furthermore, it must be noted that the village's landholdings were frequently reapportioned because of the work arrangements for higher authority (corvée). An individual's obligation to perform corvée was based on the extent of his landholdings, but in Pasuruan it was not uncommon for a person's willingness to obligate himself to corvée to determine the amount and the quality of the land which he would hold for a given year. Thus the farmers frequently were divided into three classes based upon the extent to which they wished to be subject to call – the more work, the more land. These arrangements frequently led to an annual redistribution of the village's lands.[43] Moreover, it can be accepted that the landholders did not always work their own land, but had this done for them under a family arrangement in which they were *pater familias* with rights to land and produce; often, but not always, the same land.[44] The landrent system in Java after 1813 tended to encourage the formalization of landholding for taxation purposes, and the select portion of the villagers who made up the upper social stratum gained control of fixed portions of land. In fact, it can be said that the landrent system made the village head in many districts the tenant-in-chief who adjusted the rent levy among his more important villagers. In

for the period prior to his own arrival in the district.

[39] De Vries, *Landbouw en welvaart*, pp. 94-5.

[40] Letter dd. 23 February 1831.

[41] Van Nes to the Director of Cultivations, Confidential letter, No. 1008, dd. 1 November 1833, KITLV, MS No. 92a.

[42] Letter dd. 23 February 1831.

[43] Ibid.

[44] Ibid.

Pasuruan this only partially occurred since the Regent retained immense power. This development, as well as later ones, is neatly summarized by Baud's statement of 1829 that what had been *adat* a couple of decades before had ceased to be *adat* for the villager.[45]

The Cultivation System certainly produced new pressures upon the villages of Pasuruan, but the villages' response to these pressures was a flexible adjustment just as responses to superior force and authority had traditionally always been made. The frequently stated maxim of all European officers that there must be no interference in the internal land arrangements of the village was undoubtedly closely adhered to, but did not prevent the village from making adjustments on its own initiative, or at the 'suggestion' of higher authority.[46] As the statistical report of Pasuruan for 1820 puts it, the cultivator keeps his land as long as there is no further division or partial gift.[47] As the sugar cane was grown in a single tract of village land in Pasuruan, not every farmer's plot was used, but all the villagers worked the sugar lands. In Pasuruan this method proved very successful.[48] Obviously the machinery for adjustment was always present. A variety of internal dispositions could be provided by the village depending in large part upon what was expected by higher authority and by the imposed pressures. It is not correct, however, I would say, to presume that the Cultivation System destroyed the natural configurations of the village in Pasuruan, or resulted in a social leveling through the encouragement of a pattern of communal landholding.[49] The village was far too persistent and too enduring throughout Javanese history to be so easily dislocated; the village, with rare exceptions, remains intact and integrated. New pressures beset it and would continue to do so, but the village simply did not shatter brittlely under the pressures of any system: Western inspired or not, it adjusted.

The expansion of cane cultivation in Pasuruan after 1830 was sizable.

---

[45]   Van Deventer, *Bijdragen*, II, p. 199n.

[46]   Letter from Van Nes, No. 1008, dd. 1 November 1833.

[47]   *Statistiek van Pasoeroean van 1820*, quoted in De Vries, p. 62. It is interesting to note that when De Vries, p. 97, attempts to show from this same source that the fields and villagers were subject to a permanent threefold division, he confuses the shifting arrangements for corvée, mentioned above, with a permanent socio-economic stratification. This latter was more true for other parts of Java such as Tjirebon.

[48]   Letter from Van Nes, No. 1008, dd. 1 November 1833; Van Nes points to the obvious productive advantages of this method, but it should be understood that this single tract arrangement was not applied in all parts of Java.

[49]   See De Vries, p. 97. Obviously if one assumes, as has frequently been done, that individual rights to land were clearly established in Java before the Cultivation System or even before the Landrent System was introduced, then the notice of a decline from paradise follows naturally. I do not find such an earlier condition supported by the evidence – at least not for Pasuruan.

Domis indicates that in 1830 there were 1,089 large *bouw* planted in cane, 466 of which had been added that year.[50] By 1833 the area under cultivation had, according to Baud, risen to about 2,500 *bouw*.[51] This estimate corresponds closely to the sugar cane area of 2,437 large *bouw* for Pasuruan listed in the first Cultivation Report of 1834.[52] The area under cane remains practically constant for the next decade and one half according to the Cultivation Reports. By 1851 the total area in Pasuruan under cane had risen to only 2,880 large *bouw* of which 80 *bouw* were privately owned (since 1842) and therefore not within the normal operation of the System.[53] The number of families attached to cane cultivation remained constant at about 23,000 until 1848 when it began a gradual decline over the next few years to about 20,000. The actual production of refined sugar obtained from Pasuruan rose from 107,000 piculs in 1834, to 204,000 piculs in 1839, to 345,000 piculs in 1850.[54]

Not surprisingly, the rapid growth in cane cultivation during the 1830s produced tensions. Merkus was already 'tremulous about the means whereby this expansion was obtained', in December 1831.[55] However, the Regents assured the Resident at that time 'that the planting of sugar cane is in no sense burdensome to the people [for they] obtain advantages from this cultivation which are denied them in the usual planting of rice.'[56] By whatever means this statement was obtained, it fit precisely into the government's desire for expansion of the cultivation, so this bent was followed. If the Regents' optimism had some basis in 1831, it had lost its validity by 1833 for the burdens had come to outweigh the advantages. In July and August 1833 thousands of persons involved in cane planting joined in open protest against the burdensome nature of the cultivation.[57]

The Pasuruan protest was quickly dealt with by Resident Van Nes. After hearing the grievances and promising redress, he obtained the disbandment of the protestors. The leaders were soon thereafter arrested and exiled to other parts of Java. As a result of the investigation launched by Van Nes the prices paid to the planter were raised from 160 to 200 guilders per *bouw* of first quality cane. Moreover, the cutting and transportation of the cane was

---

[50]   Domis to Van den Bosch, Letter No. 32, dd. 17 January 1831, KITLV, MS No. 92a.

[51]   Van Deventer, *Bijdragen*, II, p. 665. The figure given in the chart on p. 570 of Van Deventer is obviously incorrect.

[52]   Cultivation Report 1834, Archive Ministry of Colonies, State Archives, The Hague, Exhibit dd. October 15, 1835, Kabinet secret, No. M1.

[53]   Cultivation Report 1851, Archive Ministry of Colonies, Exhibit 4/15-53, No. 12.

[54]   Cultivation Report 1834; Cultivation Report 1839, Exhibit 4275, 8 November 1841, No. 480 Secret; Cultivation Report 1850, Exhibit 61/8-1852, No. 35.

[55]   Van Deventer, *Bijdragen*, II, p. 372.

[56]   Ibid., pp. 371-2.

[57]   This protest movement is described in *Blik op het bestuur van Nederlandsch-Indië onder den Gouverneur-Generaal Js. van den Bosch* (Kampen, 1835), pp. 100-103, and Van Deventer, *Bijdragen*, II, pp. 582-591.

now compensated for separately. These changes amounted to a sizable monetary adjustment in the planter's favor. As noted above, the evidence indicates that Pasuruan was restful and productive during the ensuing years. Such a splendid testimonial for monetary incentives in Pasuruan raises interesting speculations, also noted above, which we cannot unravel on the basis of existing evidence. What is possible is an investigation into some of the factors that fashioned the form which this movement took.

Unlike many other areas in Java and unlike many other forms of cultivation, the sugar cultivation work in Pasuruan was not accompanied by a remission of corvée for the worker and planter.[58] Corvée usually took the form of road building and maintenance, and bridge construction; it was always work done without pay for supra-village authority and was quite separate from village services. Remission of corvée wherever granted by the government was a valuable concession and may be a partial explanation of the lower prices paid for cane in areas where this was granted. But in Pasuruan the extra work created by the introduction and expansion of cane cultivation came on top of the existing corvée. As cane cultivation increased, the need for roads and bridges to move the cane to the factories and the sugar to the warehouses also grew. The increased burdens of cane cultivation after 1830 were thus accompanied by increased needs for corvée.

After 1830 the Regents and other supra-village heads in Pasuruan continued to demand and to receive personal services and free delivery of products from villagers as of old. In return for these unpaid goods and services the Regents authorized the remission of corvée for some people and some entire villages.[59] This remission was extended to family members and relatives of the individuals accorded the original concession, and was passed on from generation to generation. The result of this practice over the years was the creation of sizable body of persons exempted from corvée in Pasuruan. This meant that the heavier burdens associated with the cane cultivation after 1830 fell more heavily upon the remaining people. As early as 1832 Van Nes recognized a non-articulated reluctance to cultivate cane and attributed this to the burdens imposed on the people by services to the Regents.[60] This is probably an oversimplification for many forces in Javanese life would encourage passivism in the face of promptings to work

---

[58] Letter No. 337, dd. 28 August 1835.
[59] Letter from Domis, dd. 23 February 1831.
[60] Residency Pasuruan, General Annual Report 1832, First Section, Part A. KITLV, MS No. 104. It is with regard to this question that De Vries, p. 81, deprecates Van Nes's manner of inquiry and accuses him of stubbornly demanding the answer he desired. It is probably true, as I have indicated, that in asking questions of the Javanese one could get the answer one wished, but in this instance the continued pressures upon the villages by the services and deliveries for the Regents was also noted and described in detail by Domis, letter dd. 23 February 1831.

from higher authority. However that may be, the increased burden would probably be settled upon those persons already involved in most of the work activities and would allow them less time and energy for the performance of their previously designated tasks. In this wise the pressures of the new system would be felt within Javanese society and would create pressures for change.

On July 26, 1833, Resident Van Nes issued a decree reducing the number of exemptions from corvée in the Residency Pasuruan.[61] The intent of this decree was to reduce (not eliminate) privilege and to equalize the work burdens intendent upon the expanded sugar cane cultivation. The entire supra-village stratum and the village heads and leaders were exempted from the corvée obligation by this decree, but there is no doubt that the general purpose was to bring into the corvée obligation many persons previously exempted. De Vries feels that Van Nes fought the Heads and destroyed their social privilege by choosing the side of the *hoi polloi*.[62] Unquestionably the privileges of the Pasuruan elite were challenged, but they were far from being destroyed even under the fairly rigorous administration of Van Nes. Yet the challenge had been made and could not pass unnoticed. Another view of this decree is presented by Van Soest who felt that this specific limitation of privilege meant 'the virtual destruction of the class of substantial village members'.[63] While in theory the decree must have meant a more equitable distribution of the corvée within the village, the fact remains that the regulation and assignment of the corvée services remained with the village leaders. More appropriate seems to be the contemporaneous view of Vitalis that the system of community labor preserved the social distinctions of the village.[64] The latter is certainly what happened; the decree produced no immediate social change in Pasuruan and it is questionable if it had much to do with the gradual erosion of the authority of the Javanese elite. Such erosion could occur only under a far more effective administrative system than the Dutch had in Java in the first half of the century. What is perhaps most interesting about this decree when viewed within the total context of the Cultivation System is its divergence from the general trend of unequivocal support of the traditional elite.

Returning now to the unrest among the sugar cane cultivators in July and August 1833, it seems rather significant that the demonstrations in Pasuruan began just a week after the decree concerning corvée was issued. It

---

[61] KITLV, MS No. 92a; an abridged version of this decree is printed as Appendix F of *Blik op het bestuur*, pp. 203-4.
[62] De Vries, *Landbouw en welvaart*, pp. 80-1.
[63] G.H. van Soest, *Geschiedenis van het Kultuurstelsel* (Rotterdam, 1869), II, p. 127.
[64] L. Vitalis, *Opmerking omtrent den loop der suiker-industrie in den Ned. O.I. Archipel* ('s-Gravenhage, 1862), pp. 21-2.

is not inconceivable, therefore, that members of the supra-village sphere had a hand in organizing the latent discontent among the villagers when their own privileges were challenged. From what we know of Indonesian institutions in Java in the 1830s it would be virtually impossible for a protest movement to be organized and to proceed in orderly fashion to the seat of administration without leadership emanating from higher authority. This was no holistic peasant uprising endemic in Southeast Asian peasant society, but an organized and orderly protest directed against specific grievances. The government's analysis of the movement as being led and inspired by a few incendiaries from the upper levels of society was probably rather near the truth though the nature of the language used leaves a bad aftertaste today. The government's response of heavy-handed punishment for a few of the leaders accompanied by concessions to the planters in the form of increased payments and improved work arrangements seems to have effectively resolved the matter. This was obviously not the ideal liberal approach to these matters as indicated by both Van Deventer's and De Vries's deprecation of government statements and actions.[65] Baud's suspicion that dispossessed middlemen from the reorganized coffee growing areas of Pasuruan were seeking revenge by stirring up trouble in the sugar growing areas is not supported by any evidence I have been able to find.[66]

It remains only to add a few subsequent details about the sugar cultivations in Pasuruan. The supra-village sphere of the society came increasingly after 1833 to profit from the percentage payments on the production of the government cultivations. These payments must have gone far to balance any loss of privilege which the higher orders may have suffered under Van Nes's decree. But there is evidence that even this loss, while probably never great, was not to be permanent. De Vries has indicated that there was a high proportion of farmers in Pasuruan in the 1830s, and a marked decrease in both absolute and proportionate numbers after 1839.[67] This fact does not, it occurs to me, prove his point of a rural proletarianization,[68] but instead indicates the effective implementation of Van Nes's decree during the 1830s in keeping the privileges of the higher orders in check, and a reaffirmation after Van Nes's departure from Pasuruan of special privileges which would remove farmers from the work rolls and provide more exemptions from the work associated with the sugar cultivation. Much research would need to be done before this viewpoint could be adequately substantiated, but it is interesting to note that Vitalis

---

[65] De Vries, *Landbouw en welvaart*, p. 82; Van Deventer, *Bijdragen*, II, pp. 583-4.
[66] Letter from Baud to Van den Bosch, dd. 8 August 1833, Westendorp Boerma, *Briefwisseling*, II, pp. 122-3.
[67] De Vries, *Landbouw en welvaart*, pp. 96-9.
[68] Ibid., pp. 98-9.

speaks of a definite change in the System over all Java after 1836.[69] This change was characterized by increased formalization and routinization of the administrative tasks placed upon the European administration, and by an increased lust for material gain on the part of both the European and the Indonesian administrators. The resultant lack of actual control from the top allowed an extension of anarchy into the local levels with ensuing overburdening of the little man who increasingly lost his sources of protection. This is not dissimilar to the problems that had for centuries plagued Java.

---

[69]   Vitalis, *Opmerking*, p. 88. See also L. Vitalis, *De invoering, werking en gebreken van het stelsel van kultures op Java* (Zalt-Bommel, 1851).

CHAPTER III

The Regulation of Sugar Production in Java, 1830-1840

In midyear 1965 my family and I moved from Troy, New York, to Honolulu, Hawaii, where I took up the position of Professor of Southeast Asian History at the University of Hawaii. The University was then in a period of great expansion. Walter F. Vella had arrived in Hawaii a few years before and the interest in Southeast Asian history was so great that a second Southeast Asian historian was needed. Walter and I taught Southeast Asian history together in a team-taught course until his death at the end of 1981. Soon after I arrived, the University decided to change the Asian Studies activities on the campus by creating a program with subsections for East Asia, Southeast Asia, and South Asia; I was asked to take charge of setting up the Southeast Asian Studies activities. One of the things I organized was a multidisciplinary seminar in 1967 for the graduate students interested in Southeast Asia. Five faculty members presented papers while the students prepared their research presentations. The papers of the five faculty members were published under the title *Economic Factors in Southeast Asian Social Change* (Honolulu 1968) which appeared as No. 2 in a new publication series that I had started called 'Asian Studies at Hawaii'. My contribution to this publication is presented here as paper number 3.

In the course of doing the research for the sugar industry in Pasuruan in 1964, I had worked my way through a substantial amount of material about the introduction of sugar cultivation in other parts of Java as well. As I puzzled over the various reports which I had on microfilm from my 1960-61 sojourn in the Dutch archives, I was persuaded by the evidence that there were three general variations in the way sugar cultivation was regulated in Java. Moreover, these three variations coincided with three distinctive areas of Java. These in turn had three different historical traditions and ecologies. The more I became involved with the basic data, the more I wondered why this rather obvious set of distinctions had not been commented on before. The paper that I prepared for the seminar spelled out these three variations. Together with the previous piece on Pasuruan, it laid the basis for a revised view on the older literature on the sugar industry and its impact as represented by the writings of E. de Vries, *Landbouw*

en welvaart in het regentschap Pasoeroean (Wageningen 1931)
and D.H. Burger, *De ontsluiting van Java's binnenland voor het
wereldverkeer* (Wageningen 1939). These two papers of mine
(Numbers 2 and 3) proved transitional to later, more comprehensive, and more detailed studies of specific cultivations in
specific areas in Java. Elson's study on Pasuruan has already been
mentioned in my introduction to paper number 2. Here I should
like to mention the studies of M. Radin Fernando, *Peasants and
plantation economy; The social impact of fhe European
plantation economy in Cirebon residency from the Cultivation
System to the end of the first decade of the twentieth century*
(Monash University 1982) and the various articles of G.R. Knight,
'From plantation to padi field: the origins of the nineteenth
century transformation of Java's sugar industry,' *Modern Asian
Studies* 14-2 (1980) and 'Rice and second crops in Pekalongan
Residency, North Java, 1780-1870,' (Paper ASAA 1984). The
situation in Jepara, which is emphasized in my paper, has been
further detailed by Frans Hüsken in *Een dorp op Java* (Overveen
1988) where it has been used to draw broader social observations.
Though none of these authors is beholden to me for either their
training or their research, it has pleased me greatly to see the
extension and improvement of the type of investigation that I
was undertaking in the mid 1960s.

In the following discussion and analysis, I will consider three variations in
the pattern of arrangements for government sponsored sugar cultivation
along the north coast of the island of Java. My interest here is to describe the
fashions in which sugar cultivation was introduced under stimulation by a
colonial government in the years immediately after 1830, to look into the
fashion in which various groups were involved in this matter, to observe
the successes and failures with whatever adjustments the latter produced,
and finally to analyze the role of the indigenous population of Java in this
process. I wish it were possible to say more about the effects of the process
upon the Javanese, but good evidence is lacking and speculation is so easy
and obvious that I leave the matter to the reader's imagination.

The System of Cultivations introduced into Java by Johannes van den
Bosch in 1830 had as its chief purpose the production of commodities in
Java which would be salable on the world markets. These commodities were
conceived as agricultural items with whatever fundamental processing they
required. To be salable they had to be of equal or better quality and cheaper
in price than like commodities produced in other parts of the world. To
achieve this goal it was necessary to have the Javanese produce and process
the desired commodities at the lowest possible cost which rather rapidly
came in effect to mean productive arrangements which operated quite apart

from the self-regulating principles of the world market. In short, Java became in a sense a self-contained production area with some features of modern socialist societies. Illustrative of the manner in which this was accomplished is the introduction of sugar cane growing and sugar milling along Java's north coast. The three variations described here can most easily be separated on a geographical basis; the pattern of the central area of Tjirebon-Pekalongan-Semarang; the pattern of the Japara district; and the pattern of the eastern region of Surabaya-Pasuruan-Besuki.

Sugar cultivation was started on a very limited scale in the Tjirebon-Pekalongan-Semarang region of Java for it was not easy to find entrepreneurs interested in establishing a sugar factory under government contract. Where such an entrepreneur could be found the government made the necessary advances for the construction of the factory which could be repaid over a number of years in sugar at a fixed price. The government also provided for the growing of the cane in the vicinity of the factory, the cutting and delivery of the cane, and the supplying of firewood. The ripe cane was evaluated in the field for its estimated productive capacity and the factory owner was expected to pay the government for the value of the cane delivered to him; this sum was generally paid in processed sugar. The miller was to have free disposition over the sugar he produced over and above the amounts required to settle his obligation to the government for advances for the construction of the factory and for the value of the cane. In this part of Java the factory operators were either Europeans or Chinese most of whom had little experience in sugar milling. While little capital was needed, the business of sugar milling appealed little to most Europeans in Java at the time, and seemed rather dubious to many Chinese who could do rather well without assistance from the government. There is no indication of any Javanese being involved in a milling contract in this area.

The government's involvement with the Javanese came primarily at the level of growing, cutting, and delivering the sugar cane. For each factory the government contracted with the local population for the planting, tending, cutting of an extent of land in sugar cane, and the delivery to the factory of the cane. In the area here under consideration these contracts initially placed much of the risk on the population, later the contractual nature of the arrangement gives way to forced obligations but the risk is more equitably shared by the government. The burden of the work remains upon the population. The contracts were effected with the village headmen and local officials in the areas around a factory. The lands actually used for the growing of the cane were not assessed for landrent. Each village contract provided for a fixed number of laborers who would work under the direction of their headmen who in turn received their instructions from supervisors. Initially the value of the cane was supposed to pay all the landrent of all the villages involved in supplying land and people to the process, but as I have indicated elsewhere this did not continue long but was replaced by an equation of production with landrent owed.[1] Let us now examine the actual condition at some of the factories by 1834 and 1835.

The factory at Tjielendoek in Tjirebon had been established in the early 1830s with a promise of 600 *bouw* of land planted in cane.[2] The usual calculation for manpower in this area was four men per *bouw*; each man to work one quarter of the year. By the end of 1834 there were over 2600 families plus more than 400 village headmen and local authorities assigned to this factory. These people came from various villages in the vicinity and supplied not only their labor but also buffaloes, plows, wagons, tools, etc. The field and factory supervisors were first paid out of the value of the cane, then the total amount of landrent owed by the various villages from which the laborers came was deducted; the remainder, about 5,000 guilders, was divided among the 3,000 laborers but was hardly sufficient to cover the cost of buffaloes and equipment. The work arrangements in the field and factory had proved greater than the available manpower could handle, so the working time for each individual had been doubled; the calculation against landrent was variously calculated against the land area of the village or against the total number of men required; and for all his efforts the individual worker rarely saw a payment for his efforts. Small wonder that Vitalis reports in 1835 that the population in the area was unsettled and moving from place to place to escape the work compulsion. He also reports growing dissatisfaction among the headmen over the loss of personal work services which the system created for them; these free services seem to have been more important to them than the development of individual material gain.[3] For the average villager there was certainly nothing in this system that would have induced or stimulated voluntary efforts on his part to engage in sugar cultivation. By the end of the decade the government had ironed out a number of the inequities in the above described arrangements by transferring added responsibilities to the millers, but nothing had basically changed the unpleasant compulsive nature of the work for the villagers involved for the major incentive continued to be the mounting pressure of the traditional system of authority.

The government's side of the ledger did not, surprisingly enough, show

---

[1]   Robert Van Niel, 'The function of landrent under the Cultivation System in Java,' *Journal of Asian Studies* 23 (1964), pp. 357-375.
[2]   The *bouw* of 500 square rods was used in this area and became standard for government reports.
[3]   Report to the Director-General of Cultivations B.J. Elias from the adjunct inspector Mr. L. Vitalis on his inspection in the Residency Cheribon, 21 July 1835, Netherlands State Archives, The Hague, J.C. Baud folio 458. [Titles and quotes of Archive material throughout this paper are translated from the original Dutch by the author.]

Table I
Sugar cultivation in Cheribon (Tjirebon) 1834

Sugar Mill	Number of planters	Number of *bouw* (successful)	Estimated production*	Approx. actual production*	Payments made to planters	Landrent owed by planters
Tjielendoek	2,662	552	8,905	7,620	ƒ 28,500	ƒ 21,104
Kendang Laoet	2,775	580	4,980	5,800	ƒ 1,750	ƒ 1,993
Ardjawi-nangoen	2,091	84	977	1,600	ƒ 5,969	ƒ 20,890
Cheribon	220	162	2,380	2,200	ƒ 8,241	ƒ 2,902

* in piculs
Source: Vitalis Report, Appendix A.

the profits one might imagine, but this is partly explainable through the cost items included in the calculation and also the quality of the sugar obtained. The sugar miller had contracted to deliver sugar to the government at 10 guilders per picul to repay the evaluated cost of the cane as well as the cost of constructing the factory. Thus the basic cost of a picul of sugar was listed by the government at ten guilders, but much of this was a paper transaction for the value of the cane had actually been charged against the landrent of the population working in the cane fields. At most this value might be regarded as money which the government might have received if the villagers had grown rice instead of sugar, but the extra labor in which the villagers had been involved for the sugar was at their expense. It is not surprising, for instance, to find the workers attached to the factory Karang Anjer in Pekalongan owing the government money.[4] To the above cost of ten guilders the government added two additional cost items: an item for the remission of landrent on the fields on which the cane was actually grown; and a payment of fifty cents per picul for a so-called 'percentage payment' which was to be divided among the European and Indonesian civil servants connected with the cultivation. The latter payment accounts in part for the willingness of higher authorities to lend a hand in the system; the nature of the payment was a sort of tribute for traditional services rendered rather than a profit achieved through entrepreneurship or industriousness. All of these calculations raised the government's book value of a picul of sugar in Tjirebon to 13.21 guilders in 1834, certainly not competitive on the world markets if this were to be regarded as a cost based on normal capital investment. In Pekalongan the per picul value reached 16.74 guilders in the

---

[4]   Report by the inspector of the Cultivations L. Vitalis to the Director-General of the Cultivations B. J. Elias concerning the former's regulation of cultivations in the Residency Pekalongan, 29 October 1834, J.C. Baud folio 460.

same year. In Semarang the productions of 1833 and 1834 were so bad that the government wiped the books clean and attempted no calculations of losses.[5] Clearly this entire area needed a reorganization of the system and, as I have indicated, this was done in the latter part of the decade. In general this was accomplished by adjusting the contracts with the millers in such a way as to make them responsible for the transportation, that is, the purchase of carts and buffaloes (an item that could be well borne by the profits made by the factories) and by eliminating individualized amounts of landrent equivalents (usually 7.50 guilders) and instead basing the calculations on amount of landrent actually owed (usually about 6 guilders per family) while also gradually increasing the payments while simultaneously moving the landrent assessment on the villages upward. The peasant cultivator was again made to carry the burden of the system; for him this was little more than a new type of corvée which he sought wherever and whenever possible to avoid.

The second area to be considered here is that of Japara where a system totally different from any other part of Java was introduced for regulating sugar cultivation and production. Regretfully I have not been able to find as much detail about this system as I would like, and cannot, therefore, provide details on its eventual breakdown.[6] Some aspects of the system introduced into Japara in the early 1830s would seem to lay the basis of a greater involvement of the village and the individual in the sugar industry than in other parts of Java, but the generally poor soils of the area lowered the economic advantages of sugar production and probably led to the failure of the system. The sugar planters of Japara undertook the initial processing of their cane in small hand presses and delivered barrels of sugar water to Chinese manufacturers. The manufacturer would set up his boiling vats near the fields and would pay the planter 3.50 guilders for the sugar water needed for one picul of sugar. On average 7 barrels were needed; a *bouw* of sugar cane might produce anywhere from 50 to 100 barrels depending upon the quality of the cane. Only at the higher level of productivity did the income obtained from growing sugar surpass the comparable value of rice and a second crop, and already in 1833 the government was concerned by the sizable migrations out of the Japara area.[7] A few of the villages involved in

[5]   Report of the Inspector Vitalis on his inspection in the Residency Semarang in 1834, 30 August 1835, J.C. Baud folio 459.

[6]   The information given here on the system in Japara is drawn from the notations made by Governor General J.C. Baud on his inspection trip across Java, May 1, 1834-August 9, 1834 (folio 462). It is interesting to note that the final, official report of this trip is printed in S. van Deventer, *Bijdragen tot de kennis van het landelijk stelsel op Java*, vol. 2 (Zalt-Bommel: Joh. Noman en Zoon, 1866) [Ch. 14] but that this published source contains none of the information on Japara which I found in J.C. Baud's handwritten notes.

[7]   Letter and appendices from Resident De Vogel to J.C. Baud, Pattie, 30 June 1833, J.C. Baud

sugar cultivation in Japara undertook to manufacture the sugar themselves, and where this occurred the payment of 8.50 guilders per picul by the government made the sugar production far more profitable than rice cultivation. Statistics available for 1833 indicate a higher level of productivity per unit of land in those areas where the Chinese sugar boilers were operative, but a higher level of payment in those villages which milled their own sugar.* The pressure of the Chinese entrepreneur who seems also to have advanced money to the villagers and consequently kept them indebted to him seems to have been a necessary ingredient in stimulating production. Not only do the figures for 1833 speak clearly of a low efficiency ratio in those villages producing their own sugar, but government reports from later in the decade express problems about the quality of the sugar produced by the villages. By the end of the decade the limited sugar production still carried on in Japara was operating through a system of factories similar to that of other areas of Java.

The statistics in Table II do not include the extent of *tegelan* fields which were most extensive in the villages of the Regency Japara, but they do show that already more than one-fifth of the sawah land area of many villages was being used for sugar cane growing. When Governor-General Baud visited Japara in 1834 he reported that several regents felt that the common man did not care for the system of delivering sugar water to the Chinese sugar boilers, but that either the headmen and officials were in the obligation of the Chinese or the existing contracts could not be changed to the system of village manufacturing. Everyone seemed quite aware of the greater profitability of the village's involvement in the processing of sugar yet little seems ever to have been done to increase the number of villages operating in this fashion. The trend is in the other direction for reasons already indicated. While admittedly unable to probe the details of the Japara system of sugar growing, one is left with the impression that there would have been greater opportunities to develop entrepreneurship and economic incentives here than in the first region discussed. Taking account of the rather mediocre agricultural conditions in Japara, one is struck by the fact that profits were undoubtedly being made, but not in most instances by the Javanese villager. Yet the opportunities were present in certain instances,

---

folio 462. A summary of the evidence here would indicate an excess of 3,300 persons moving out of the Residency Japara during the four-year period 1829-1833. Examination of the detailed evidence indicates that the bulk of these came from the districts Selowessie, Glongong, Bogorame, Passelian, Oendean, and Mergotoe which were involved only to a minor degree in government cultivation.

*NOTE 1989. Frans Hüsken, *Een dorp op Java* (Overveen 1988), p. 56 ftnt. 24 disagrees about the productivity part of this sentence. I have checked the figures in the document that we both used and I stand by my analysis and conclusions.

Robert Van Niel

Table II
Production of sugar water and rice plantings, Japara, 1833

Regency	Village	Area of sawah bouw	Area in sugar bouw	Barrels sugar water	Monetary value paid village	Total landrent village
Pati	Pladen	251	52	2,131	ƒ 1,031	ƒ 1,623
	Jawik	145	42	816	ƒ 408	ƒ 1,068
	Klaling	232	68	2,168	ƒ 1,084	ƒ 2,138
	Palelessan*	304	62	228	ƒ 1,872	ƒ 1,263
	Tepoos*	85	21	172	ƒ 1,41	ƒ 555
Kudus	Dapoor	16	10	658	ƒ 364	ƒ 159
	Tumpang	53	27	1,243	ƒ 621	ƒ 411
	Prokowinong*	88	27	74	ƒ 594	ƒ 537
	Krapiek*	66	16	185	ƒ 1,489	ƒ 579
Japara	Banju putih	80	16	1,269	ƒ 715	ƒ 634
	Pelang	48	12	989	ƒ 495	ƒ 307
	Siengorodjo*	71	14	169	ƒ 1,453	ƒ 306
	Gebok*	94	22	121	ƒ 995	ƒ 990

* Villages manufacturing their own sugar.
Source: Letter from De Vogel to J. C. Baud, 30 June, 1833. J. C. Baud, folio 462.

but the villager, for reasons that can vaguely be described as cultural, seemed unable to take advantage of the potential profits of the situation.

The third part of Java to be considered is the area of Surabaya-Pasuruan-Besuki which ultimately became the most successful sugar growing area in the island. Sugar cane had already been grown in the Pasuruan-Besuki area before 1830 though it had not developed into a major export commodity. I have described the growth of government sugar production in Pasuruan after 1830 elsewhere so that I will limit myself to considering Surabaya and Besuki here.[8] For the entire area, however, it can be said that the existence of an experienced body of Chinese and European sugar producers and unusually favorable soil and climate made sugar cane growing more profitable for the Javanese cultivator than was true in the areas of Java previously discussed. The regulation of sugar growing and production in this area was similar to the arrangements in the Tjirebon-Pekalongan-Semarang area with some modifications. The population seems to have been already more densely concentrated here than in other parts of the north coast and as a consequence the labor supply could be drawn directly from the same village whose lands were being partly used for sugar cane. Landrent was from the first levied on the fields used for cane growing, but at

[8]   Robert Van Niel, 'The introduction of government sugar cultivation in Pasuruan, Java, 1830,' in *Proceedings of the Conference on Asian History, Hong Kong, 1964,* ed. by Brian Harrison (Hong Kong: University of Hong Kong Press, in press). [This refers to the previous article in this collection.]

a rate usually reserved for *tegelan* fields which was lower than for *sawah*. Income from the sugar cane was initially deducted from the total landrent assessment of the village and only the balance was paid to the village collectively. Communal style land holding seems to have been more prevalent here than in other parts of Java.

By 1835 the regulation of sugar cultivation in Surabaya did not appear much more satisfactory than that of the region to the west of it already described. Floods at the beginning of the year had destroyed about one-half of the 4600 *bouw* planted in cane, and left about one-half of the 35,000 families involved in sugar cane growing without payment for their efforts (though their landrent was remitted on the cane fields.)[9] In future years, however, improved irrigation facilities would reduce the hazards and allow an expansion of both area and profit in this crop. In spite of an apparently disastrous sugar crop in 1835, the sugar millers or entrepreneurs made great profits for the successful fields and produced far more sugar than had been estimated and charged to them. This aspect of sugar production in the entire area under consideration here is a special feature of the production from the very first. It results from the system of estimating the productivity of sugar cane.

In the entire sugar cane growing area of Java the value which a village was to receive for a field of ripe sugar cane was based upon an estimation of the productivity of that cane. A *bouw* of cane that was estimated to produce 20 piculs of sugar was qualified as first sort and the village was allowed a payment of 75 guilders. Second quality cane estimated to yield 15 piculs had a value of 56 guilders per *bouw*, and third quality estimated at 10 piculs was paid 37.50 guilders. This estimation system was used throughout Java though the actual payments might vary somewhat. One of the problems in the Tjirebon-Pekalongan-Semarang area was that the millers often did not obtain the number of piculs of sugar from the cane that had been estimated; this was in part due to inefficiency and inexperience on their part, but essentially the cane was not too good. But in Surabaya-Pasuruan-Besuki the opposite was the case; the sugar mill operators might obtain more than double the amount of sugar from the cane. Ament indicates that this was quite definitely the case in Surabaya in 1835, and there is ample evidence to indicate that this became ever more the case throughout this area as the techniques of sugar manufacturing were improved.[10] There is a rapid rise in the value of sugar contracts in this area. Until the government extended its control over the entire sugar production here and raised the price paid the

9   Report of the Inspection of the adjunct inspector of the cultivations in Surabaya, 20 December 1835, No. 91, J.C. Baud
10   Ibid. Later cultivation reports found in the archive of the Ministry of Colonies, Netherlands State Archives, support this view.

manufacturer for sugar in excess of the amounts needed to repay advances
and the cost of the cane, the manufacturers were allowed to sell their
surplus sugar on the open market where handsome profits could be made.
In fact, by the 1840s private sales were again permitted on a limited scale and
we find a greater degree of individual entrepreneurship entering the
Cultivation System at this time than is frequently recognized. Again,
however, this had little bearing upon the Javanese cultivator who, while
not badly off compared to other areas of Java, was receiving a smaller
portion of the profits made on the sugar grown in his area than was the case
elsewhere. Some effort was made to improve his lot by raising the price paid
for first quality cane, but these increased payments were in nowise
commensurate with the increased quantity of sugar obtained by the
manufacturers. Never did the government raise the incentives to the
cultivator in an effort to involve him in cane production as an industry or
source of total income.

In the Besuki area where the overproduction of the estimated yield was
similar to Surabaya, Ament calculates that the sugar planter was actually
losing about 50 guilders per *bouw* (a larger *bouw* of approximately 1200
square rods was used here) on the price he could obtain from growing padi
on his fields.[11] He feels that a payment of 3.50 guilders for each picul of sugar
produced by the miller would be the only way to make sugar cultivation
more profitable than rice for the cultivator. But never did the government
or the millers institute this system; the gains made through increasingly
more efficient milling processes accrued to them, not to the planter. By 1835
the *bouw* of sugar cane in Besuki produced an average of 57.5 piculs of sugar
while the estimate for first quality cane was only 40 piculs and the average
estimation throughout the district was about 30 piculs. In short, there was
almost twice as much sugar produced as estimated, and with the planter
paid on the basis of the estimate rather than the production, there is little
difficulty in ascertaining who was subsidizing the production and who was
reaping excessive profits.

An interesting feature of the sugar regulation in Besuki was the
individualization of the payments to the planters. By 1835 individual
payments seem to have been instituted in favor of lump payment to the
village. Where this occurred – we know of its happening in diverse areas for
various crops throughout the life of the Cultivation System – it seems to
have been introduced by European civil servants who hoped to create more
individual interest in the cultivations and who also hoped to implement a
more immediate sense of participation in the gains of the system. Appended

[11]   Report of the Adjunct Inspector of the Cultivations Ament in the Residency Bezoeki,
No. 87, 30 November 1835, J.C. Baud folio 457.

Table III
Sugar cultivation, Probolingo, Bezoeki (Besuki), 1835

Sugar Mill	Number of planters	Number of *bouw* (planted)	Estimated production*	Approx. actual production*	Payments made to planters	Landrent owed by planters
Bayoman	1,123	208	5,590	11,000	ƒ 25,706	ƒ 16,550
Oemboel Wonno	1,087	215	5,898	12,000	ƒ 26,997	ƒ 17,890
Langan	1,254	197	4,890	10,000	ƒ 22,418	ƒ 16,464
Gending	957	210	6,187	13,000	ƒ 28,555	ƒ 14,634
Pedjarakkan	1,972	252	6,580	12,000	ƒ 31,206	ƒ 26,013
Phaiton	447	80	2,598	4,500	ƒ 12,308	ƒ 6,436

* in piculs
Source: Report of Ament in Bezoeki, 1835, Appendix 2.

to Ament's report of Besuki in 1835 is a chart of one village in the district indicating this method of payment.[12] In the village of Dringolor in 1835 payment was made to 78 villagers in varying amounts based on the extent of land which each had planted in cane and the quality of the cane produced, the payment was reduced by the amount of each individual's landrent on his *sawah* and *tegelan* planted in other than cane as well as the landrent on the fields planted in cane. The remainder was paid to him in cash. It is interesting to note that 13 of the 78 villagers still owed additional landrent, the remainder received payments ranging from 51.78 guilders for the village headman down to one-half cent each to some half-dozen of the smaller producers. Underlying this method of payment are certain socio-economic factors such as individualized, permanent holdings which could possibly not apply in other areas, but the eventual socio-political implications of the extension of this system raise many interesting questions about the impact of the new cultivations and increased government interference upon the nature of the Javanese village.

One or two further points of interest concerning the regulation of the sugar cultivation and production in the Surabaya-Pasuruan-Besuki area might be noted. Diverse sources have commented upon the greater energy and effectiveness of the European civil servants in regulating the cultivations in this area. I have noted this previously when describing the situation in Pasuruan,[13] but it bears repetition here, for it seems that the Controleurs in many of the districts of this part of Java were concerned not only with the direct individual payment to the cultivator, but also the immediate supervision of the planting, irrigation, etc. We do not hear of the

[12] Ibid, Appendix 1, Payments to individual agriculturists of the desa Dringolor in 1835.
[13] Robert Van Niel, 'Sugar cultivation in Pasuruan, Java' (in press).

same massive labor recruitments directed by headmen and notables as occurred in Tjirebon and Pekalongan, instead the work seems to be more closely supervised by the European officials.

The sugar millers in the Surabaya-Pasuruan-Besuki area were chiefly European and Chinese entrepreneurs who operated under contracts not dissimilar to those in the Tjirebon-Pekalongan-Semarang area. However, there are Javanese entrepreneurs noted in the East Java area, but there is too little known about them to draw conclusions about their social position.[14] Unfortunately the records give us no indication of the success or failure of these Javanese entrepreneurs, for the documentation does not attempt to trace the fortunes of the millers. I have been unable to find later references to Javanese sugar manufacturers in this area and see little point in speculating on what might have happened to their enterprises. The fact that some Javanese were involved raises many intriguing avenues for further investigation when and if further information is uncovered.

In what has been said here about the regulation of sugar cultivation under government control during the 1830s, a few guarded conclusions seem evident. For the village cultivator under any system there seem to have been minimal incentives. With the possible exception of Japara the cultivator was neither expected nor encouraged to develop an industry of the sugar cane cultivation; he was instead expected to produce the cane under traditional conditions of obligation and compulsion. Moreover, while he was not left unprotected in the face of natural and man-made hazards of production as some late nineteenth century detractors of the System have contended, he was expected to give an inordinate amount of his energies and resources to the cultivation in comparison to the share of the profits he received. To the designers of the System, the common man's labors and time do not seem to have been regarded as a normal economic commodity; experimentations, stupidities, and organizational failures were at the expense of his energies regardless of where the fault lay. While it can be argued that the social and cultural conditions of the Javanese did not afford him much scope for the development of incentives needed to promote a sense of industry, it must be said with equal force that the system (again perhaps with the exception of Japara) did not allow or encourage him to break out of the confines of his traditional patterns. The situation in Japara raises more questions than it answers and one would like to have more detailed information about it. On the surface it would appear to allow either individual or village-wide industry, but beneath this there seems a

---

[14] Ament notes 'Chinese and native contractors' in the district Jengollo, Surabaya, but mentions no names. In the Gunung Kendeng district, '40 *bouw* were planted for the native Soemodiwirio'. Report of inspection in Surabaya, 1835.

problem of meager soil compounded by an indeterminate role of the Chinese sugar dealers who conceivably might have been working with credit advances which limited the profitability for the Javanese. In any event, the Javanese does not emerge as a potential entrepreneur in this one instance which might have acted to encourage economic incentives on his part.

If the common Javanese villager did not develop a sense of enterprise about the sugar cultivation, we might have expected something more from the upper class Javanese, but here again there is little indication of involvement beyond the traditional role and function of this group. It is difficult to maintain that the Dutch administration did not allow Javanese notables to engage in sugar production contracts, for there is no evidence of either overt or covert nature that Javanese were officially excluded from such contracts, and we do have infrequent occurrences of their involvement in a contract.*

The time period under consideration in this paper precedes many of the cultural changes that occurred within Javanese society during the past century, but we see many of the same problems faced in Indonesia at a later date. Though no one will deny the economic inequities and disincentives of a colonial system, these were inequities not completely foreign to the supra-village portion of Javanese society. Their failure to undertake a greater measure of developmental activity probably has its root causes in social and cultural factors within Javanese society itself. The continuance of the traditional cultural forces within this society into the present day operates as a brake upon development now as in the past.

*NOTE 1989.   I am incorrect here. Subsequently I discovered that the priyayi were explicitly by law excluded from engaging in such entrepreneurial activity.

CHAPTER IV

Measurement of Change under the Cultivation System in Java, 1837-1851[*]

This piece appeared in the journal *Indonesia* No. 14, October 1972, which is published by the Cornell Modern Indonesia Project and is reprinted here with permission. In the years between the publication of the previous paper in 1968 and this one in 1972 a number of things happened to me that impacted on me personally, but more importantly, had bearing upon the development of Southeast Asian studies. Since arriving in Hawaii I had been pushing for the preservation of Southeast Asian source materials and the upgrading of libraries and archives. I saw this within the context of advancing the training of scholars in history and the social sciences in the United States and Southeast Asia. In these years (1965-1968) I was one of several Southeast Asian scholars who felt that local research in Southeast Asia was needed and could be used as the venue for the training of younger scholars.[1] When I met Marnixius Hutasoit, who was visiting senior scholar at the East-West Center, in 1967-68, I was persuaded to put together a plan for the in situ training in a sort of team project of historians and social scientists in Indonesia.[2] As it turned out, this was an idea whose time had not yet come, but I didn't know that then. In midyear 1968 I went to Indonesia for a year with a Fulbright research grant to work in the archives on the Cultivation System and to promote the projects of the preservation of source materials and the training of young scholars.

What started out as a year of hope and constructive development had within a few months turned to disillusion. Efforts to

[*] The collection of the basic data from archives in the Netherlands was made possible by a grant from the Joint Committee on Asian Studies of the ACLS/SSRC; assistance in collating and transcribing the information came from the University of Hawaii Research Council; preparation and programming for computerization was assisted by the Social Science Research Institute of the University of Hawaii. I am indebted to Miss Karen Essene for assistance in programming.
[1] See my 'Nineteenth century Java; An analysis of historical sources and method,' Asian Studies, Vol. 4 (August 1966) and 'Techniques and approaches to local history and its role in the development of Malaysian history,' *Foram sejarah pertama universiti sains Malaysia,* 1971.
[2] The project is described in 'Proposal for training Indonesian historians', *International Educational and Cultural Exchange* (Summer 1967), pp.35-8.

interest US foundations in the preservation of Southeast Asian
retrospective materials were unsuccessful. Eventually a small
amount of money with which to hold a conference of librarians
and archivists of Southeast Asia was found. With the assistance of
LIPI, the Indonesian Council of Sciences, I was able to organize a
conference in early 1969 at the Puncak Pass in West Java. It
became the one bright spot in an otherwise totally frustrating year.
The Southeast Asian Librarians Association grew out of this
conference, and the American Committee on Southeast Asian
Resource Materials (CORMOSEA) also developed out of this
meeting. Both of these have continued into the present day
though I have had little to do with their continued existence and
successes.

The idea of multidisciplinary team research encountered
obstacles that I, as a foreign scholar in Indonesia, could not
surmount. Everyone liked the idea but no one was prepared to do
anything with it or to take the initiative. Some years later a
similar project was launched with foundation and government
support and has had very interesting results.

My own research in the Indonesian archives was stopped when
the permission that I had obtained to consult materials proved
worthless in the face of the resistance by the then archivist. The
only thing left to do was to survey local archives throughout Java
for which the then secretary general of the department of internal
affairs, Sumarman, gave me permission. I shall forever
remember his kindness for I was able to accomplish something,
however limited, which I wrote up in a monograph *A Survey of
Historical Source Materials in Java and Manila* (Asian Studies at
Hawaii No. 5, 1970).

Being unable to do everything that I had hoped to accomplish, I
had time to visit many parts of Java and to reflect upon life as I
found it and to talk with many older persons and to learn of the
changes in their lives. Quite indirectly these observations and
talks created in me a stronger sense of the dynamism of Javanese
life than I had had before, and this growing perception on my part
also influences the way in which I thought about the past. More
strongly than previously I came to realize how the materials that I
had been working with on the Cultivation System gave me a top-
of-the-heap view on the events of the nineteenth century. How
was I going to find out about the impact of the System on the
Javanese cultivators? How was I going to get any inkling of their
life and how it was affected? I knew no answer to these questions.
My survey of local archives in Java had shown quite convincingly
that there were virtually no nineteenth-century documents
scattered around the countryside. From an intellectual point-of-
view it was not a good year.

Before leaving Hawaii in mid-1968 I had undertaken to put
information from the Cultivation Reports which were issued

annually from 1836 onward onto computer punchcards. These Cultivation Reports were statistical compilations on many diverse matters but principally on government cultivations, and I had them on microfilm since my days in the Dutch archives. Once the task of completing the entry of this vast amount of material onto the punchcards had been completed and the results were printed out, I discovered that I could make virtually no sense of these heaps of numbers. That was where matters stood when I went to Indonesia for the year. When I returned to Hawaii in mid-1969 I picked up these sheets of numbers again and concluded that the only way to draw meaning out of them was to study relationships between various categories of information rather than attempting to extract meaning out of absolute numbers whose accuracy was oftentimes questionable. To do this I obtained the help of Karen Essene, a most patient programmer, who was able to get the computer to link up and interrelate the categories of information that I thought could be most fruitfully juxtaposed. What I was trying to get at was the impact of the Cultivation System on the Javanese cultivator and I think I had some success in the paper that follows. The overall results are certainly not revolutionary; the Cultivation System put a much heavier burden on labor than it had on land, but this methodology put it in a way that made the point very strongly.

After I completed this piece on the measurement of change, I did not again work with a quantitative approach to nineteenth-century history. Quite frankly, I am not enamoured of using statistics which I feel can be manipulated to bring about whatever one wants to show – though I hasten to say that I have tried not to employ this cynicism in this paper. But I was really diverted from the crunching of numbers by a number of other issues that this paper raised and which for me offered more interesting avenues of future research. Some of these issues were: the beginnings of the bureaucratization of the civil administration; the local adjustments at various levels to the Cultivation System; the aggregation of labor under the System and the relationship of corvée to cultivation services; the control over land in Java and the relationship of landholding to corvée, cultivation service, and social status; and the growth of a capital base for expansion of agricultural enterprises under the government controlled Cultivation System. In my future writings I will turn to these matters rather than pushing ahead with quantitative analysis.

This paper is an attempt to determine some of the social and economic impacts of the Cultivation System in Java through the use of statistical information contained in reports prepared by government officers at the time the System operated. Such information has not hitherto been used in this way. This paper is meant as an exploration of the possible uses of this type of information. The nature of this information, and the fashion in which it is used, will be made clear as the paper progresses.

The Cultivation System was introduced in Java in 1830 with the arrival of its enthusiastic creator, Johannes van den Bosch. In the previous year King William I had charged Van den Bosch with putting into operation the scheme he had devised for making the island of Java produce commodities which would be salable on the world markets.[3] The Netherlands' government had been singularly unsuccessful in extracting profit from Java since its return from British control in 1816. Now Van den Bosch's scheme promised to change all that. It was a plan of ingenious simplicity that recommended itself to the King, and Van den Bosch had been dispatched to Java as the new Governor-General.

Unlike earlier schemes which viewed the economic productivity of Java in terms either of individual enterprise on the part of the Javanese or of stimulation by European entrepreneurs, Van den Bosch's notion was essentially a governmental-administrative enterprise. Traditional patterns of authority, obligation, tribute, and service were to be harnessed into a productive pattern which would be guided by the traditional Javanese administrative elite with some advice and control by a small corps of European administrators. Despite Van den Bosch's protestations that participation in the scheme would be completely voluntary on the part of the Javanese villagers, many of his compatriots entertained grave doubts about the freedom of choice which would be allowed under such control in Java. Before he even arrived in Java, Van den Bosch was being criticized for reintroducing the old VOC system of monopoly and rigid mercantile control. This criticism was highlighted by the resignation of the Minister of Industry and Colonies, C.Th. Elout, a strong proponent of liberal economic principles.[4] But Van den Bosch's blandishments had persuaded the King that coercion would not be the keystone of the System and that it would provide the long anticipated profits while actually raising the welfare of the Javanese.

Van den Bosch's plan was simply that the Javanese village set aside a portion of its land, normally one-fifth, for the planting and tending of a crop

---

3   Van den Bosch's original advice to the King, dated March 6, 1829, is reprinted in an appendix of D.C. Steijn Parvé, *Het koloniaal monopoliestelsel getoetst aan geschiedenis en staatshuishoudkunde, nader toegelicht* (Zalt-Bommel: Noman, 1851), pp. 294-328.

4   Extensive powers were given Van den Bosch by the King in a secret decree of June 9, 1829; at that time Elout submitted his resignation. Elout had been the highest placed critic of Van den Bosch's policies, and during the months of March, April, and May 1829, the two had waged a memoranda debate. The King's decision to support Van den Bosch was taken at a conference on May 23, 1829, at which time a new fundamental law for the Indies was drafted. See further, J.J. Westendorp Boerma, *Een geestdriftig Nederlander; Johannes van den Bosch* (Amsterdam: Querido, 1950), pp. 70-1.

or crops designated by the government. The produce of this portion of the village's land was to be delivered to the government at a fixed price. This price should, according to Van den Bosch's calculations, have been sufficient to pay the landrent owed by the entire village. Since the landrent was normally calculated at two-fifths of the yield of the village's major crop (usually rice), and since Van den Bosch constantly asserted that the new crop would require no more work than rice, the logical conclusion was that the village would have more lands for its own use and would benefit from the application of the System.[5]

Van den Bosch also made reference to a commitment of work which the Javanese was expected to devote to the System. The labor component of the plan was most vague. It is generally assumed that this labor would be used in planting, tending, and cutting the crop planted for the government as well as in preparing the land, opening new lands, and extending the areas of irrigated land. It would also seem that this amount of labor was the equivalent of traditional corvée services. Obligatory labor of various sorts is, and was, a complicated matter in the Javanese context; the exact dimension of the additional or equivalent labor under the Cultivation System has remained one of its most obscure aspects. Van den Bosch said little enough about it, for he was sensitive to the allegation of compulsion. Moreover, he probably had little idea what was actually happening at the local level.[6]

The products delivered to the government by this scheme were to receive sufficient processing in factories or mills established with government loans to make them exportable. The processing plants were in the hands of Europeans and Chinese and worked with paid labor, although probably not entirely free labor. The processed commodities were shipped to the Netherlands in ships chartered by the Netherlands Trading Company (NHM), a government concern founded in 1825 in an unsuccessful effort to compete with English shipping. Slowly Van den Bosch's System brought life into the NHM as the transportation, insurance, and marketing profits began to mount. Within the Netherlands itself the products of Java were auctioned

[5]   The best general accounts in English of the System are found in Clive Day, *The policy and administration of the Dutch in Java* (New York: Macmillan, 1904), pp. 249-342, and J.S. Furnivall, *Netherlands India, a study of plural economy* (Cambridge: Cambridge University Press, 1944), pp. 115-73. These two accounts differ in interpretation rather than substance. My emphasis and interpretation is slightly different from either, but the basic facts remain much the same.
[6]   In the report of his accomplishments, *Mijne verrigtingen in Indië* (Amsterdam: Muller, 1864), pp. 423-37, Van den Bosch continuously speaks of four men (i.e., four families) per *bouw* of sugar or indigo, but there must have been much more labor than this drawn into the System. W.Ph. Coolhaas, 'Nederlands-Indië van 1830 tot 1887,' in: *Algemene geschiedenis der Nederlanden* (Utrecht: De Haan, 1955), vol. X, pp. 238-43, states that the Javanese was supposed to give up one-fifth of his land and one-fifth of his labor time for the cultivation of exportable crops.

into international channels. Gradually a new prosperity began to be felt; it was a prosperity that was supposed to have benefited everyone from the Javanese peasant to the Amsterdam merchant.

The functioning of the System above the level of the Javanese producer is not the primary concern of this paper, but it is well to keep in mind that Van den Bosch's scheme comprised rather wide-ranging goals. In practice, there was too little concern with high ideals at the lower levels of the System, and the growing criticism of the System after the mid-1840s probably reflects with some accuracy the baleful effects which the System was having on Javanese society.[7] Since much of the writing about the System has been by its opponents these failures were often drawn out of context, and there has never been an attempt (nor perhaps has it been possible) to measure the extent and form of the impact of the System.

One of the chief problems in understanding the Cultivation System derives from the fact that critics and proponents have taken it literally as a *system*. Actually from the moment of inception it began to function as a series of local arrangements designed to get production moving. Van den Bosch was most sensitive to the criticism that in the early years his System derived its profits from coffee cultivation which had been the mainstay of the export economy before his arrival.[8] As a matter of fact, coffee remained the most profitable single export throughout the life of the System, but not for lack of efforts to raise the production level of other crops, especially sugar and indigo. To change agricultural production patterns is not easy, and the early years of the System saw intensive efforts to make adjustments in the administrative and productive arrangements on Java. This was not always successful, and compromises were continually made. In the years when Van den Bosch himself was in Java (1830-1834) and when his close associate J.C. Baud succeeded him as Governor-General (1834-1836), there was a great deal of innovation, experimentation, and variation allowed. Later efforts to regularize the System never overcame this beginning, and those who tended to see the System as a unit invariably found discrepancies which were then viewed as abuses or corruptions of the basic plan. Much of this

---

[7]   G.H. van Soest, *Geschiedenis van het Kultuurstelsel*, 3 vols. (Rotterdam: Nijgh, 1869-71), is a rather thorough compilation of mistakes and abuses. The broader implications of the System as well as the mounting pressures upon the Javanese cultivator are discussed in W.M.F. Mansvelt, *Geschiedenis van de Nederlandsche Handel-Maatschappij* (Haarlem: Enschedé, [1926]), vol. II, esp. pp. 48-50.

[8]   The anonymous book *Kort overzigt der financiele resultaten van het stelsel van kultures* (Kampen: n.p., 1835), makes this point. As I have shown in my 'Function of landrent under the Cultivation System in Java,' *Journal of Asian Studies*, XXIII, no. 3 (May 1964), n. 27, p. 362, the book was authored by P. Merkus who was at the time a member of the Council of the Indies. He carried this argument forward in the 1840s in a letter to the Minister of Colonies, April 22, 1844, Geheim, Kabinet no. 85, at the time he was Governor-General.

pragmatism was of Van den Bosch's creation and probably quite necessary to effect change. It may also have been necessary thereafter to bureaucratize the operation of the System.

Two essential elements of Van den Bosch's arrangements to get the production of various crops started were the introduction of percentage payments and the establishment of an Office of Cultivations. To involve the Javanese and European administrators, a percentage of the value of the crops produced in their district was paid to them; in some areas this came to amount to more than the substantial salaries paid these officials.[9] The Office of Cultivations under a Director with a number of Inspectors in his charge was to supervise, regulate, and control the production of export crops, and also to make certain that the rural population was not unduly burdened, that is to say, in the parlance of the time, received proper benefits from the System.[10]

When Van den Bosch created the Office of the Director of Cultivations in 1831 the purpose was probably somewhat less clear than stated above. Perhaps it was to be little more than an agricultural experimentation agency. The first Director of the Cultivations, J.I. van Sevenhoven, was an old Indies hand whose chief role may have been making the new chores palatable to some of the old time Residents and Regents. His agricultural advisers bordered on being charlatans, and the period he held office (1831-1833) witnessed unchecked latitude in local experimentation and/or indifference. It was under his successor, B.J. Elias, that the Office began to assume force and vigor in implementing new cultivations and at the same time inspecting for abuses while allowing local variations. Elias had been Resident in Tjirebon prior to being selected as Director of Cultivations (1833-1836). He envisioned his new function as one of maintaining an equitable balance between the interests of the government and the welfare of the population: a view which caused no small amount of disagreement with various Residents, including his eventual successor to the Directorship, W. de Vogel.

After 1836 the Office of the Director of Cultivations began to change. Partly this was the result of the passing of the creative period and the beginning of bureaucratized procedures. The annual Cultivation Reports which had started in 1834 became more standardized after 1836, the Directors

[9]   R. Reinsma, 'De kultuurprocenten in de praktijk en in de ogen der tijdgenoten,' *Tijdschrift voor Geschiedenis* 72 (1959), pp. 57-83, provides an initial excursion into the question of the percentage payments.
[10]   The function of the Director of Cultivations is officially described in *Staatsblad van Nederlandsch Indië*, 1833, No. 73. He is to see that the System operated in accordance with the basic plan, protect the Javanese against abuses and make certain that they receive the benefits planned by the System, and direct all local efforts toward lightening the labor and increasing the income of the population.

constantly complained about being burdened with paper work and having less and less opportunity for first-hand observations, and the reports issuing from the office grew ever further in arrears until by the 1840s the annual reports appeared as much as two years late. These surface phenomena would tend to indicate that the Office of Cultivations became less and less of an integral part of the productive process in Java and grew increasingly detached from the controls and regulations which it had originally been designed to oversee.

Behind this change lay a devolution of authority within the System to the local administrators. Van den Bosch's efforts to retain all decision-making power in his hands after his return to the Netherlands and elevation to Minister of Colonies in 1834 may have made it difficult for the colonial administration in Batavia to act forcibly. Also the mounting revenue needs in the Netherlands caused by the Belgian War forced all caution aside in an effort to expand the System. But possibly more decisive than either of these was the gradual development of convenient arrangements, in the various areas where exportable crops were grown, between Javanese administrators, European civil servants, and European and Chinese entrepreneurs and supervisors. Among these groups fortunes were made through percentage payments, underestimations of yields, and private sector export of goods. Persons in these groups had fewer and fewer qualms about evading the rules of the System, in putting heavier pressures on the cultivator, and in bypassing the Office of Cultivations.[11]

In practice after 1836 there was little possibility of the Director of Cultivations doing much to affect local cultivation arrangements. This is most cogently illustrated by the secret instructions issued to the Director of the Office of Cultivations in 1840. The Director was told not to interfere in existing local arrangements but instead to learn from the local authorities; moreover, he was to refrain from even discussing local landrent arrangements and to avoid actions affecting work services or the socio-economic life of the Javanese villages. At most he might look about for areas in which government cultivations, especially indigo, might be expanded.[12] Clearly the locus of regulation and control over the productive aspects of the System had devolved to the European and Javanese administrators in the

---

[11]   L. Vitalis, *De invoering, werking en gebreken van het stelsel van kultures op Java* (Zalt-Bommel: Noman, 1851), pp. 21-3, takes note of the changes in the System after 1836 much in the way that I have done in this paper. Most later writers on the System have made little use of Vitalis' writings, feeling him perhaps to be too intimately tied to the founder of the System, and sharing too directly in the profits of the System, since he was assisted by the government in buying two sugar mills in Semarang in 1838. See Besluit Gouverneur-Generaal, February 12, 1838, No. 11. Actually Vitalis' function as inspector of cultivations made him an astute and critical observer of many aspects of the System.

[12]   Geheim Besluit van den Gouverneur-Generaal, July 17, 1840, La Ya.

residencies and regencies of Java. Local variations were perpetuated and expanded, and the 'System' became in actuality an interlocking set of local accommodations.

If the information and method applied in this paper have merit, it should be possible to discern differences in the operation of the System from one residency to the next, as well as variations in impact. To test this I have taken information from the annual Cultivation Reports from 1837 through 1851. In these years the content of the reports was standardized. They are to be found in complete form in the Archive of the Ministry of Colonies.[13] The fact that the reports probably had little influence upon production policies during these years does not diminish their historical value. The information they contain is no more or no less accurate because of this fact; the candor of some of the statements contained in the reports was indeed probably due to the fact that the reports had ceased to be feared as instruments of discipline or control.

The Cultivation Reports have been little used in any description or analysis of the Cultivation System. Primarily this is because they were classified up to 1839 and available only to high officials in the Ministry of Colonies thereafter. After 1851 some of the essential bits of information from the Reports were incorporated in the *Koloniaal Verslag*, but the earlier reports were not opened to the public until about the time of the Second World War. Gradually scholars began to locate them and use them. Then another problem arose; the size and detailed nature of the statistical information made it difficult to manipulate. To resolve this difficulty I had most of the information for the years 1837 through 1851 punched on computer cards. This information was then programmed to produce the various charts, tables, and ratios with which this paper works. This paper, however, uses only a fraction of the total information.

Before turning to the actual data, I shall add a few words about the overall nature and content of a typical Cultivation Report. A Cultivation Report was an annual summary of the state of cultivations in Java, and was divided into sections dealing with: Agricultural Establishments, Cinnamon, Cloves, Coffee, Corvée, Forestry, Gunny Sacks, Indigo, Livestock, Nopal and Cochineal, Pepper, Rice, Silk, Sugar, Tea and Tobacco. These sections do not necessarily appear in this order, or in any other order, and not every section appeared each year. Each section consists of text and statistical tables. The text, normally only a few pages, summarizes advances and declines, notes particular problems, and/or indicates future plans and projections. The

---

[13] The Cultivation Reports are scattered in various folders of the Archive of the Ministry of Colonies which, for the years under consideration here, is located in the Rijksarchief, The Hague. Folio 3205 of this Archive contains a listing of the Cultivation Reports with their locations.

Table I

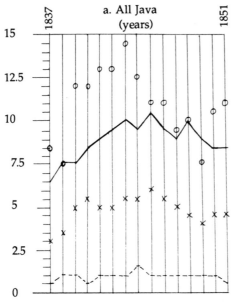

a. All Java (years)

Purchase price paid to population for:

o   all government cultivations;

x   all government cultivations except coffee.

Gross landrent assessment:

—— on all cultivated fields (incl. govt.);

--- on fields planted for the government only

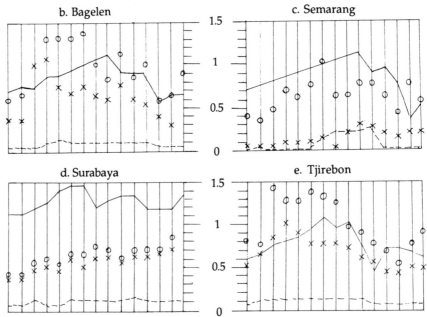

statistical tables contain information on a residency basis. It should be noted that the residencies of Batavia (Jakarta), Buitenzorg (Bogor), Jogjakarta, and Surakarta were never incorporated into the Cultivation System and are, therefore, not included in any of the figures (including totals) used in this analysis. The statistical tables contain information on such matters as: the number of individuals and/or families involved in a particular cultivation or type of work, the land area and types of land used for a particular crop, the payments made to the population for crops grown for the government, the landrent assessment on government fields as well as other fields, the costs of processing and transportation, and percentage payments to administrators, to mention but a few of the more important items. The charts accompanying the Rice sections provide the most comprehensive information on land, population, production, taxation, prices, etc. for each residency.

The set of charts in Table I shows relationships between landrent assessments and the payments made by the government for crops. These charts are first for Java as a whole (chart Ia), and then for four selected residencies (charts Ib, Ic, Id, and Ie). The landrent was the largest tax item for the rural Javanese as well as for the government; it was not the only tax, but it was the one most directly related to the cultivations. Payment for crops grown for the government was far from being the only source of monetary income for the Javanese villager, but it represented, more than any other source, the benefit which the System was supposed to bring to the Javanese.

It will be immediately apparent that the total landrent assessment for the whole of Java on all cultivated fields generally ran below the payments made for all crops, including coffee, which were grown under the government's Cultivation System. The four selected residencies show markedly diverse patterns, and two of them, Semarang and Surabaja, have landrent assessments which continually exceed the total payments for crops. The assessment on fields planted for the government ran continuously below the payments made for the crops grown on these fields, principally sugar and indigo, and, with the exception of Semarang, this was a rather large difference. This difference *should* represent the profit to the Javanese population directly involved in the cultivation of government crops on their lands if only the two elements represented on these charts are taken into account.

It will also be seen from Table I that the landrent assessment rose during the late 1830s and early 1840s, and began to level off, and even dip, after the middle of the 1840s. The payments made for government cultivations except coffee show a similar, albeit less pronounced, tendency. The inclusion of the coffee payments tends to diffuse this correlation, for coffee yields ran in natural cycles quite independent of governmental action. The charts reflect statistically what every account of the Cultivation System has already indicated: namely, that the System ran into trouble in the mid 1840s. These troubles are generally attributed to overextension, and their solution was sought in adjustments of landrent assessments and reduction of areas in government cultivation. The charts for Bagelen (Ib), Semarang (Ic), and Tjirebon (Ie) show a sharper than normal adjustment; this corresponds with the reported severity of the problems in these particular residencies.

The charts in Table II are both more complex and less precise than those in Table I. Essentially they represent a graphic relationship between the number of families and the area of land involved in government cultivations. To present this relationship graphically, the number of families liable to cultivation services and the extent of land used in the government cultivations are expressed in percentages of the total number of agricultural families and the total area of cultivated land respectively. The charts are for all of Java and for the same four selected residencies, and provide information for total crops as well as separately for indigo, sugar, and coffee. Since coffee was not grown on land otherwise cultivated, there is no line on the coffee charts for the percentage of cultivated land.

The imprecision of these charts is caused by the difficulty in obtaining accurate information about numbers of people or families and areas of land under cultivation in Java at the time with which we are concerned. Census and cadastral surveys were unknown; all figures were based on reportings from village officials to higher authorities. Virtually everyone who has used nineteenth-century Javanese figures has expressed cautions and doubts, and quite correctly so. It appears from my work with these statistics and by comparing them with spot checks and demographic regressions that a fairly constant divergence factor of 25 percent below the actual amount can be applied to both the total number of families and the total area of land. The basis of this correction factor is explained in the appendix to this paper (see below, pp. 87-88). Suffice it to note here that the charts in Table II are based on the actual figures as given. If the correction factor were applied it would lower the percentage of families and land used in government cultivations below that shown in the charts.

From the graphs in Table II it will be evident that the portion of cultivated land used for government cultivations was not a large portion of the total. Throughout the period government cultivations remain at about 5 percent of the total land under cultivation. This is probably on the high side since this land was apt to be more accurately measured than was general village land in cultivation. The proportion of land in government culti-vation runs higher in Bagelen and Tjirebon, a feature which is accounted for by the extent of land used in indigo cultivation.

What appears remarkable in light of the small land area is the high

Table II

—— Percentage of agricultural families involved in government required work for particular cultivations.

---- Percentage of sawah and tegalan fields used for cultivation of government crops.

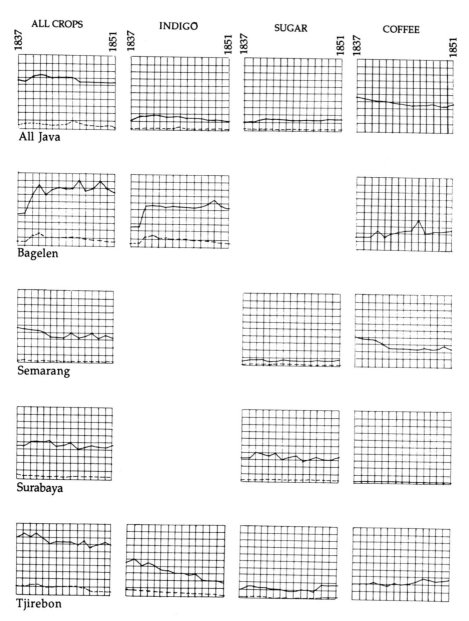

percentage of agricultural families involved in government cultivations. It will be noticed from the upper left hand chart in Table II that the percentage of agricultural families involved in government cultivations for all of Java is in excess of 70 percent for much of the period. For all of Java somewhat more than one half of these families were involved in coffee growing. But in Bagelen and Tjirebon the involvement in indigo production was also large, and in Surabaja sugar cane cultivation accounted for the largest portion. This high human involvement in the System begins to shed some light on the hitherto rather obscure element of labor service. However it was managed, there was a heavy concentration of labor brought to bear upon rather limited areas of land. Accounts of the time would lead to the conclusion that this labor force did not all appear at once, that there arose a group of people who for payment performed work services for others, and that not all the persons or families listed actually did field work. In general, the poor and propertyless seem to have borne the brunt of the work, but this had compensations which were not always expressed in monetary terms.[14]

The high proportion of agricultural families involved in government cultivations would tend to provide some explanation for the extremely low per capita payments made under the System for produce from government fields, for not only was the labor input far too large for even the most optimistic production schemes, but the large labor force was often wastefully used. Somewhat less directly evident, but probably true nonetheless, is the frequently made observation both during and after the years of the Cultivation System that it encouraged communal landholding rather than individual holdings. Both the high human involvement in some villages and the rotation of lands in sugar, indigo, and tobacco areas would support this tendency, which was in any event a rather normal state of affairs for many parts of Java.[15] Whatever the truth of these contentions, it seems quite evident that the numbers of persons involved in the System, directly or indirectly, were extremely large, and that it is obviously in this area, rather than in the extent of land used, that the System had its most noticeable effect in Java. Where these figures run especially high, as in Bagelen and Tjirebon, there are noticeable social effects as will be shown presently.

It would probably be useful to bring these labor figures somewhat into perspective by providing a brief explanation of the manner of cultivation

---

[14]   Day, *Policy and administration*, p. 267, speculated on the emergence of a destitute class under the System. His evidence for this seems to rest entirely on Van Soest's *Geschiedenis*, which would certainly indicate that all was not right with the System, but which would not give a very positive notion of the emergence of such a class at this time.
[15]   A most perceptive insight into the nature of communal landholding and the regulation of village affairs in the middle of the nineteenth century is given by J.H.F. Sollewijn Gelpke, *Naar aanleiding van Staatsblad 1878, No. 110* (Batavia, 1901), pp. 7-9 and 24-8.

and delivery used in the three major crops listed here: coffee, indigo, and sugar. The various forms of labor activity and possible extra compensations will not alter the figures, but may make them more understandable.

Coffee deliveries for little or no compensation had been imposed upon various districts in Java long before the Cultivation System was introduced, and in a strict sense coffee was not included in the schemes of Van den Bosch. However, in a practical way it was not possible to exclude the largest revenue-producing crop from a total economic plan, and the Director of Cultivations included coffee in his reports from the outset. Van den Bosch did undertake to reform the existing system of coffee deliveries first by making monetary payments immediately upon delivery and directly to the cultivator or person who delivered the coffee rather than to headmen, and second by increasing the number of collection-payment stations, thereby reducing the transportation distance for the coffee growers.[16] Almost all persons, however they felt about other aspects of the Cultivation System, regarded these reforms as beneficent and clearly in the economic interest of the Javanese villager. In portions of the Preanger Regencies the custom of delivering coffee in lieu of the paddy assessment continued.

Coffee was grown in three ways, namely, in gardens, forests, and hedgerows. Only the agricultural families designated for work in gardens and forests are included in the totals of the Cultivation Reports and in the charts in Table II. Coffee gardens were planted in foothill and upland areas on land not used for other cultivations. Forest coffee consisted of plantings in the midst of forested areas, where the coffee often did very well. For the planting and maintenance of more than 200,000,000 coffee trees in Java during the 1840s there were between 400,000 and 500,000 families designated as laborers. Constant planting was necessary, and between two and ten million new trees were planted annually, either to replace old trees or on newly opened areas. Whole families worked in various phases of the coffee growing; the work was generally seasonal. The remoteness of the coffee gardens and the primitive transportation system made the work more arduous than it would otherwise have been. The payment of seven to ten guilders per picul was great enough to provide some profit for most families, though this varied: in some areas as few as 75 trees would yield a picul of coffee, while in other locations it took more than 300. Hedgerow coffee was grown along roads and paths in kampong areas as an extra source of income for villagers throughout Java.

---

[16]   The basic coffee reforms came about through a resolution of August 8, 1832, No. 35, and later decrees. In the formulation of this policy Van den Bosch had worked closely with Merkus; this was one of the few occasions on which the two men cooperated in these years. See S. van Deventer, *Bijdragen tot de kennis van het landelijk stelsel op Java* (Zalt-Bommel: Noman, 1865-6), vol. II, pp. 526-7.

Small amounts of indigo had been grown in Java since time immemorial, but extensive cultivation and preparation for export were
introduced during the Cultivation System. The indigo plant was grown on
non-irrigated fields, frequently those otherwise used for dry rice or
secondary crops. From all reports, indigo growing and preparation became
the most detested of the cultivations for the Javanese. There are three
obvious reasons for this. The indigo plant exhausted the soil. After a few
years neither indigo nor any other crop would grow on the land, and new
areas, further from the village, had to be opened. Second, the preparation in
small factories involved a fermentation process which required wading and
sloshing in the vats with resultant discoloration of the skin. While such
work was paid extra, it was not free of compulsion. Third, the payments to
field workers were small to begin with, but the vast numbers of persons
used in the cultivation made the individual payment minuscule. Indigo
was not very profitable to the government either, and by the mid 1840s the
area in cultivation was cut back – many of the workers were turned into
coffee growers – and gradually indigo planting was almost totally
abandoned.

Sugar, also, had been grown in Java before 1830, chiefly around Batavia
and in a few areas of East Java. The Cultivation System, however, extended
the crop throughout the northern coastal plains of Java. Where it flour-
ished, as in the Surabaja-Pasuruan area, sugar provided the basis for some
prosperity for Javanese and great wealth for European and Chinese millers
and exporters. Where it grew with difficulty and with low yields, as in
Central Java, it created much work and less than the anticipated profits.
Where it failed to grow, as in Bantam, it was soon abandoned. So far as the
Cultivation System was concerned, the only obligation of the villager was to
plant, tend, and cut the cane; it is this much of the process that is shown in
both the payment and the number of families in the charts of Tables I and II.
But clearly more had to happen before sugar could be exported. Such
processes as transporting the cane from the field to the factory, working in
the factory, and again transporting the refined sugar to the wharf, were all
compensated, over and above the payments for the raw cane. These
additional payments do not appear in the figures used here. Generally,
transportation was arranged on a contractual basis with individuals, and an
independent group of transport entrepreneurs began to appear. Factory work
was not always voluntary, even though additional pay was given; frequently
factory labor was supplied through arrangements with village headmen, not
unlike the compulsion used for field laborers.

Sugar cane was grown on irrigated rice fields which were taken out of
production for a year to eighteen months in order to accommodate the new
crop. In many areas, the growing cycle came to be accommodated within the

rice pattern of production, and as village lands were extended and new areas brought into irrigation vast tracts of land on which alternating paddy and cane cultivation occurred became common. In such areas more than one-fifth of a village's lands were devoted to cane; this brought about very complicated land swaps. Also in these areas the villages became heavily dependent upon the extra monetary income from the various stages of growing and processing the sugar; this dependence produced social and economic changes within the village that were difficult to control.

To carry forward our analysis of the charts in Tables I and II, I would like to introduce two further sets of relationships based on the statistical data from the Cultivation Reports. Table II shows the percentage of agricultural families employed in various cultivations during the years 1837 through 1851, but the charts tell us nothing about the absolute total of agricultural families as it might have changed over the period in question. If we express this rise and fall of the number of agricultural families at the beginning, mid-point, and end of our period as percentages of the numbers at the beginning of the period, we are presented with the following figures:

	Beginning	Mid-Point	End
All Java	100%	109%	103%
Bagelen	100%	98%	69%
Semarang	100%	115%	7%
Surabaja	100%	116%	140%
Tjirebon	100%	107%	80%

Nor do the charts in Table II provide us with information about the relationship between the total number of agricultural families and the total amount of land in cultivation. Using again the beginning, mid-point, and end of our fifteen year period, and dividing the total units[17] of land in cultivation by the total number of agricultural families (obtaining thereby the average amount of cultivated land per agricultural family), we obtain the following set of figures.

	Beginning	Mid-Point	End
All Java	1.13	1.14	1.42
Bagelen	0.9	1.0	2.0
Semarang	1.5	1.6	2.8
Surabaja	1.7	1.5	1.4
Tjirebon	1.0	1.5	2.0

---

[17] The unit of land measurement was the *bouw* (bau or bahu) which varied in size from one part of Java to another, but which was standardized in the Cultivation Reports as an areal measurement of 500 square rods.

These figures give an indication both of rising population and increased amounts of cultivated land for all Java. Contemporary accounts constantly refer to the opening of new lands through the extension of irrigation channels, the draining of coastal swamps, and the clearing of new lands. It would appear that the amount of land in cultivation increased somewhat more rapidly than the number of agricultural families, but not too much should be made of this because of the difficulty in enumeration. The labor involved in opening and improving agricultural lands was in large part included in the cultivation work for which the families in Table II were designated. This could be extremely hard work, and was reflected in the compensation and production patterns only at a future date if at all.

The number of agricultural families seems to have increased slowly for all of Java, but to have decreased in three of the four residencies examined here. Contemporary accounts frequently speak of villagers, sometimes whole villages, moving, so the trends shown here need not be surprising. Part of this mobility was undoubtedly into towns and cities, which would mean statistically that the migrant family would drop out of the agricultural count but would eventually be picked up again in the total population count. Some of the movement was into unoccupied or formerly abandoned areas, principally in East Java, which had been depopulated in the wars of the late eighteenth and early nineteenth centuries culminating in the Java War of 1825-1830. The population line, like the landrent line in Table I, moves slowly upward to the mid 1840s and then declines slightly. The poor harvests and accompanying epidemics of the 1840s, especially severe in the Semarang-Demak-Rembang area, are generally cited as a cause of this trend, and they undoubtedly had an effect. The extent of family mobility, however, probably also put a strain on the primitive counting methods of the time.

From an examination of the trends of population and land in the four selected residencies, it appears that Surabaja runs counter to the other three. In regard to the number of agricultural families it is the only residency to show an increase during the period. Semarang and Tjirebon show a rise into the mid-1840s, then a decline below the beginning point. Bagelen displays a constant decline throughout the period.

These trends tend to confirm, and to be confirmed by, the charts in Tables I and II as well as by the reports of the time. In Bagelen, for instance, the burdensome nature of the indigo cultivation has already been noted. It is not surprising that families and villages left the area or made themselves scarce. The continuously heavy labor involvement shown in the Bagelen charts in Table II meant, of course, a steady decrease in absolute numbers since the number of agricultural families was absolutely decreasing. The decreasing land area devoted to indigo in Bagelen (Table II) reflects this trend too, but the over-all decline in the number of agricultural workers is less than would be anticipated in Bagelen because of transference out of indigo into the expanding coffee cultivations.

One feature of the Semarang chart, Table Ic, which needs some clarification, is the unusual rise in the assessment of fields planted for the government in the mid-1840s. Coming at a time when epidemics and famine were prevalent in the area and total agricultural families were declining, this may seem very strange indeed. Indeed it should, for it reveals a clear case of maladministration in which the local Resident and his staff were attempting to cover up a mismanaged situation by throwing additional burdens on the assessments on government fields. Assessments on government fields rose to 27 percent of total assessments with less than 2 percent of the total cultivated area planted for the government. This was a desperate effort to cover losses on abandoned fields caused by population movements and deaths, and to offset losses from a futile and costly effort to introduce tobacco cultivation. Chart Ic shows some rather hasty readjustments in the residency after 1847; tobacco areas were reduced, landrent assessments were lowered, large irrigation schemes were undertaken, and the labor involvement in sugar cane cultivation was slowly increased. The local administration, both European and Javanese, was also shaken up.

In both Semarang and Tjirebon the statistical patterns and the contemporary reports have a certain similarity. The introduction of indigo in Tjirebon and sugar cane in Semarang did not go especially well. Extensive draining of swamps along the coast and opening of new lands occurred in both areas. Lack of profit and heavy labor requirements drove people off the land and out of compulsory government service. Apparently the movement off the land was principally into the major towns and city of each residency, for the total population in both regions remained rather constant despite the marked decline in agricultural population. This is quite unlike the Bagelen situation where both total population and agricultural population declined.

Only in Surabaja does the number of agricultural families increase constantly and sharply, so sharply that an inward migration can be the only explanation. The lighter than average involvement in government cultivations, as shown in Table II, and the prospering sugar industry would appear to be significant contributing factors. The lack of any reported food or disease crisis in the Surabaja area during this period must also be noted. The increase shown in Surabaja is similar to the patterns for the residencies of Pasuruan and Besuki, both expanding sugar areas. The residencies of Kediri and Madiun also show a similar, albeit less pronounced, trend. By contrast, all residencies in Central Java seem to have lost agricultural population.[18]

---

[18] The statistical information for all residencies has been worked out, but is not included in

Turning to the relationship between the area of cultivated land and the number of agricultural families, we note from figures on p. 79 that the area of land per family was gradually increasing throughout the period for all Java. This increase is reflected in exaggerated fashion in three of the four sample residencies; only Surabaja is moving in the other direction. The over-all increase for all Java is about 125 percent while that for Semarang is 185 percent, Tjirebon 200 percent, and Bagelen 220 percent. This is naturally related to the movement off the land in these three areas which, along with the addition of newly opened lands, meant that there was increasingly more cultivated land per family. Or, seen from another perspective, there were less people to work more land as time went on. Surabaja shows the steady decrease in the area of cultivated land per agricultural family to be expected in light of the inward migration. Also the actual expansion of cultivated lands in Surabaja was less than in the other three residencies. Moreover, the growing reliance of agricultural families in the sugar producing areas upon land rentals to sugar producers and upon paid work in the sugar industry, may well have made it possible to concentrate more people on smaller amounts of land.

From all of this it would appear that the amount of land available was perhaps less important to an agricultural family than the amount of imposed labor required by the government and/or the profitability of particular types of work. The availability of agricultural land in Bagelen, Semarang, and Tjirebon may have been a contributing factor in the individualization of landholding which is noted in these areas later in the century. While the interpretation of the data produced by the investigation launched in the 1860s into Javanese rights in land awaits careful analysis, it is quite evident that communal holdings were strongest in East Java and the interior regions of Central Java, while individual landholdings arrangements prevailed in West Java and along the central north coast.[19] The rather easy availability of land in Bagelen, Semarang, and Tjirebon may have led to concentration of landholding by families which could either escape or manage the imposed services that accompanied control of land. Admini-

---

this paper. Where reference is made to contemporary accounts, the text portion of the Cultivation Reports is generally meant. However, such accounts as Van Soest's *Geschiedenis* and Van Deventer's *Bijdragen* are compendia of details about famine and disease (attributed to the System), abuses, brutalities, and stupidities which led to the abandonment of certain areas as well as less sizeable movements of populations.

[19] [W.B. Bergsma], *Eindresumé van het [...] onderzoek naar de rechten van den Inlander*, 3 vols. (Batavia: Ernst, 1876, 1880, and 1896), makes the local variations in landholding arrangements quite explicit. The report was so long in preparation that it had little effect upon the land conversion arrangements toward individual holdings which the government started in the late nineteenth century. The wealth of substantive data contained in this report has hardly been touched by scholars.

strative families as well as village headmen were freed of such obligations, and it is possible that for such groups their privileged position would allow a gradual shift in economic patterns.

An interesting question which our data does not touch upon but which seems relevant to understanding the relationships expounded here, is the extent to which cultivation services were turned to other ends and the extent to which other service obligations continued. Technically both were violations of the System as originally conceived, but both happened and seem to have become regularized. Large government projects such as road works, factory construction, and the building of fortifications continued to draw on labor which was levied under corvée arrangements supposedly equated with, not imposed in addition to, cultivation work. Forced labor imposed by village headmen and higher officials, except for village guard duty and local maintenance, was supposed to cancel out cultivation obligations, and to be specially provided for from particular villages which were freed from cultivation work. But there are many indications that large amounts of labor were used on personal projects by both European and Javanese civil servants. This question is too complex to be unravelled here. Suffice it to note that the burden of obligatory service could mount up considerably in some areas, and, quite apart from any particular crop or type of land usage, the personal quirks of the local administration which had virtually a free hand in such matters was of considerable importance in determining the quality of life of the agriculturist.

A number of observations should be made to clarify certain aspects of the problems raised here. Van den Bosch had assumed that his plan would bring increased welfare and prosperity to the Javanese. In the main, despite shortfalls in some areas, the System did that. By all material bases of calculation such as area of land under cultivation per family, amount of livestock per family, and availability and price of basic food commodities it would appear that material well-being was growing more rapidly than the population during the period under consideration here. But this is a very generalized observation and says nothing about the manner in which these material gains were distributed among the population.

From Table I it is clear that the payments made to the population for crops grown for the government were more than enough to pay the landrent assessment on the lands on which government crops were grown. But that was not the purpose of the System; it was supposed to provide enough to pay the total landrent assessment. In a few localities this occurred, but it was more the exception than the rule. Moreover, if we view the amount of payment for crops in relation to the number of agricultural families involved, then the payment per family was minuscule. But it is not at all clear that payments were made on a per family basis. In some areas such individualized payments were introduced by European administrators, but much more common was payment on a village basis, or, to put it differently, a reduction in the landrent owed by the village by the amount of the crop payment. In actuality, then, many families received no benefits unless they were included among the village landholders. There are indeed indications that in many villages landholding rights were extended to a broader segment of the population under the Cultivation System than had previously been the case. Such indications lie behind the assumption, probably correct, that the System encouraged communal landholding arrangements in many areas.

It is perhaps not surprising that the landrent assessment on fields planted for the government was on the average higher than on the remaining fields. Chart Ia shows that the landrent assessment on government fields ran at about 12 percent of the total, while the extent of such fields, as shown in the upper left hand chart of Table II, was generally less than 6 percent of the total cultivated area. The statistics are again confirmed by contemporary observations which tell us that fields planted in sugar cane were always assessed at the highest rate regardless of what their classification might have been when planted in paddy.[20] It also follows logically that since fields planted for the government were more accurately measured and supervised the assessment discrepancy would be even greater.

There is probably little doubt that such matters as described here ran counter to the original plan of Van den Bosch, but they did exist and did grow worse as time went on. They form an essential aspect of the pressure of the System upon the Javanese cultivator and the tendency of the System to effect social changes in Javanese society. Van den Bosch undoubtedly succeeded in raising the material level of Javanese society. The System in its own way undoubtedly bestowed privilege and benefit upon a small segment of Javanese society, but there was very little done to promote the sense of enterprise and personal endeavor among the Javanese. That was not, of course, Van den Bosch's purpose. Javanese society was supposed to remain constant and content; it was not meant to develop any dynamism. Moreover, there was an underlying assumption that the Javanese cultivator was not influenced by normal economic stimuli – an assumption that would appear rather far off the mark if the evidence presented in this paper has any validity. Whatever the aims of the System in preserving Javanese society in stasis, they were not successful. Javanese society did change, did develop new social and economic relationships, and did apparently undergo population shifts. It is also a fact that the profits from the cultivation of

---

[20] R.W.J.C. Bake, *Kunnen en moeten veranderingen gebragt worden in het kultuurstelsel op Java?* (Utrecht: Dekema, 1854), p. 22.

crops for the government which the Javanese did not make were being made by others, namely the European and Chinese mill owners, importers and exporters, and especially, of course, the government itself.

The period of the 1830s, just prior to the years covered by the statistical evidence used in this paper, seems to me a most critical time in the development of the System. In the early 1830s there had been some efforts to involve the Javanese cultivator more directly in the System. Labor arrangements, for instance, were originally conceived as contractual rather than forced. This did not work well, partly due to impatience and pressures for money from the European side, partly due to socio-economic disabilities among the Javanese. In some areas, such as Djepara, there were early efforts to involve the Javanese in the processing side of the System. These efforts too were soon abandoned, owing to stronger Chinese capital, on the one hand, and, on the other, failure to maintain quality control.[21] Schemes to involve some of the Javanese *prijaji* upper class in milling and production contracts also failed. After 1836 no further efforts were made in this direction, and the role and function of the Javanese was relegated to what seemed to work best, namely traditional authority controlling unthinking labor. The System, as I have said above, became entrenched in local arrangements, and as it began to show profits, it became less and less possible to tamper with its production features. There was by now no longer room for the Javanese, other than the administrators, to seek a future within the cultivation aspects of the System. There was no device within the System for absorbing the socio-economic or cultural changes which emerged. Only in fringe areas was this possible. Transportation contracts, arrangements for delivery of subsidiary materials, supervisory functions in fields and mills, and other types of jobs developed around the government cultivations. For many others movement into the towns and cities provided an entry either into paid employment or into an expanding internal commercial sector which provided commodities for the growing market economy in Java. This market economy was in large part expanded through the growing communication network and the increased monetization of economic life made necessary by the System.

From an economic point of view the growing profits to individuals and to the government produced by the System came largely from more efficient processing of sugar and the continued marketability of coffee. This could occur without altering arrangements for cultivation or payment with the population. The charts in Table II indicate quite clearly that the area of land

---

[21]   R. Van Niel, 'The regulation of sugar production in Java, 1830-1840,' in R. Van Niel (ed.), *Economic factors in Southeast Asian social change* (Honolulu: Asian Studies Program, University of Hawaii Press, 1968), pp. 91-108.

under government cultivation was diminishing, while the number of families with an obligation for cultivation service remained constant. It would appear that the size of the labor force bore little relationship to the economic functioning of the System. I suspect that the amount of available labor that became tied to prestige functions of Javanese and European administrators became ever greater. By the end of the period which we are considering here there was probably more abuse in the area of diverting services to personal ends than there was in the way of overwork in the actual cultivation of crops.

Conclusion

Most of the statistical evidence presented in this paper has tended to confirm and substantiate the accounts of the Cultivation System as obtained from other sources. We have certainly not presented a radical revision of the generally accepted story. Moreover, this type of evidence seems most convincing and is most illuminating when used in conjunction with other kinds of material. At most, the data has highlighted certain developments such as the extent to which the population was involved in the System and the degree of population mobility in Java. These are not new concepts, but the fashion in which they are presented here may make them more rigorous, and by so doing may place some of the changes in Javanese society in sharper perspective. This type of supporting and reinforcing role is probably the most that should be hoped for or expected.

It is my feeling that this is sufficient to warrant a continuation of the method of inquiry. Information on rice prices, paddy yields, wages, livestock, and many other items are available in the Cultivation Reports for the period covered in this paper. Much of this type of data continued to appear in later periods in the *Koloniaal Verslag*. Some records below the residency level may still be in existence and may become available to future historians.[22] Such records can provide exciting insights into local variations, and can perhaps advance our understanding of the process of social change. Historians will hopefully be able to use the records as a whole to tell a story of social, economic and cultural change in Java which will include the Javanese population whose own records of mundane events scarcely exist. The present effort to do this is rather gross, in keeping with the nature of the evidence, but one can hope for future refinements.

---

[22] R. Van Niel, *A survey of historical source materials in Java and Manila* (Honolulu: University of Hawaii Press, 1970), p. 12.

Appendix

The Cultivation Reports for the years covered here (1837-1851) contain figures on total population on a residency basis. The total population for all reported residencies rose from 6,282,848 in 1837 to 7,386,802 in 1851. These figures were derived from village and district reports compiled by local officials whose interests lay in under-reporting, but whose capacity to do this was limited by sight estimates by European and higher Javanese officials. The residencies of Batavia (Jakarta), Buitenzorg (Bogor), Jogjakarta, and Surakarta were not included in these figures. It was customary among officials at the time to estimate the population of these excluded areas at about two million persons. If this amount is added to the population figure for 1851 we achieve a total population for all Java of about 9.3 million persons which is very close to the officially reported figure of 9.5 million given in the *Koloniaal Verslag* for 1850.

I cannot explain why Dr. P. Bleeker, whose investigations into the population of Java began in the mid-1840s and whose figures are used by all demographers for this period, made no use of the figures in the Cultivation Reports.[23] The Cultivation Reports do not show as high a rate of growth as Bleeker and others tended to assume, but this more moderate growth rate for the period under consideration seems to accord more closely with the feelings of contemporary demographers about Java's population during the early nineteenth century.

No one, then or now, would regard any of the nineteenth century figures as accurate. The question is, how inaccurate are they? Through working backwards from later data, Breman estimates that the population of Java in 1850 must have been about 12.5 million, while Peper prefers a figure closer to 13.1 million.[24] The difference is attributable to various estimates about the rate of population growth in the latter half of the nineteenth century. Widjojo prefers to make no estimates for lack of accurate evidence (for which he cannot be blamed), but questions any population growth to speak of in the nineteenth century. This latter supposition is completely unsupportable. It seems to rest on nothing more than an exaggerated reading of Gonggrijp, whose already exaggerated account of the effects of the Cultivation System is generally recognized as an overreaction by an economic

[23]   P. Bleeker, 'Statistisch-ekonomische onderzoekingen en beschouwingen op koloniaal gebied: Over de bevolkingstoename op Java,' *Tijdschrift voor Nederlandsch Indië*, Nieuwe Serie I (1863), pp. 193-4.

[24]   J.C. Breman, 'Java; Bevolkingsgroei en demografische structuur,' in: *Drie geografische studies over Java* (Leiden: Brill, 1963), pp. 252-308, esp. 267-9; Bram Peper, *Grootte en groei van Java's inheemse bevolking in de negentiende eeuw* (Amsterdam: Anthropologisch-Sociologisch Centrum, 1967), esp. pp. 112-9.

liberal to a system of restriction and state control.[25] The fact is that the studies of Breman and Peper provide us with some estimates which, if used cautiously, can give us a working model of Javanese population configurations in the nineteenth century.

If we accept Breman's figure of 12.5 million persons as the approximate population of Java in 1850, and take the figure of 9.3 million as the sum of the total obtained from the Cultivation Reports and the uncounted residencies, for about the same date, we note that the latter figures are about 75 percent of the former. Van der Wijck reports on a population reassessment check in Tjirebon in 1844 in which the population proved to be 145,000 instead of a reported 105,000; this would mean that in this instance only 72 percent of the actual total had been reported.[26]

The Cultivation Reports also provide information on the extent of land area under cultivation. Again these figures are derived from village headmen and local officials, and again there were clear advantages to underreporting. Dutch officials in Java at the time were quite aware of this practice, and made some spot checks to determine how far off reported land areas were from the reality. One such check in Tjirebon in 1842 led Governor-General Merkus to report that the 1,515,436 *bouw* reported in that residency was about 500,000 *bouw* short of the mark.[27] The reported amount was thus about 75 percent of the actual total. In 1836 a random sampling of villages in Tjirebon, Pekalongan, and Tegal showed that a reported cultivated area of 990 *bouw* was in actuality 1380 *bouw* – meaning that only 72 percent of the true amount of cultivated land was reported.[28]

It should be noted in both instances that this factor of underreporting ranging from 72 to 75 percent of the rechecked totals for both population and cultivated land, works only for rather large aggregates. It is often not relevant to figures for a single village. For the large aggregates, however, I have found it to be fairly consistent for the period covered by this paper.

Whatever the merits or demerits of applying any such factor to the adjustments of statistical errors in the pertinent data contained in the Cultivation Reports, it should be noted that this was not done in the present analysis; here all calculations are based upon figures exactly as contained in the Cultivation Reports.

---

[25] Widjojo Nitisastro, *Population trends in Indonesia* (Ithaca: Cornell University Press, 1970), Chapter 3.
[26] H.C. van der Wijck, *Eenige beschouwingen over Java* (Arnhem: Nijhoff, 1851), pp.42-8.
[27] Letter from Gouverneur-Generaal P. Merkus to the Minister of Colonies, dd. Buitenzorg, April 22, 1844, Geheim, Kabinet no. 85. Archive, Ministry of Colonies.
[28] Van Deventer, *Bijdragen*, vol. III, report of P.F. Clignett, pp. 45-63; see esp. the chart on p. 64.

CHAPTER V

Government Policy and the Civil Administration in Java During the Early Years of the Cultivation System

From mid-1971 to mid-1973 I served as foundation Dean of the School of Humanities of the Universiti Sains Malaysia in Penang, Malaysia. Upon my return to Hawaii in 1973 I returned to my research on the Cultivation System. The questions raised by the previous paper were still much on my mind, and having been part of the Malaysian bureaucracy, I was naturally enough drawn to questions related to civil service. This was, I should hastily add, a general interest and not one based on comparisons between British-style administration in Malaya and Dutch administrative development in colonial Indonesia. In any event, when John Smail asked me to participate in a Conference on Modern Indonesian History to be held at the University of Wisconsin in Madison in July 1975, I chose to write on government policy and public administration under the Cultivation System. This paper was published in the proceedings of that Conference. These proceedings had only limited distribution, so for many readers this paper will be quite new.

While I was preparing this piece I had my first contact with C. Fasseur who was putting the final touches on a dissertation at Leiden about the Cultivation System. It was the first indication for me of serious scholarly interest in the System and a great boost to me to find other scholars showing concern for this aspect of Indonesian history. Professor Fasseur and I have kept in touch with each other over the years and have benefited from our mutual interest. This was the beginning of a wider research interest into nineteenth-century Indonesian history, which had by the 1980s blossomed into an extensive area of historical research.

In characterizing the legalistic aspects of the Netherlands Indies civil administration in the years before 1854 – the year of the last in a series of fundamental laws (Regeerings Reglementen) which were supposed to lay the foundations of colonial government – Logemann uses the term 'police state.'[1] Seen from the point of view of legal certainty and consistency for the

---

[1] J.H.A. Logemann, 'Over Indië's staatsorde voor 1854,' *Mededeelingen der Koninklijke*

years from 1816 to 1854, the term is not incorrect. My personal preference would be to say that civil administration and governance in the East Indies rested on a system of men rather than laws. However you choose to express it, the image to be conveyed is of an administration in which individual administrators exercised wide personal latitude in interpreting and applying rules and regulations.[2] The word arbitrary springs easily to mind. The civil administrators from the governor-general down to the lowest ranking inspector and *contrôleur* shared in diminishing measure the sovereign rights of the Netherlands monarch in his absolute rule over the land and people of the colony. At each level independent judgments could be, and were, made; these judgments in turn might or might not be confirmed afterwards by decrees, proclamations, or edicts.[3] Any later wisdom might countermand or amend any former judgment and might be partially or totally 'legalized' through formal action by higher authority. This resulted not only in varied interpretations of basic rules and regulations but also produced local variations in application from one administrative circle in Java to another.[4]

If one attempts to characterize the Netherlands Indies civil administration on the basis of political institutions as Furnivall does in his classic study, then one must conclude that looking at the fundamental laws will not suffice to produce an accurate insight into the workings of the administration in Java.[5]

Both Logemann and Furnivall – the former with regard to legal practices, the latter with regard to political institutions – make the point that things did not change in 1854, though this date did mark an alteration in the presuppositions about the rule of law in the system which slowly impregnated the operation of the administration throughout the remainder of the century.[6] During the first part of the century the government had imposed six fundamental laws in 1815, 1818, 1827, 1830, 1836, and finally in

---

Akademie van Wetenschappen, Afdeeling Letterkunde, vol. 78, Serie B, No. 5 (1934), p. 140.

[2]   Clive Day, *The policy and administration of the Dutch in Java* (New York, 1904), p. 225; B.R.P. Hasselman, *Mijne ervaring als fabriekant in de binnenlanden van Java* ('s-Gravenhage, 1862), p. 3.

[3]   Logemann, *op. cit.*, p. 141.

[4]   One example of local variation will suffice here. The landrent assessment in Kedu had been imposed on a district instead of a village basis as regulated in N.I. Stbl. 1819 No. 5. A decree of April 12, 1820, sought to remedy this, but correspondence with the Resident in 1833 indicated that the 1820 order had never been implemented; the landrent in Kedu continued to be collected in a unique fashion. A government decree of December 19, 1833, instructed the Resident to continue in the existing fashion and not to change. S. van Deventer, *Bijdragen tot de kennis van het landelijk stelsel op Java* (Zalt-Bommel, 1865-66), II, pp. 11-12, 580-1, III, pp. 78-81.

[5]   J.S.Furnivall, *Netherlands India, a study of plural economy* (Cambridge, 1944), pp. 187ff.

[6]   Logemann, *op. cit.*, pp. 131-2. Furnivall, *loc. cit.*

1854. Each is, in large measure, a copy of the former with some elaboration. Yet none of these explains what was actually being attempted at the time. The Statutes (*Staatsbladen*), next in order of sanctity, prove equally useless in shedding light on the actual operation of the government and administration. One looks in vain, for instance, for a statute creating and defining the famous Cultivation System[7] though statutes will help in indicating what the government hoped to have happen at any given time.

Moreover, an examination of the regulations and instructions, by which civil administrators at various levels were supposed to function, shows a similarity and continuity throughout the century. Furnivall correctly points to the continuity of basic theme and purpose in the European administrators' instructions in 1818, 1837, 1855, and 1872 – each in a sense being a more elaborate and more detailed copy of the former.[8] One looks in vain for a marked shift in the guidelines presented to the European civil administration.

Furnivall's one effort to show how the function and position of the *contrôleur* were altered in the 1830s when forced cultivations were introduced is based on a misinterpretation of a text written by the Minister of Colonies J.C. Baud in 1842. Furnivall's statement to the effect that the *contrôleur* was not allowed to be sympathetic with the people during the 1830s is incorrect. This in turn makes incorrect his feeling that the work of the *contrôleur* changed after 1850 when he became an agent for promoting welfare and removing abuses; actually he had always been this and continued in the same pattern. A reading of the instructions for the *contrôleur* bears this out.[9] Throughout, he had the role of developing intimate relationships with the people and their heads. He kept a watchful eye on local affairs to see that extortion and oppression did not occur.

Whatever new duties the instructions of 1837 imposed with regard to checking on the state of the government cultivations, they did not remove or change the *contrôleur*'s fundamental duty of cozying into Javanese society, helping along the prevailing policy of the government, and

---

7 C. Fasseur, *Kultuurstelsel en koloniale baten* (Leiden, 1975), p. 11.
8 Furnivall, *op. cit.*, pp. 189-90.
9 Furnivall, *op. cit.*, p. 193, writes, 'Baud would not allow "the tender feelings of a few younger gentlemen" [het gerief van eenige Heeren Kontroleurs] to affect the profits of the Culture System.' In S. van Deventer, *Landelijk stelsel, op. cit.*, III, p. 122, the complete reference is to be found. This shows that Baud was writing a reply to a proposal by Governor-General Merkus that government funds be used to support a fifty kilometer postal route out of Demak so that a couple of *contrôleurs* could get their mail delivered. In keeping with the thrift measures of the time, Baud wrote the following (which is my translation), 'The convenience of some gentlemen *contrôleurs* should not be the cause for abandoning the only system by which Java can remain the cork upon which the Netherlands floats.' Furnivall has mistranslated the word 'gerief' and has taken the statement out of context, for it has nothing at all to do with the *contrôleurs'* sympathy toward the Javanese people.

guarding against abuse of the population.[10]

For the European government in Java the period up to 1830 saw numerous changes of policy. Recalling only such key names as Daendels, Raffles, Van der Capellen, and Du Bus will bring to mind new efforts at developing a strategy for making the colony profitable. But within all these policies there were certain fundamental principles which did not change. These principles could be broadly termed liberal, as that word was then understood. Private enterprise, self-regulating markets, reduction of governmental restrictions, and protection of private property were at the core of all the policies which were attempted. Yet none of them succeeded in making Java profitable. In fact, the largest part of whatever profits Java did produce for the motherland was drawn out of anachronistic holdovers of an earlier age when non-liberal principles such as forced labor, compulsory delivery, and the use of traditional Javanese channels of authority had prevailed. It was public knowledge that government profits before 1830 were largely drawn from coffee produced under forced cultivation which had been continued in the Preanger and introduced in disguise in Cirebon.[11]

In May 1827 the Commissioner-General Viscount Du Bus had proposed the latest liberal solution, the sale of Javanese lands – unused but near centers of population – to Europeans with sufficient capital to colonize and develop these lands in products suitable for profitable export. It was this plan which the King asked J. van den Bosch to comment upon. His response of 1829 was the first sketch of the Cultivation System which he was then asked to introduce into Java. Du Bus's plan was never put into operation. Though it was praised by liberals throughout the remainder of the nineteenth century, there is no reason to believe that Dutch capital would have responded to its challenge at that time. Also there is little doubt that the plan would not have succeeded without force and compulsion in obtaining labor and land from the Javanese.

Throughout the years up to 1830 the European administration in Java became more uniformly liberal in attitude. Especially after 1816 the recruitment of young secretaries, destined to rise upwards, came through family recommendations from some of the leading liberal, middle-class, patriot families of Holland. The failure of various policies to make Java profitable did not result in a widespread rejection of liberal principles, just as the continuation of traditional patterns of force and authority in parts of Java did not lead to general acceptance of these devices as solutions to Java's

[10] The instructions are found in N.I. Stbl. 1837, No. 20. For the continuing moral motivations of the European administrators see: R. Nieuwenhuys, *Tussen twee vaderlanden* (Amsterdam, 1959), pp. 162-3.
[11] D.H. Burger, *De ontsluiting van Java's binnenland voor het wereldverkeer* (Wageningen, 1939), pp. 98ff.

economic ills. The upper levels of the European administration were filled with an optimism that liberal concepts would prevail if only the proper touchstone could be found.

Meanwhile, life in Java was comfortable. For those at the top in civil administrative positions, for some of the private landowners, and for some who had leased estates in the Princely lands, life had a sort of seignorial quality.[12] At all levels there were opportunities for advancement and gain – moderate to great. The number of full-blood Europeans was small, probably no more than a few hundred in civilian and governmental positions, and a few hundred more in the military. Administrators worked their way up in the hierarchy, having been brought into the service through personal contacts and then provided with certification by the King. The total corps was quite international, though the greatest number was made up of Hollanders. Some, especially in the lower ranks, had been recruited from military personnel who chose to retire in Java. For most the administration was a channel of advancement through which personal adherence to liberal principles would yield its reward. The European administrator lived among the Javanese – usually with a native woman – in a style that adopted many of the trimmings of Javanese life. If there was a prevailing attitude toward the Javanese, it was that they were indolent and long-suffering of the abuses imposed upon them by their own heads. And if there was a prevailing attitude toward their own European presence, it was that they must protect the ordinary Javanese from such arbitrariness, abuse, extortion, and exploitation his own heads would subject him to.[13]

This civil administration and its personnel carried on its vague paternalistic, liberal, autocratic style through all the changes in policy. To the extent that it seemed necessary, possible, and profitable, they applied each policy as they understood it in the area under their administrative control. And each did this within his understanding of the instructions and guidelines for his function. All of these matters were subject to interpretation and colored by local circumstances. This is to say that the European consulted and worked with the local Javanese elite who provided the agency for advancing new policies. They also made it possible for the European civil administrator to survive in his function.[14] The civil administrator, in turn, quickly learned to accommodate and to fit the vague

---

[12] Nieuwenhuys, *op. cit.*, pp. 6-7.

[13] W.F. Wertheim, 'Havelaar's tekort,' *De Nieuwe Stem* 15 (1960), p. 372, quotes from a letter of J.C. van Leur to the effect that in the middle of the nineteenth century Java was 'a beautiful, uniform, closed, patrimonial bureaucratic state,' with a knightly bureaucratic ideology, with an interconnected culture, and with a gentry-court civilization. This translates rather awkwardly into English, but the description strikes me as extremely apt.

[14] Day, *op. cit.*, pp. 218-9.

instructions and imperfectly understood policies to what was possible. Naturally there were misunderstandings or errant behaviors on both the European and Javanese side, and so there were discharges and transfers. But by and large the system functioned smoothly, if not too profitably; life had its comforts and pleasures, prosaic and unexciting as they were.

The arrival of J. van den Bosch as governor-general in 1830 heralded a significant change in the underlying policy of the preceding years. Van den Bosch had promised the King he would make Java profitable. He had conceived a plan for doing this; it involved using the traditional patterns of Javanese authority by controlling the elite in order to gain control of land and labor, which would in turn be used to produce crops that were salable on world markets. In 1829 there were still few specifics, but Elout, the liberal-minded Minister of Colonies, saw the direction which things had to take, and, after remonstrating unsuccessfully, resigned.[15] It is generally believed that the King had been given some insights into the non-liberal aspects of Van den Bosch's plan, but decided to go along with it.[16] His need for money, his inability to make the NHM (Netherlands Trading Company) profitable, and his growing disenchantment with the lack of entrepreneurial spirit displayed by his countrymen probably made him decide to let Van den Bosch have his chance.

Van den Bosch believed that he could use the traditional authority patterns in combination with the authority of the Dutch colonial government to get the Javanese peasant involved in the production of marketable commodities. Beyond the well-known concept of using one-fifth of the land and one-fifth of the labor supply, few details were spelled out. This vagueness was due, I suspect, in part to the fact that Van den Bosch did not actually know or particularly care how the detailed application of his conception would work, and in part to his realization that both in Holland and in Java the prevailing liberal frame of mind would not accept some of the implications of what he had in mind. As a result, the statements made by Van den Bosch for members of the government in Holland and for public consumption are best viewed as propaganda pieces or wisps of wishful thinking rather than serious plans of action. This was true in 1829, and remained true throughout Van den Bosch's time in Java, which lasted until February 1834. His famous memorandum of 1834 which was supposed to set forth the guidelines of the Cultivation System is fraught with misstatements which he simply must have known were wrong since he himself had ordered other arrangements.[17]

[15] R. Van Niel, 'Measurement of change under the Cultivation System in Java, 1837-1851,' *Indonesia* 14 (1972), pp. 89-90.

[16] F.W. Stapel, *Geschiedenis van Nederlandsch Indië*, vol. 5 (Amsterdam, 1940), p. 235.

[17] R. Van Niel, 'The function of landrent under the Cultivation System in Java,' *Journal of*

What can one conclude about Van den Bosch on the basis of this evidence? Some have seen him as a gross prevaricator, others as an overly zealous patriot. I think the latter is closer to the truth. He seems to have been fanatically desirous of serving his King and country. With regard to his truthfulness, I suspect he was honest enough in his own context; it was just that his context was always at the vague, 'big picture' level. His vision was of prosperity – a prosperity that would involve Dutch ships and merchants, markets for tropical produce in the Netherlands, and in Java a busy and industrious people whose life would be secure, intimately traditional, and increasingly prosperous. All of this would redound to the glory of King and Country. Anything that seemed to move in the right direction was acceptable to him. In Java he was prepared to make whatever accommodation seemed necessary in order to put his schema into operation. The result was a series of local, interlocking arrangements. It was called a 'System,' but it never was that.[18]

Having indicated what Van den Bosch did not do, it is perhaps appropriate to indicate what he did do. To achieve his profitable goals, he was prepared to turn away from the prevailing liberal principles, which had envisioned changing the nature of the Javanese, and instead to use for his purposes the traditional attachments and patterns of authority long known in Java. Without dwelling upon the specifics of how Van den Bosch's plan worked, it is clear both in profession and practice that he intended to use the Javanese Regents (*Bupati*) and lesser elite. These persons were regarded by most Javanese as chiefs who had always – even in the liberal years – been functioning as the local-level administration in Java. This Javanese elite had been only momentarily (and ineffectively) displaced by Raffles. Restored in 1816 to the positions which they had never really left, they lived through some desultory years during the 1820s, when many of the European administrators looked upon them with little respect and when their positions were less secure than they might have wished.[19] Van den Bosch set out to change this immediately.[20] Beginning in 1830-31 the Javanese Regents were accorded hereditary rights (something they never formally had before), were granted lands and people for their personal services

---

Asian Studies 23 (1964), pp. 372-5. Also N.I. Stbl. 1834, No. 22.

18   R. Van Niel, 'The introduction of government sugar cultivation in Pasuruan, Java, 1830,' *Journal of Oriental Studies* 7 (1969), p. 261.

19   H.R. van Delden, *Over de erfelijkheid der regenten op Java* (Leiden, 1862), p. 31. Day, *op. cit.*, p. 224, feels that administrative irregularities had increased the influence of native officials during the 1820s.

20   Day, *op. cit.*, pp. 219-20, makes note of a change of spirit of the government after 1830 which he regards as a lamentable partial abdication by European officials of their power and which in turn resulted in the abuses of the following years.

(which they had always had, at least covertly),[21] were allowed to display all the accoutrements of their rank and status (only begrudgingly allowed earlier), and were reinforced in their physical presence by exclusive right to a special guard unit or *barisan* (which they might have had earlier if they could manage it financially). In return for all this, they were expected to introduce the government cultivations and garner support for them in their districts. Translated into practical terms this meant that they were to use their authority to convey the government's requests to the village heads, who would either carry them out or not long enjoy the privileges of their office.[22]

The early years of Van den Bosch's administration were difficult. European administrators in Java were not persuaded of the efficacy or righteousness of his plans. One of the members of the Council of the Indies, P. Merkus, contested the new governor-general in a lengthy memoranda exchange which by 1832-33 began to spill over into public awareness through books and pamphlets.[23] By mid-1833 Van den Bosch found it necessary to end the debate by using his special power as commissioner-general to change rules on the spot.[24] Whatever the extent of Van den Bosch's authority had been earlier, it was now exposed in full measure. Merkus was obliged to accept an assignment outside Java and was forced off the Council of the Indies, later downgraded from its earlier co-executive position and reduced to that of a separate advisory body. Van den Bosch was firm and unrelenting in implementing his general scheme. From the Residents and other European administrators he expected full cooperation and energetic application. If this was lacking or if incompetence was evident, immediate dismissal followed. A few examples sufficed to convey this message to others.

Soon the cultivation of products for the government began in virtually all Residencies; in many the management was stupidly or inappropriately handled, while in others the soil and climate were wrong for a particular crop. The results were often far from good and in some areas the cultivations had to be abandoned. For the European administrators, unless there was patent malfeasance, there was little punishment for such failures; it was the local population who bore the brunt of them by having labored for no gain. For Javanese administrators the same principles were applied,

---

21 Burger, *op. cit.*, pp. 74-5.
22 Van den Bosch writing to Baud, April 20, 1832, put it rather interestingly by stating that the industry of Java was not expanded by high prices, but only by the influence of the government on the people. J.J. Westendorp Boerma, *Briefwisseling tussen J. van den Bosch en J.C. Baud* (Utrecht, 1956), I, p. 143.
23 Van Niel, Function of landrent, *op. cit.*, p. 362, esp. fn. 27.
24 On the effect of using the powers of commissioners-general in 1816, 1826, and 1832-3, and commissioners in 1824 (Celebes) and 1825 (Palembang), see Logemann, *op. cit.*, pp. 145-53.

except that they were less easily dismissed and almost never transferred. Finally, with the decision in 1832 to pay a percentage of the value of the crop production to both the European and Javanese administrators, the System began to win warmer support from them and slowly to take hold and expand.

Van den Bosch within a very few years managed to gain with some pressure and profit-inducement rather widespread acceptance of his ideas in Java. In large measure his success with the European civil administration must be seen as directly related to his forceful autocratic stance. He had ultimate authority over the positions of these men and had indicated that they would either have to participate in his scheme of forced cultivations or be expelled from their posts. To supervise cultivation operations he had created a new Office of Cultivations under a Director with a battery of Inspectors. These persons not only advised the Residents on ways to experiment with new crops and on areas to open to new cultivations, but also inspected the results. Local variation in mode of production as well as in financial arrangements was permitted.[25] The cultivation percentage payments in the more successful areas might almost double an administrator's salary. For some crops, especially sugar, processing arrangements were contracted out to private entrepreneurs who had been advanced government money and in return agreed to sell their production to the government. These contracts proved within a few years to be lucrative arrangements, and were increasingly awarded to civil administrators, their families, or friends.

Thus there were profitable reasons for European administrators to support Van den Bosch's plans. By the time that Van den Bosch finished his tour of duty as governor-general in 1834 and his close confidant J.C. Baud had carried on his ideas for another two years, there remained very little overt opposition from the Europeans in the civil administration. Many in fact had come to realize the value of the plan and had, like P. Merkus, overcome their earlier doubts about making Java profitable through forced cultivations. For many the new System also opened paths to personal profit.[26]

Before moving on to the second thesis which I wish to develop in this

---

[25]   See the example in footnote nr. 4 above. Also R. Van Niel, 'The regulation of sugar production in Java, 1830-1840,' in: *Economic factors in Southeast Asian social change* (Honolulu, 1968), pp. 91-108.

[26]   Throughout the years of the cultivation system there was a private sector in both production and export. J.P. Cornets de Groot van Kraaijenburg, *Over het beheer onzer koloniën* ('s-Gravenhage, 1862), pp. 151-3, provides figures on the amount of this private production. This production could result from private lands and factories or from overages in government factories. With the exception of coffee after 1832, the cultivations show a generally increasing private production from 1830 to 1860.

paper, it seems appropriate to review briefly the argument thus far. In 1830 Van den Bosch, in autocratic fashion introduced a concept that was in principle different from the earlier liberal system. This was done, not by altering the fundamental laws, statutes, and the like, but instead by using the type of arbitrary persuasion and personalized adjustment that had always functioned in the East Indies. It was also done without changing the instructions or guidelines of the European civil administration but rather by extending them. The personnel of the administration, with very few exceptions, was left intact. With a bit of thundering and a bit more personal profit inducement, Van den Bosch was able to get government cultivations introduced.[27] More to the point, perhaps, he was able to win the cooperation and support of the Javanese administrators who were, more than the Europeans, the instruments through which the System had to work. Again this was accomplished by applying both the stick and the carrot: prestige, profit, power, and physical persuasion were present in varying degrees.

In short, what we have during the early 1830s is a rather dramatic alteration of principles and policy at the top imposed upon the people of Java without seriously changing many of the basic precepts of the personnel who helped the system function. What made this possible and successful to the degree that it was, was the fact that localized arrangements allowed the internal administration to adjust this to their area and to fit the new cultivations into the traditional patterns of district and village authority structures.[28] The European and Javanese administrators were not disinterested in profit, but neither were they inspired by the patriotic fervor for funneling revenue to the motherland which so impelled Van den Bosch. The Belgian revolt and war (1830-1839) had so drained the King's coffers that Van den Bosch grew ever more frantic in trying to meet his demands. Java's contributions were expected to increase each year, but the operating costs of the System were to remain static.

At this point I wish to introduce my second thesis. Beginning in 1836, these arrangements began to fall apart. The reasons for, and symptoms of, this change comprise the remainder of this paper. Central to this change, as one will quickly suspect, are the departures of Van den Bosch and Baud from Java. Even though they succeeded each other as Minister of Colonies in The Hague (Van den Bosch from 1834 to 1840 and Baud from 1840 to 1848), both their absence from the scene and their great efforts to keep intimate control over actions in Java from afar, set the stage for the natural dissolution of the autocratic control which they had maintained in the early

---

[27] Baud writing to Van den Bosch, October 7, 1834, says, 'the aim of my most consistent efforts is to keep alive all the institutions you set up, which takes constant attention and effort [for] one does not like to be restricted here [...].' Westendorp Boerma, *op. cit.*, II, p. 139.
[28] Burger, *op. cit.*, p. 119.

1830s. I say 'natural dissolution,' for one element of my thinking is that the fundamentally liberal nature of the European civil administration, combined with the insensitive and excessive demands of Van den Bosch, together led to a change of spirit and style in the administration. Again this occurred without any noticeable change in guidelines or instructions and was made possible by the fact that there never was a 'system' based on consistent principles for the epigones to follow.

During the 1850s and 1860s the plans and actions of Van den Bosch were subjected to strong liberal attack on many grounds. At the heart of this critique was a feeling that legal certainty and consistency were lacking and that the system worked outside a body of laws and regulations.[29] Today, and for the past forty years, the Cultivation System has been seen as the first step in a comprehensive development scheme involving the future economic growth of both motherland and colony.[30] Both views are correct from their respective standpoints and with their hindsight visions. But both attribute to Van den Bosch and his system more integrated planning and control than he was capable of attaining. The events of the 1830s and 1840s when seen in their own context do not fit easily into these retrospective views, though both views contain revelations about the ultimate nature of the system.

Van den Bosch was constantly scheming and planning to raise money for the King. He often spoke favorably of liberal solutions, sometimes advocating statist solutions, often trying makeshift arrangements that were little more than manipulative, and many times mixing these all together.[31] It is amazing in retrospect that his actions achieved the success they did in Java. Multatuli, who hated the colonial-exploitative arrangement under whatever policy, saw the answer to this quite clearly when he wrote, 'The Cultivation System is nothing other than the translation of Javanese morality into statutes.'[32] The system very much fit the basic realities of life in Java. The fact that the arrangements were arbitrary and almost sometimes whimsical made little difference in the personalized autocracy that existed in both the European and Javanese spheres; that is rather as things had

[29] Van Deventer, *Landelijk stelsel, op. cit.* makes the point consistently. For example, in volume 2, p. 581, he charges Van den Bosch with extra-legal operations for the incident cited in ftnt. nr. 4 above.

[30] W.M.F. Mansvelt writing during the 1930s advances this thesis in his excellent study of the NHM and later in his statistical studies prepared for the Central Statistical Bureau in the Netherlands Indies.

[31] Archive Ministry of Colonies, folio nr. 4277, contains an interesting decree, July 26, 1841, ordering an investigation into a series of proposals made by Van den Bosch which would have extended private contractual arrangements into more cultivations, allowed importation of foreign labor on private lands, and extended the scope of land rentals to private persons.

[32] Multatuli, *Nog-eens: Vrye-Arbeid in Nederlandsch-Indië* (Delft, 1870). [Het *Kultuur-stelsel* is niets anders dan *de Javaansche zeden overgezet in staatsblads-termen.*]

always been. No training was instituted for either European or Javanese administrators during Van den Bosch's time; that was hardly needed in an arrangement which required only the application of natural sentiments and prejudices as these existed in both societies.

With Van den Bosch as Minister of the Colonies and with the departure of his trusted confidant J.C. Baud from Java in 1836, some method of controlling Java at a distance had to be found. In order to make the new governor-general dependent for advice and action on The Hague rather than upon various parts of the European community in Java, three devices were applied. On Baud's advice, a man without previous Indies experience was selected; this was repeated in 1845.[33] Van den Bosch also provided the new governor-general with an elaborate set of instructions which committed him to support the system of government cultivations. Third, a new fundamental law was promulgated in 1836 which removed the Council of the Indies from its co-executive role, in which it had given Van den Bosch so much difficulty, and reduced it to an advisory board.[34]

These devices for controlling Java at a distance were not totally unsuccessful for the flow of profits from Java in the form of salable crops magnified over the years. The new governor-general was D.J. de Eerens, a meticulous bureaucrat who prided himself on always following orders and doing what was expected of him. He seemed just the right person to carry out the wishes of Van den Bosch and Baud. The events of the next few years were to show how wrong such calculations could be. De Eerens died in office in 1841. For some years before this he had every reason to feel badly used and unnecessarily abused by Van den Bosch and Baud.[35] What had happened to cause this? Various answers come to mind, but two seem especially pertinent. First it was not possible to send to Java a man without colonial experience and expect to be able to dangle him at the end of a slow and uncertain communication system. Correspondence took on the average three months to move from The Hague to Batavia, and another three for a reply. Obviously, immediate decisions could not wait on this and not even the application of larger plans could proceed under such limitations. It was therefore essential for the governor-general to use his judgment and

[33] Letters from Baud to Van den Bosch, June 19, 1834, in Westendorp Boerma, *op. cit.*, II, p. 136.
[34] Cornets de Groots, *op. cit.*, p. 160.
[35] The tensions that developed between De Eerens, on the one hand, and Van den Bosch and Baud, on the other, are reflected in both the private and the official correspondence of these years. The private correspondence has been published by F.C. Gerretson and W.Ph. Coolhaas, *Particuliere briefwisseling tussen J. van den Bosch en D.J. de Eerens 1834-1840* (Groningen, 1960). The introduction of this book contains a biographical sketch of De Eerens. The official correspondence is in the Archive of the Ministry of Colonies in the State Archives in The Hague.

understanding of the broad policies and to confirm his opinions with the persons near at hand who had more experience in these matters than he. Second, the European civil administration in Java at the governor-general's call was composed of men who were essentially liberal in viewpoint. True they had come to appreciate the benefits of government cultivations, but their natural instincts tended toward private profit and private enterprise for themselves and for their family and friends.

An immediate and noticeable change was the increased paper work at the center of the East Indies administration. This was a direct result of the obligation to send information back to The Hague in enlarged measure, but was exacerbated by the rather natural tendency of the new governor-general to keep himself at the administrative center of affairs in Bogor (Buitenzorg). The burden of this additional work fell upon the General Secretariat which Baud had already in 1835 found incapable of supplying the needed information to the governor-general. But once back in The Hague he refused to allow it to serve the newly separated Council of the Indies.[36] This almost senseless retraction was undertaken as part of the prevailing parsimony of the time.[37] Every *duit* was to be squeezed out of Java while expenditures there were to be kept level: no increase in administrative costs could be tolerated. In the case of the General Secretariat the resultant squeeze not only cut back on the information which the governor-general might be expected to obtain from the Council of the Indies, but also prevented any effort to provide broader information through a statistical bureau and a geographical section. Instead only basic correspondence and essential reports could be handled to keep The Hague satisfied.

The consequence was a growing gap in communication between the central administration in Bogor, on the one hand, and the local administration in the Residencies, on the other.[38] The Residents had always been fairly independent autocrats, but they now more than ever cast upon their own local resources and devices.[39] Their chief channel of contact with the central administration was through the Office of Cultivations, a change which they found little to their liking because it reduced their influence at the center and because it caused them to deal with persons whom they regarded as inferior.[40]

The Office of Cultivations, headed by a Director, had been created in 1833

---

[36]   *Geschiedkundige nota over de Algemeene Secretarie* (Batavia, 1894), pp. 19-23.
[37]   Cornets de Groot, *op. cit.*, pp. 162-3.
[38]   *Geschiedkundige nota, op. cit.*, pp. 30, 37ff, 47. In 1842 (p. 49) GG Merkus laments the lack of time and energy to undertake any development or reform.
[39]   Hasselman, *op. cit.*, p. 4.
[40]   Private and official correspondence of the time abound with references to problems with various Residents most of whom resented the Director of Cultivations, De Vogel, and the influence he exercised over the governor-general.

by Van den Bosch as the administrative device charged with introducing the government cultivations into Java. In 1834 B.J. Elias, former Resident of Cirebon, became Director. With a group of inspectors he was largely responsible for the introduction of many new cultivations during the next two years. He left Java about the same time as Baud and became part of the team at the Ministry of Colonies in The Hague. He was replaced in 1836 as Director of Cultivations by W. de Vogel, former Resident of Japara. Why De Vogel was selected for this post remains as much a mystery to me as it clearly was for many persons associated with the cultivations at that time. He had distinguished himself in Japara with a badly bungled administration of the cultivations in which local Chinese entrepreneurs stole the local cultivators' meager profits – one assumes without the knowledge of the Resident. Vitalis suggests that he was selected because he wrote pleasant reports.[41] That seems as good an explanation as any.

Two things can be said about De Vogel. By his own admission he spent all of his time in his office writing reports and collecting information. By his own advices and actions he showed himself to be one of the most profit-hungry, self-seeking administrators in Java, finally succeeding in parlaying his Directorship into a re-assignment as Resident in one of the most prosperous Residencies as far as percentage payments went. The Cultivation Reports, which began in 1834, became more elaborate and detailed after 1837, but they also became more tardy in their submission. These reports should have provided the government with information on the state of the cultivations in Java. Since they were submitted two or three years late however, it was clear that no planning or projections affecting the cultivations could be made with them.[42] Neither the central government in Bogor/Batavia nor the ministerial staff in The Hague was any longer making decisions on the nature and extent of particular cultivations. This was now being done at the Residency level.

In addition to the increasing formalism at the center which brought in its wake an ever looser control of the local areas, there was also a change in spirit and attitude once the strong personality of Van den Bosch was moved to a distance. This change was, of course, little more than the prevailing and constantly underlying liberalism which had been cowed into submission and then persuaded of the profitable nature of the new system. For Van den Bosch and Baud, much of their concern and many of their directives over the next dozen years from 1836 to 1848 were devoted to limiting this liberal

---

[41] L. Vitalis, *De invoering, werking en gebreken van het stelsel van kultures op Java* (Zalt-Bommel, 1851), p. 45.
[42] A list of the Cultivation Reports with their date of receipt in The Hague is in Archive Ministry of Colonies folio 3205.

spirit among the civil administrators in Java.[43] At the center of the East Indies government, that is at the level of the governor-general and the directorates and secretariats around him, they were able to exert enough influence to hold intact the general patterns of government control of productions and to force a continual increase in these productions. The profits which flowed to the motherland during these years were also bolstered by a prevailing rise in prices for East Indies products. But at the Residency and district level there was almost no way in which the cultivations could be controlled from The Hague. At this level the Resident became increasingly autonomous and often self-seeking, if not directly for himself (which was illegal), then for members of his family and friends.[44] Alliances among Indies families had always existed, but they now became more extensive and more intimately tied to various aspects of government or private cultivations and assorted exporting arrangements.[45]

When in 1848 in the motherland the autocratic control of the government was brushed aside in a liberal revolution which placed greater control of political affairs in the hands of the Dutch parliament, the local influence in determining matters in Java was already well fixed and had already made its accommodation with liberal interests. The changes in Java during the 1850s and 1860s were, therefore, often much slighter and more subtle than would be realized by reading the debates and pamphlets. Multatuli again saw more clearly than most, or perhaps had more courage than most in saying it, that the apparently dominant issue of 'free labor' was no real issue at all but merely disguised moves for economic control by various cliques within the establishment.[46]

---

[43]   This is most clearly illustrated in Baud's hesitation to name Merkus as governor-general until a supplementary set of instructions were accepted in 1842. These instructions are printed in Cornets de Groot, *op. cit.*, pp. 163-4.

[44]   The decree of November 26, 1838, No. 4, established new regulations governing the awarding of sugar contracts. The *Overzicht van de voornaamste algemeene administrative aangelegenheden van Nederlandsch Indië over het jaar 1838*, Archive Ministry of Colonies, folio 4265, p. 93, says the following about the decree. 'In framing this regulation it was taken as a principle that only Europeans or their descendents would be acceptable for agricultural enterprises, and even these only if they were permanent residents of the colony [...]. Also a special preference was given to anyone who discovered and was first to point out a possible enterprise.' Since the interior of Java was open only to civil administrators and some private contractors, no one else than they could ever hope to be in a preferred position with regard to obtaining a contract in the cultivations.

[45]   The number of European civil administrators who retired or resigned in order to take up contracts with the government grew during the late 1830s and 1840s. What is more difficult to determine is the interrelations between some officials and contractors of various sorts. The A.A. Reed papers give one example whereby the daughters of Resident Van Son were married with private contractors, export-house representatives, and administrators, with active economic connections between all of them.

[46]   Multatuli, *Over vrijen arbeid in Nederlandsch Indië* (Amsterdam, 1862). Though favoring free labor over forced labor, Multatuli argues that free labor is impossible without

It is not my purpose here to pursue the question of the European civil administration in Java beyond the 1840s. Enough has been said to indicate what my opinion might be, namely, that the spirit and style of the administration was largely a continuation of the patterns laid down during the period already discussed. As changes occurred, they developed slowly and took the form of alterations of what existed, stopped by the pressures of subsequent events. I would, however, like to return to the period 1836 to 1848 and illustrate with a series of examples how the attitude and spirit of the administration then differed from those of the early 1830s.

A critical area in which private interests confronted governmental involvement in cultivation was the cession in lease, rental, or sale of unused lands (*woeste gronden*) in Java to non-indigenous private entrepreneurs.[47] Such cessions had occurred earlier, sometimes on a large scale, in both the government and princely lands in Java.[48] Du Bus had sought to make them a cornerstone of his colonization scheme. Van den Bosch, however, downgraded the role of private entrepreneurs, even though article 109 of the fundamental law of 1830 spoke of the possibility of ceding such lands, and the same paragraphs, slightly amended, became article 94 in the fundamental law of 1836.

Van den Bosch had persuaded the King to limit the ceding of lands by giving the determining power in such matters to the Indies government and by declaring that cessions had to be related to the cultivation of essential crops. The latter point was the essence of the changed 1836 law. In practice, there were very few land cessions after 1830. The government's attitude was summarized in the resolution of December 31, 1835, No. 9, stating that no fixed requirements would be established for ceding lands to private persons, but instead each case would be considered separately to determine the essential nature of the cultivation to be undertaken as well as the interests and rights of the nearby population which might be affected. While in Java and also later when in The Hague, Baud and Elias argued in favor of full consideration being given to a village's rights to all land in its vicinity. Put

---

free will. This latter does not exist in Java, nor do the various liberal groups want it to exist. Everyone concerned really needs and wants the authority of government on their side in Java.

[47] The correspondence and advices on the question of unused lands for the period of this paper are to be found in the Archive Ministry of Colonies, folios 2589, 4277, 4290, 4420, 4431, and 4432. The facts of the following three paragraphs are drawn from these materials.

[48] Baud felt that the destruction of native institutions in these private lands of an earlier date had led to all sorts of problems and so warned the new governor-general Rochussen in a political note of March 12, 1845, Archive Ministry of Colonies, folio 2955. A political overview of the years 1839 to 1848 recently published by the Indonesian National Archives, *Ichtisar keadaan politik Hindia-Belanda, tahun 1839-1848* (Jakarta, 1973) also gives indications of tensions on the private lands around Batavia. Unfortunately the Indonesian and English summaries provided in this volume lift the statements of unrest and popular disturbances out of context thereby giving a distorted picture of conditions in Java at this time.

simply, they believed that there was no such thing as unused land anywhere near populated areas. It was thus virtually impossible for a private entrepreneur to get any land ceded to him in Java during these years unless it was far distant from any population. Land of this type, however, had little attraction to entrepreneurs since people were required to make it productive and profitable. The government had no wish to see the population drawn off government lands to fill these desolate stretches, for these people were regarded as essential for government cultivations.

Almost immediately in 1836 the whole scene changed. Governor-General De Eerens was prevailed upon by local administrators to accept the fundamental law in a literal sense. His Director of Cultivations, De Vogel, was especially persuasive, though he and the others must have known that this ran counter to the interpretation of Van den Bosch and Baud. They were, however, interested in promoting private interests. At best this motivation was based on a belief that private enterprise could produce more crops more efficiently; at worst it involved a personal interest to advance private gain for self or close friends. It is unclear how much of this was known in The Hague until early 1839, for it was only with the public decree of December 25, 1838 (N.I. Stbl. No. 50) that the change in attitude toward the cession of unused lands became openly known. Essentially this statute established guidelines for ceding lands for the cultivation of essential crops. At first glance the announcement may have appeared to be nothing more than a beneficial standardization of practices which had earlier been arbitrary, but actually it gave notice that henceforth the Indies government was prepared to encourage land cessions. The decree also provided that the Resident would be charged with determining the validity of each request, and that further regulation of private land would also be left in his hands.

The governor-general's action became known in The Hague in early 1839 and produced immediate adverse reaction. It was Baud and Elias who reacted most negatively, and it was they who convinced Minister Van den Bosch that the new regulation posed a serious threat to government control of the cultivations in Java and to the profits which these provided for the treasury. Their argument was strengthened by the circumstance that some of the earliest requests for land cessions had been for private coffee estates in the Salatiga area.[49] Since coffee was one of the most successful revenue earners for the government and since private coffee growers had, in times past, been known to engage in illegal purchases of government coffee, there was plenty of reason for suspicion. There is some reason to think that Van den Bosch was less adamant on this subject than his advisors, since his

---

[49]   The correspondence relative to the Salatiga requests in 1836 and 1837 and involving a number of European civil administrators is located in Archive Ministry of Colonies, folio 4432.

family had for some years owned private lands near Batavia, and since he had grown increasingly to feel that such crops as tea and tobacco which had been grown by the government but processed by private contractors might be more advantageously handled in a totally private way. As in an earlier day, he was willing to try whatever would work. It is to his credit to note that before 1850 both tea and tobacco were being produced under private arrangements.

But for the moment, in the late 1830s, the advice of Baud prevailed, for uncontrolled granting of lands to various types of entrepreneurs could cut into the government's labor supply and thereby undermine the government cultivations. The governor-general was told to stop all further ceding of lands until the King had given his approval. With the communications of the day it was almost three years before that approval (or rather disapproval) came, the decision being that no lands could be ceded for sugar, indigo, or coffee since these crops were the mainstay of government profits. At about the same time Baud, now Minister of Colonies, made it clear that no foreign labor should be imported into Java to provide labor on unused lands.[50] These decisions from The Hague were a setback for the liberals whose desire to take over all areas of cultivation from the government grew in direct proportion to the government's profits from the system. They would have to be satisfied with working on the localized, personalized basis in Java and await a change in the home government before moving toward total control of the key government cultivations.[51]

Another example of drift away from the plans laid down in the early 1830s is to be found in the action initiated by the Resident of Madiun, L. Launij, in July 1838 to turn over the government operated sugar mills in that residency to private entrepreneurs.[52] Again the proposal was supported by the Director of Cultivations and was approved by the governor-general in a decree of October 25, 1838, No. 2. Van den Bosch's reaction was immediate and negative; on April 3, 1839, he wrote the governor-general to say that with the King's approval he was ordering him to hold off on the transfer of the Madiun factories. If any had already been transferred the arrangements

---

[50] The correspondence between Baud and Merkus in 1842 gives clear indication that the idea of some persons, specifically Van den Bosch, to import cheap labor from southern India into Java, would not be implemented. Archive Ministry of Colonies, folio 4290.

[51] The liberal position on the land question is eloquently stated in W.R. van Hoëvell, *Bedenkingen tegen de mededeeling van den Minister van Kolonien [...] omtrent den verkoop van landen op Java* (Groningen, 1849). Private ownership of land is regarded as not only economically profitable but also a useful way to spread Christianity, thereby improving the Javanese people.

[52] The obituary notice on Lodewijk Launij – July 29, 1849, *Tijdschrift van Nederlandsch Indië*, 11-2 (1849), pp. 363-4, provides an insight into the latitude accorded capable administrators under the crown administration.

were to be undone.[53] While Van den Bosch felt that private entrepreneurs might be able to get the factories to produce more sugar, he made it very clear that he did not see that such additional profits would in any way benefit the government. He was completely unswayed by the arguments of the Resident and the Director of Cultivations that the Madiun sugar factories were being inefficiently operated by civil servants. (This system, incidentally, was quite unique to Madiun and Kediri.) He specifically told the governor-general that this was yet another instance of deviation from the working arrangements which he had started. The change in the status of the Madiun sugar factories would have to wait for a change in the home government, but it is clear that the attitudes of the European civil administration in Java were already moving away from Van den Bosch's views of government control.

A changed attitude toward the Javanese administrators on the part of the European administrators also began to be noticed after 1836. In 1839, after more than two years of deliberations and consideration, De Eerens decided to reduce the number of Javanese Regents in one of the Residencies – it happened to be Madiun again, but the argument of greater efficiency which was used could have been applied in any number of places.[54] Van den Bosch was most irate on this occasion and let De Eerens know it. He wrote that what was done could not be undone, but he made it clear that any further action relative to the status of Javanese administrators would have to be approved in the motherland.[55] On a closely related matter, Van den Bosch warned the governor-general away from the recent decision (October 1838) to place the Javanese police forces under the ultimate authority of the European public prosecutor.[56] Van den Bosch saw this, quite rightly, as a transgression against the authority and position of the Javanese Regents – a position which he had carefully strengthened after 1830. These two examples will serve to illustrate the gradual erosion of the position of the Javanese administrators vis-à-vis their European counterparts. We can discern a gradual slippage back to the earlier stance of the 1820s when the regents were often treated more coolly.[57] This tendency, I would suggest,

[53]   Archive Ministry of Colonies, folio 4423, contains all the correspondence on this issue.
[54]   In 1840 the Resident of the Preanger Regencies usurped from the Regents the authority to appoint native officials of lower rank; this practice was legally confirmed in 1847. J.W. de Klein, *Het Preangerstelsel (1677-1871) en zijn nawerking* (Delft, 1931), p. 86. N.I. Stbl. 1847, No. 25 places appointment of native officials fully in the hands of various levels of the European administration.
[55]   The correspondence on this matter can be found in Archive Ministry of Colonies, folio 4428, and Archive J.C. Baud, folio 530. Van den Bosch's letter dd. December 31, 1839, LaY19 Kabinet to De Eerens is most explicit.
[56]   Van den Bosch to De Eerens, dd. June 22, 1839, LaK8, Archive Ministry of Colonies, folio 4424.
[57]   The Director of Cultivations G.L. Baud (no relation to the Minister) writing to acting GG

becomes more noticeable in the period after 1850 when the European administration began dealing more directly with the lower ranks of the Javanese administration.

These examples should suffice to illustrate the change in spirit and attitude which came to characterize the European civil administration in Java after 1836. The change was subtle in that it is only partially recorded in statutes or regulations, but it is nonetheless very real and clearly antecedent to the styles and modes of administration in Java for the next three decades. The implications of the views set forth in this paper on the conceptualization of nineteenth-century Indonesian, especially Javanese, history seem to me to be both interesting and fundamental. In one sense I have argued for a greater stress on continuity than has generally been the case. But more importantly, I have tried to show that when changes did take place, they occurred at different levels and in different ways than earlier accounts would have us believe. Moreover, they centered around different issues than those traditionally emphasized.

The patterns and trend which I have formulated here are supported by an impressive amount of data, but I feel that a great deal more needs to be done, especially with regard to understanding developments at the Residency and district level. The limited resources currently available to us on this subject seem to support my suspicions concerning the role of the local administration in the process of introducing and operating the cultivations which enriched them as well as the government. The operational and attitudinal changes at the center of the East Indies government seem more clearly supportable despite their novelty. Hopefully the arguments made here will recommend themselves to other historians of Indonesian history for future research and consideration. To my way of thinking they explain the process of change in government and administration in a fashion more compatible with the nature of both Javanese society and European bureaucracy.

Merkus, dd. Buitenzorg, June 17, 1842, No. 1934/4 secret, says, 'Even the European administrators have, as a result of the introduction of the system, been gradually forced to protect the population against the arbitrary actions of the heads more than formerly. Thus, they have taken over the influence and authority of the heads in somewhat diminished form, for through this influence they can for the moment achieve much, but eventually they will not be able to demand such extensive labor as the cultivations demand.' Archive Ministry of Colonies, folio 4290.

CHAPTER VI

The Labor Component in the Forced Cultivation System in Java, 1830-1855

Ever since my article on the 'Measurement of Change' (Paper number 4), I had been interested in learning more about how the vast amount of labor needed for the government cultivations had been aggregated. At the 30th International Congress of Human Sciences in Asia and North Africa held in Mexico City in 1976 I presented a paper on my findings. That paper was published in that Conference's *Proceedings: Southeast Asia 1*, published by El Colegio de Mexico in 1982. The subject of labor under the Cultivation System was more complex than I was able to handle in this paper and I have felt more ambivalent about this paper than the others in this volume. Since 1976 I have made further efforts to extend my insight into the question of labor under the Cultivation System, but I have felt little fulfillment in my achievements. In 1983 I presented a paper at the annual meeting of the American Historical Association on 'Coerced and Free Labor in Indonesia' which covered a much broader area of labor relations than I am covering here. Some of the research for this later paper did bring about changes that I felt should be noted. Therefore, I have included a Notation for Clarification at the end of this paper that briefly presents some of the points that relate to the matter of labor under the Cultivation System. This does not, however, allay my feeling that this subject does not have the rigor that I would like.

Recently, others have become interested in this topic and will perhaps be able to provide a more satisfying portrayal of it. R.E. Elson of Griffith University, Australia, has sent me a paper on 'The Mobilisation and Control of Peasant Labour in Java in the Early Cultivation System' (Asian Studies Association of Australia, 1988) which throws additional light on this matter.

That the introduction of the Cultivation System into Java in 1830 brought with it new and unusual pressures upon Javanese society is generally conceded. However, the extent and nature of these pressures has not been analyzed or the nature of the response fully considered. It is the purpose of this paper to make a preliminary exploration of these matters and in so doing to raise some tentative ideas about the peasantry of Java in the mid-nineteenth century. Central to the pressures brought about by the Cultivation System is the labor requirements imposed by that System. Due to lack of precise information the magnitude of the labor requirements has been little studied, though from the 1840s onward it was generally known to be large. Persons working within the System in Java tended to write few specifics about the labor requirements of the cultivations. Persons outside the System stressed the burdens imposed by the System, but generally had only limited access to detailed information and tended to focus on systemic reforms which missed the heart of the labor problem. The most popular remedy proposed by the opponents of the System for the labor component was to institute 'free', that is, wage, labor, for the existing forms of compulsion. From the moment it was advanced in the mid-1840s, the concept of 'free' labor had about it an aura of remoteness from the economic forces at work in Java at this time.

A reassessment of the extent and impact of the labor component is made possible at this time through the use of new evidence, or more accurately stated, the use of evidence not previously explored. Specifically I refer here to the annual Cultivation Reports which provide statistical data as well as narrative descriptions of various aspects of the System including the organization, payment, and extent of labor.[1] This information entered the public domain almost a quarter of a century ago, but it is extremely detailed and difficult to manipulate. The discovery, more recently, of the local details of the surveys undertaken by the Umbgrove Commission in the mid-1850s, provides additional insights into the nature of the labor element within the System. These materials have been brought to light by Dr C. Fasseur whose forthcoming article makes extensive use of the data provided by these surveys which were never published as part of the Commission's Report.[2] His statement that 'The Cultivation System was less a claim on the land than a tax in labor; many persons shared in the cultivation services who paid no land rent,' serves as a convenient summary and point of departure for some of the arguments which will be made in this paper. In light of our present knowledge about the System this statement may seem somewhat bold, but I believe it to be essentially correct, certainly in its first part, and possibly in its second part also. Additional support in this reassessment can also be drawn from the Final Report (*Eindresumé*) of the investigation into landrights in Java launched in the 1860s.[3]

---

1   A list of the Cultivation Reports can be found in C. Fasseur, *Kultuurstelsel en koloniale baten* (Leiden dissertation 1975), p. 269.
2   C. Fasseur, 'Organisatie en sociaal-economische betekenis van de gouvernementssuiker-kultuur in enkele residenties op Java omstreeks 1850,' *BKI* 133 (1977), pp. 261-93.
3   [W.B. Bergsma], *Eindresumé van het bij Goevernements besluit van 10 Juni 1867 No. 2 bevolen onderzoek naar de rechten van den Inlander op den grond op Java en Madoera*. 3 vols.

Before proceeding with an analysis of the data supplied by these sources it seems appropriate to strike a note of caution about nineteenth-century data. In the main it is highly inaccurate and biased. In an earlier article (1972) I have discussed this; here I wish to reiterate the warning and also point out that my analysis is not so much dependent upon the positive value of the numbers as upon the relationship between various sets of numbers.[4] These numbers, however scattered they may presently be, were derived from a common source, namely the reports of local administrators and village headmen in Java. Whatever manipulation occurred at the time and place of reporting would have had to maintain rather obvious relationships which could not have been lost on either Javanese or Dutch administrators. Failure to do so would certainly have raised some questions over the years covered by these reports by persons intimately associated with the cultivations in Java. Such questions did occur, but not with respect to the figures dealing with the labor imposition which I will be using here.

When in 1829 Johannes van den Bosch set forth his scheme for making Java profitable by exporting products which would be salable on the world markets he spoke in generalities about how these products would be grown, processed, and otherwise handled. Five years later when he left Java after four years as governor-general and commissioner-general (1830-34) he continued to speak in generalities which he must have known to be different from the actual situation in Java.[5] His statements tell us more about his devotion to king and country, his strong sense of self-righteousness, and his penchant for social engineering, than they tell us about the manner in which the Cultivation System was operating in Java. All this might have been of little consequence if the realities of Java had become otherwise known, but this was hardly to be the case with the closed imperial system of the time when the colonies were not subject to public scrutiny. When this situation changed after 1848 – more specifically after 1854 – and the public came to hear more about actual conditions in Java through newspapers, journals, and parliamentary hearings, it was difficult to reconcile these revelations with those of the founder of the System. Whether one chose to regard Van den Bosch as a scoundrel or as a victim of the wiles of those who succeeded him in Java, did little to affect the nature of the tirades against a System which had deviated so mightily from its professions. So easy was it to turn the argument against this ready-made figment, that one could appear brilliantly destructive and subsequently

Batavia, 1876-1896.

[4]   Robert Van Niel, 'Measurement of change under the Cultivation System in Java, 1837-1851,' *Indonesia* 14 (October 1972), Appendix pp. 107-9.

[5]   *Mijne verrigtingen in Indie. Verslag van [...] J. van den Bosch over de jaren 1830, 1831, 1832 en 1833 [...]*.(Amsterdam, 1864).

constructive without having a much firmer basis in fact than did the strawman that was being tarred and demolished. Since the attacks on the System were prompted by ideological outrage of either a humanitarian or economic sort, partisan and tendentious arguments were rife. There was, however, relatively little grasp of the underlying realities of life in Java and of the problems that beset the Javanese peasant. It is a mark of the genius of Multatuli (Eduard Douwes Dekker) that he was able to cut through much of the hollow rhetoric of his time and expose the central issues starting in 1860.[6] It is one of the sadder commentaries on his time to note that it could not or would not understand what he was really saying.

Van den Bosch conceptualized using one-fifth of the village lands to grow exportable crops. This one-fifth of the villages' lands, with one-fifth of the villagers' labor effort expended upon it, should have produced enough of whatever crop was designated to cover the amount of the landrent for the entire village. Thereby leaving the village with four-fifths of its land and labor-time to raise its own necessities for home consumption or local sale. In this way, it was believed, the System would raise the welfare of the Javanese peasant while at the same time providing exportable crops which would keep Dutch ships occupied and provide a profit for the Netherlands government when sold. Coffee, sugar, and indigo became the most important commodities to be grown, processed, and exported under the System. None of these was new to Java with the advent of the System in 1830, but the manner in which their production was organized and compensated was. If the founder's ideas had taken hold as he proposed them, one could easily envision villages having a patch of their lands planted in a crop for the government and one-fifth of the men of the village working on this patch (or alternatively all of the villagers working one-fifth of their time on it). From the produce of this land the village would earn enough money to pay its landrent, making up shortfall or keeping the excess.

From the first it never worked this way. The reasons for this are complex and cannot be dealt with fully in this paper, but in the main the local conditions in Java were extremely varied both as regards the disposition and experience of the various villages and as regards the natural conditions of the land and the crops. Production was, of course, the central principle, but

6   Eduard Douwes Dekker (Multatuli) wrote the book *Max Havelaar* in 1860. This book exposed the suffering of the Javanese, principally at the hands of his own headmen and chiefs. His essays *Over vrijen arbeid in Nederlandsch Indië* (Amsterdam, 1862) and *Nog-eens: Vrye-Arbeid in Nederlandsch Indië* (Delft, 1870) are the most relevant of his writings to the points being made in this paper. For a further assessment of his perceptions of the time see my 'Government policy and the civil administration in Java during the early years of the Cultivation System,' in: *Conference on modern Indonesia history* (Madison, Wisconsin, 1975), pp. 61-79.

the way in which it occurred varied greatly. One feature that stood at the heart of the production, however, regardless of local variation, was the mobilization of labor. Labor was what did the planting, tending, transporting, and processing of the government crops. The manner in which workers were induced to undertake their chores was a key aspect of the success of the System, for there is little doubt that the crops grown for the government required more labor and, frequently, a different type of labor, than was needed for the peasants' normal crop, rice.

The labor requirements of the Cultivation System were imposed on the villages through the medium of using the authority of the supravillage Javanese elite. This elite group, consisting of a hierarchy of authority figures generally culminating in the Javanese *Regent* or *Bupati*, was held in high regard by the Javanese peasants. These elite persons were privileged under the Cultivation System by according them hereditary status and providing them with personal militia units. Their loyalty to the Dutch authorities was further assured by paying them a substantial salary and awarding them percentage payments of the value of the crops produced in their districts. In turn they placed their authority behind the System. The labor required of the peasantry was enforced in the same manner as traditional obligations such as corvée and village services. It was in no wise a voluntary labor contribution or even in first instance one that was performed for money, but instead one that was levied as part of the traditional social obligations long known to Javanese peasants. By present-day standards we could think of it as corvée, but at the time the term was applied to unpaid traditional service to higher authority. Since the labor requirements needed by the Cultivation System were compensated *either in remission of landrent* or more frequently in monetary payment, the required cultivation service was not called corvée but was seen as separate. This distinction was lost on the nineteenth-century Javanese peasant; to him it was all work for the government. Work that he was obliged to perform or suffer dire consequences. To the government, however, cultivation service was regarded as different from corvée and was, therefore, not registered as corvée or forced labor.

The number of peasants involved in labor service for the cultivations is an extremely large proportion of the total population; this proportion is remarkable in light of the limited use of village lands by the System. About five percent of the cultivated land in Java was used for government crops, but between 65 and 70 percent of the agricultural households in Java worked in government cultivations. Since the impact of the System was uneven it might be useful to cite a few examples drawn at random. Jepara, for instance, is close to the overall average in land usage, namely 5 percent, but shows only about 45 percent of its families involved in the cultivations. In

Pasuruan the land area was closer to 12 percent with about 90 percent of the families involved in cultivation service. In Banyumas the portion of the cultivated lands used for government crops dropped from 15 percent to about 8 percent from the 1830s to the 1850s while the labor involvement remained at about 95 percent of the families. In Kedu between one and two percent of the land was used, but the population involvement was close to 100 percent. Surabaya, to complete our sample, had about 5 percent of the cultivated land in government crops and between 35 and 40 percent of the families involved in cultivation service.

Some explanation will help to make these relationships more under-standable. Coffee, to which the largest number of families in Java were assigned, was not grown on the villages' cultivated lands, but instead on newly cleared upland gardens or in forests or as hedgerows. In Kedu, where only coffee was grown for the government, almost everyone was assigned to this cultivation, but it took almost none of the villages' lands. In Jepara, Surabaya, and Pasuruan sugar was the chief government crop and coffee and indigo less important. Lands suited to the growing of sugarcane often were used on a short-term basis and rotated every year or two; the labor for this crop was drawn from the same vicinity but not always from the same village as the land. The location of the sugar mill often determined the location of both land and labor. Indigo was regarded as the least profitable and most difficult of the government crops. Its area of planting was reduced sharply after 1840 as is shown in the example of Banyumas, but families removed from assignment to the indigo were generally reassigned to coffee cultivation. These explanations of local circumstances in nowise reduces the large disparity between the proportion of land used compared to the amount of labor demanded by the cultivation services. These statistical relationships provide strong evidence of the extent of the demands made upon the labor of the Javanese peasantry.

Since it was not Van den Bosch's intention to alter in any way the traditional pattern of village life he thought it best to deal with Javanese authorities down to the village headman. At first he thought that contracts could be closed with villages to undertake the government cultivations; since the landrent assessment was also negotiated at the village level this would make a rather natural arrangement. But that did not work, so increasingly the traditional elite hierarchy had to be used as a stimulus to the village, and the labor component required by the cultivations was arranged through the traditional channels of other work services, namely the corvée and village services. But these duties and obligations of the Javanese village were in most places related to rights to the village's lands. Everyone with a share in the village lands, regardless of the size of the share, also had a share in the work services. In Javanese villages, then as now, only a portion of the village families shared in the rights to the agricultural lands. This was generally true regardless of whether land was held communally or individually. Villagers with rights in the land usually controlled village affairs of all sorts. Some villagers owned only a house and yard, others owned nothing; these persons were usually dependent upon one of the nuclear villagers. Since the village tended to structure itself along patron-client lines, it was not unusual for the better-situated nuclear villagers (those that controlled larger plots of land and were often in the village administration) to arrange with others to perform services of various sorts for them, often in return for some form of recompense. Thus it was quite possible that within the Javanese village persons without land and without a tax obligation were doing work services of various sorts. Van den Bosch was aware of these socio-economic relationships in the village, but was inclined to let the village regulate in its own way the new obligations put upon it. The village was thus expected to absorb the cultivation services in field and factory and to adjust somehow to these new demands. In the main this is what happened.

At this point I wish to introduce another set of statistical relationships which provided added meaning to the extent and manner of the villages' adjustment to the increased work obligations. This data, derived from the annual Cultivation Reports provides figures for the total number of agricultural families in the various districts and the total number of men liable for corvée and other work services in each district. If these work services were related to landholding rights, as they ideally should have been, the number of corveable men who were heads of households with rights in the land would be only a fraction of the total number of families making their living through agriculture. This is not the case. In general these statistics indicate that the number of men liable for corvée and other work services was larger than the number of agricultural families. Again there are variations. In the north coast areas such as Tegal, Pekalongan, Semarang, and Jepara the figures are about equal, that is to say about 100 percent of the agricultural families were liable for work service of one sort or another. In Bantam, where the Cultivation System was reduced after the 1830s the number of persons liable for work service declines from about 100 percent to about 80 percent. In Cirebon, Banyumas, and Kedu the corveable number is in the neighborhood of 125 percent of the total number of agricultural families, while in Surabaya and Pasuruan the relationship is over 130 percent. These are not just casual or onetime figures, but consistent relationships covering almost two decades. As indicated above, these statistics are easily comparable and represent a relationship that was clearly understood and accepted by both Javanese and European administrators.

A positive and totally satisfactory explanation for these figures is not easily achieved, but certain plausible and partial explanations emerge through the various reports mentioned earlier. Fasseur has already stated that there were persons who shared in the work services who paid no landrent, i.e., were not shareholders in the village lands. As noted earlier this is quite probable, and it is therefore likely that they came to be eligible for cultivation service under the Cultivation System. Many villages increased the number of workers by giving more people rights to some land. The *Eindresumé* compiles instance after instance of villages in which either the number of shares in the land was increased to include virtually every family, or minor householders were included in the land division so as to include them in the work service. Sometimes landholding shares were alternated on two or three year cycles to increase the labor pool, or villagers were forced by higher authority to accept shares in the land against their will so they would be corveable.[7] It is interesting to note that this Report avoids speaking of any work obligation without a share in the land in whatever attenuated form, but it was after all the purpose of the Report to unfold landholding rights, not labor service. On the basis of the statistical data available to us it is not possible to be more specific about the various ways in which villages handled the additional labor burden.

The problem is not greatly helped by looking both forward and backward in time from the time of the Cultivation System. There is little precise information of the villager's labor obligations before 1830 and its precise relationship to land rights. The *Eindresumé* indicates that it was the pressure of the System that led to this heavy work obligation which affected the internal village arrangements. Its investigators were told on more than one occasion that work obligations were less in the days before the System. This certainly seems likely. In the later nineteenth century, after the Cultivation System ended after 1870, it was popular to assume that the village structure readjusted to a pattern of an earlier day once the heavy obligations imposed by the System were removed. That is to say, the control over land returned to a limited group of nuclear villagers, though individualization of landholding became more prevalent in some areas. All information available for the later period points to a decrease in the pressure of labor services in the village along with an increase in individualization of both land and labor. This trend was in conformity with the economic pressures of this later day and made the villages' adjustment to this new period more possible. It could be argued, though it falls outside the scope of this paper, that for the majority of the peasantry the new patterns after the 1860s were neither more advantageous nor more free than the earlier System for the private entrepreneurs used the same authority

---

7   *Eindresumé*, I, viz. Titel I and II.

patterns as had the government. It was certainly less in conformity with traditional authority patterns than the government controlled System.

One of the more remarkable phenomenon of the mid-nineteenth century was the acceptance of the Cultivation System by the Javanese; if they did not accept it willingly or gladly they certainly did not protest as much or as vehemently as in the later period. Generally speaking the period of the 1830s to the 1850s saw little protest of a violent sort associated with the System.[8] The most notable movements of the time occurred in areas where the System was not operative. The reasons for this acceptance are manifold. Some of these reasons such as the possible demoralization following upon the Java War (1825-30) are difficult to document though probably had an effect. More influential, I think, was Van den Bosch's conscious effort to maintain traditional authority patterns, which in turn involved enhancing the prestige of the traditional elite and reinforcing their positions. Also the monetary rewards offered administrators and village headmen for their cooperation with the System made it workable. Finally, I would point to the monetary compensation made by the System as a possible device for equalizing the burdens and providing a stimulus, however limited, to many of the individual peasants. This latter point of payment for labor services will occupy the remainder of this paper and should be seen as part of the overall nineteenth-century trend in Javanese society to move from a traditional, authority-bound nexus to a more individualized, cash nexus.[9]

As pointed out above the cultivation service imposed upon the villages by the Cultivation System was viewed as a social obligation by the Javanese peasantry, not distinguishable from corvée. The government viewed cultivation service as a paid, contractual arrangement which in most instances involved payments to the village that would be subtracted from the assessed landrent. The role of the village, specifically in the form of the village headman, was important in this financial arrangement. Within a very few years, however, it became impossible to maintain this because of inequity between the labor obligation and the landholding arrangements within the village. In some places the villagers, in others the administration (especially the Europeans) began to recommend making payments directly to the individuals involved in the work services connected with the

---

[8]   Fasseur, *Kultuurstelsel*, p. 47. See also for contemporary supporting evidence *Ichtisar keadaan politik Hindia-Belanda, tahun 1839-1848* (Jakarta, 1973) which is an Indonesian edition of a N.E.I. government report prepared by E. de Waal at the request of GG Rochussen to analyze the partial failures of the System. The original Dutch version makes it very evident that there was almost no protest activity of any significance in Java during this period.
[9]   The best overall account of social changes in Java during the nineteenth century is D. H. Burger, *De ontsluiting van Java's binnenland voor het wereldverkeer* (Leiden dissertation 1939).

System. By 1837 this became the rule. Van den Bosch from his position as Minister of Colonies protested but found he was unable to affect the situation in Java. For the administrators on the scene, many of whom were more liberal than the founder, this payment for cultivation service was the only way to maintain some sense of equity in the heavy labor burdens imposed on the Javanese peasantry. This practice was partially, but not totally, in conflict with the traditional patterns of Javanese life.

The payment to the individual cultivator for his labor service in the government cultivations was in proportion to his work effort and not in relationship to his part in the village's lands. The exact mode of this payment varied from place to place and from crop to crop. In fact, sometimes it was not made at all but continued to be manipulated by Javanese elite or village headmen, and this becomes a continuously sore point with European administrators and potential reformers of the System.[10] However, where it was made, it was made directly to the cultivator or processor and had the effect of providing a direct reward for the work in the cultivations. Part of the later confusion about these payments undoubtedly stemmed from the fact that they were made only for cultivation services, not for corvée or village services, and since it was difficult to disentangle the various forms of obligatory service it was often not clear what was being done in one category and what in another.

In the coffee cultivations, for instance, the arrangements after 1832 called for a payment directly to the individual or his representative when the coffee was delivered to the local warehouse. This payment, standardized throughout most of Java except for the Preanger Regencies which remained under the old system, was twenty-five guilders per *picul* from which was deducted ten guilders for landrent on the coffee lands which the peasant tended and three guilders to cover the cost of transportation from the local to the central warehouse. The peasant thus received twelve guilders in cash for each *picul* of coffee. This may seem a small recompense but it put more money into the peasant's hands than had previously been the case when local middlemen profited at his expense. In the indigo areas the grower was supposed to be compensated when he delivered the leaves to the small factory in his vicinity, but, as previously indicated, the payments in this crop were small and often less certain. In the sugar areas the payment of the assessed value of the cane in the field was paid directly to the cultivators who actually tended the cane. A fixed rate which varied locally but was generally about three and one-half guilders for each *picul* of sugar (later a

---

[10] Fasseur, *Kultuurstelsel*, p. 99, and *Ichtisar*, pp. 82-3. The fundamental law of 1854 attempted to regulate services in article 57, but this was no simple matter and was subject to varied interpretations for the remainder of the century.

fixed minimum of 75 guilders per *bouw* was set) was sometimes paid long after the work had been done and thus left room for manipulation. In general, however, the sugar payments were made to the individuals involved in the various chores involved with the government cultivations. Their payments were usually reduced by the amount of landrent owed on the land on which the cane was grown, but the mode of such reductions varied locally since the cultivator of the cane was often not the landholder of the plot on which the cane had been planted.

Additional work associated with the cultivations was compensated separately. Factory work in the sugar mills and indigo factories, cutting and transportation of cane, provision of firewood, stones, lime, timbers, etc., packing and loading of the processed item for export, and other activities were all regarded as cultivation service and was paid. Such payments, which sometimes included provision of minimal food allowances, were always paid directly to the individual. In some cultivations such as tea and tobacco the laborers were often obtained through using the traditional authority channels, but they were paid individually since these were not fully under government control. Ideally these duties should have all been performed by voluntary labor recruited by the processor in direct negotiation with the individual peasant. But in actual fact this was hardly possible since there were very few 'free' laborers in Java and only a small portion of this work could be managed by them. There did indeed come to be some persons who were totally dependent upon their factory work for their income. In some areas local Javanese undertook transportation contracts with factory owners and managed to be freed from some of their obligations to the village. But in the main it was necessary to seek labor through the intercession of the village and supra-village administration. This fact of life in Java remained true after the Cultivation System was dismantled in the 1860s, altering only slowly and not totally.

Was this compensation for cultivation services somehow involved in easing or adjusting the labor burdens imposed by the System? It is difficult to say with certainty in the light of our present knowledge of the details of life in Java. The amounts of such compensation were generally enough to cover the amount of the landrent in most places, but one must not conclude too much from this for the payments were often made to persons other than those who were obliged to pay the landrent. The amounts of the individual payments were never great since the number of persons was extremely large, and there is little to indicate that any Javanese peasant was totally proletarianized by the cash inducements offered in this form. Moreover, the manner in which the labor was recruited and the multifarious obligations with which most Javanese peasants lived, did little to change society in this direction. The general impression that one obtains is that the village and supra-village administrators managed through fair means and foul to win advantages for themselves through special payments, official landholding rights, and petty extortions at the expense of the peasant-laborer. In a social sense one can feel, though not easily documented, the formation of a more solidly privileged group in the rural areas of Java with resources that distinguished it from the mass of the overworked and overburdened peasantry. But this has only a minimal relationship to the individualization of payment for cultivation services. Very possibly these payments fooled very few people. The Javanese peasant may have submitted to the burdens of the System because he had no real alternative. But it is also possible, and again not readily documented, that the System, for all its shortcomings, provided a certain basic prosperity in most parts of Java. This peasant prosperity was based upon material holdings of livestock and land, both of which were increasing faster than the population at this time, and was adjusted and spread about through the increased use of money.

The evidence presented in this paper has clearly raised more questions than it has answered. It will have succeeded in its purpose if it serves to focus the attention of future historical researchers upon the importance of the labor component in the village arrangements of nineteenth century Java. Rural labor was then, just as earlier and later, the foundation of Javanese society and civilization. The fashions in which it was mobilized, stimulated, and rewarded is of fundamental significance in understanding the nature of and changes in this society. The relationships which this paper has brought forward will leave little doubt about the magnitude of the labor services imposed upon the Javanese peasants. The paper will also have provided some positive ideas about how that labor was organized and mobilized. But it leaves for future consideration the form and extent of the impact of all this upon the various levels of Javanese society.

Notation for Clarification, 1989

The legal justification for demanding cultivation service from the peasantry was contained in article 80 of the Fundamental Law (Reegerings Reglement) of 1830 which was framed by Van den Bosch and the King. By this article, timbering (*blandong*) operations which had been conducted as forced obligatory labor for compensation were used as an example of labor coercion that could now be extended to other cultivations. Previous Fundamental Laws had regarded timbering operations, birds' nest crags, salt flat operations, Preanger coffee, and spice gardens as subject to special regulations because of their importance to the Government. The Fundamental Law of 1830 (article 80) speaks of timbering operations as being done for the account of the Government for either a wage or in partial remission of landrent.

Then it goes on to say that arrangements of this sort can now be made for other labor services for the Government and for special cultivations whose expansion is considered important. This same wording was repeated in the Fundamental Law of 1836 (article 68).

The extent of the cultivation service was calculated by Van den Bosch at 66 days per year per person. It is not totally clear to me how he derived this figure. I assume that since he thought that each village should plant one-fifth of its land in a crop of use to the Government, then one-fifth of the village's labor should also be available to the Government.

The question quite often arises about the relationship of this new cultivation service to the corvée (herendiensten) which had existed since time immemorial. This relationship was left obscure in Government regulations for a long time and thereby this matter became a source of much confusion. Only with the Fundamental Law of 1854 is an effort made to clarify the issue, but then only partially and the confusion dragged on into the twentieth century. To Van den Bosch and Baud there seems to have been a clear distinction between corvée and other services mentioned above, and that distinction was based on the simple fact whether the work was compensated or whether it was done for no compensation. Corvée was uncompensated, though some of the corvée laborers in Government service might receive a ration of salt and rice. The other labor such as cultivation service, *blandong*, etc. was compensated whether that compensation took the form of money or remission of landrent. If one sees the matter in this light, then it becomes obvious that cultivation service was different from and in addition to corvée. When seen in this light it becomes obvious why the labor burden on the Javanese population was dramatically increased after 1830.

One additional point can be suggested here though this matter will be considered more fully in later papers in this volume. Labor aggregation in the traditional Javanese corvée arrangement was generally based on landholding rights. The labor under this arrangement was calculated through a system known as *cacah* and was based on households; the household head who had rights to land was also obliged to perform corvée (whether he did the actual work or whether he called upon a member of his household to do it made no difference). This *cacah* system was still in operation in 1830. Interestingly enough, the *cacah* system seems to have been phased out by Van den Bosch and Baud for after 1838 there seem to be no further references to it. The reason for this is obvious. To aggregate the largest possible labor supply it was necessary to call up labor service on an individual basis, not on a household basis. As a consequence there were many persons involved in cultivation service who had no rights to land. In many villages it became necessary to make adjustments that gave people the use of some land in order to get them to cooperate in the required labor arrangements. I suspect that this land use arrangement was not a full empowerment in landholding rights in many cases.

CHAPTER VII

The Effect of Export Cultivations in Nineteenth-Century Java

From mid-1978 to mid-1979 I spent a year at the Netherlands Institute for Advanced Studies (NIAS) in Wassenaar, for me most fortuitously located between the Netherlands State Archives in The Hague and the Royal Institute of Linguistics and Anthropology (KITLV), now situated in Leiden. I was again able to immerse myself in the documents and books of nineteenth-century Java. About midway in this year (January/February 1979), I was invited to spend a month at the Rockefeller Foundation's Bellagio Study and Conference Center on Lake Como, Italy. There I was able to lift my eyes and my thoughts above the source materials and reflect on some problems facing me in my understanding of the Cultivation System. The result was this article on export cultivations which I tried out in an abbreviated form at a conference at Cambridge University later in 1979.

It will be quickly evident to the reader that this paper deals with much more than export of crops, though that is certainly an important aspect of what it is about. My concerns have carried me into the pre-nineteenth-century nature of the Javanese village and into the impact of the West upon it. This theme will recur in later papers, but in this 1979 paper, which was published in 1981 in *Modern Asian Studies* 15,1, I am obviously trying to resolve a number of problems that have been raised in papers (nos. 4, 5, and 6) in this volume. In this paper I am taking a different tack and by so doing find the beginnings of a resolution to some of these problems. By the time of this paper I have come to see the introduction of the Cultivation System as less of a radical departure from earlier patterns of life in Java than had been generally assumed.

Of all the pieces that I have written about the Cultivation System, this is one of the most extended and comprehensive. More than any previous paper in this volume this paper will provide the reader with my overall view of the System. Toward the end of this paper I raise the question about the nature of the Javanese village before 1800 in order to approach an understanding of how the institution of the village evolved. This issue will be raised again in later papers.

When in 1913 Count van Hogendorp edited the letters and papers of his ancestor Willem, who had served in Java as one of the secretaries of the Commissioner General Du Bus from 1825 to 1829, he characterized the early nineteenth century in Java as a time of 'systems.'[1] His use of this word was not meant to be complimentary. Ancestor Willem had taken great pride in being the inspirational genius behind one such 'system'; one, incidentally, which was not adopted. The characterization of the time seems to me particularly relevant as an opening wedge into the contents and theme of this paper, for all 'systems' relative to nineteenth-century Java had at their core the stimulation of export commodities derived from the agricultural process. A *system*, as I use the term here and as it was used by nineteenth-century policy planners, was an orderly and logical arrangement of thoughts and objects into a complex whole according to some scheme which drew its inspiration from fundamental economic and social principles. Such systems for Java were devised by persons in positions of high authority either in Europe or in Java on the basis of what they had seen or heard about Java. Invariably the purpose of the system was to make the island of Java profitable to its European 'possessor'; the prevailing colonial theory holding that through treaty and conquest the European power had gained sovereign rights over the land and its people and should make use of them in accordance with its best judgment. Such judgment was embodied in a 'system' which hopefully provided benefits for both the possessor and the possessed.

The 'system' was a statement of European policy and drew its importance from that fact more than from its astute insights into conditions in Java. It was couched in idealized terms, based upon theoretical views of human nature, and premised upon the belief that it could succeed where its predecessor had failed. Each system showed what Europeans thought was possible in the way of improving the value of Java for the motherland. It showed what Europeans thought they were up to in Java and should not be confused with what they were really up (or down) to. The system always seemed to have more reality in the government centers of Batavia (Jakarta) and Buitenzorg (Bogor) than anywhere else. Policy was frequently not reflected in practice.

The early nineteenth century was indeed a time when the Dutch needed a good 'system' to make Java profitable. After 1795 when French armies moved into the Dutch Republic, the Dutch East Indies Company was abolished and its assets and liabilities taken over by the government of the

---

[1]   H. Graaf van Hogendorp (ed.), *Willem van Hogendorp in Nederlandsch-Indië 1825-1830* ('s-Gravenhage, 1913), p. 4.

Batavian Republic.[2] The Company had been the agency of Dutch contact with Java and the East Indies for some two hundred years. The general public in Europe knew very little about the Company, its mode of operation, or the territory it controlled. The new Dutch government inclined toward a liberal political economy and was, therefore, tilted against monopolistic trading companies controlled by a privileged elite. This inclination along with the apparent bankruptcy, widely proclaimed corruption, and self-righteous arrogance of the Company conspired to end its life. The Company 'system' seemed inappropriate for the time and no longer seemed profitable. The power and wealth of the Company remained a legend in the East Indies longer than in Europe.

The fate of the East Indies Company was not a matter of primary concern to most people in the Batavian Republic. Institutions closer to home were being swept away by the Dutch Patriots who were applying the ideas of the Enlightenment and the Revolution to the Dutch provinces. Everything in the Low Lands seemed to be changing, and not always for the better. As Dutch control slipped into French hands the economic and political pressures became increasingly unbearable and the country went into a downhill slide that reached its nadir in 1810 with the French annexation. For the next three years there was no independent Dutch state.[3] Alongside the political chaos was an economic collapse which had started earlier in the cities of Holland and ultimately carried away with it the mercantile prosperity of the oligarchical Regent families of Amsterdam and other trading and manufacturing cities. The East Indies along with other former sources of prosperity were certainly thought about in these years in terms of the good old days. In a practical sense, however, there was little the Dutch could do beyond think, for both their merchants and their governments were cut off from practically all contact with the former Company's territories.[4] When, with great joy for most, the Kingdom of the Netherlands appeared upon the scene in 1813, the new Government had to tread a careful political path and set about to overcome a queasy economic situation. Guided by a paternalistic and hard-working King, it needed all the help it could get. Of its former overseas territories only some were returned, and of these Java seemed by far the most promising as a source of profits to the motherland.

---

[2]   The charter of the East Indies Company was terminated by the Estates General of the Dutch Republic at the end of 1795 but was then extended by the National Assembly of the Batavian Republic to the end of 1799. In 1800 the Company's territories were brought under the administration of the State.
[3]   For the history of the Low Lands during this period see: Simon Schama, *Patriots and liberators; Revolution in the Netherlands 1780-1813* (New York, 1977).
[4]   For ideas and plans for the colonies at this time see: G.J. Schutte, *De Nederlandse Patriotten en de koloniën* (Groningen, 1974).

Meanwhile in Java the arrangements of the East Indies Company had continued without alteration until 1808 when Marshal Daendels arrived to sweep the stable clean. During the few years he was in Java, he changed the administrative and judicial systems in the direction of rationality, bureaucratization, and central control. Economic prosperity eluded him, however. It could hardly have been otherwise, given the disrupted state of the world's mercantile channels. In 1811 the British conquered Java to keep it from falling under further French control. It was now the turn of the British Lieutenant Governor T.S. Raffles to apply his 'system' to Java. The system which he introduced was a further step on the road to liberal change which had been started under Daendels, but it was meant to be more thorough and consequential, especially in its impact upon Javanese society. This system was perhaps the most influential of all the nineteenth-century systems in Java because it provided a pattern with which later systems were forced to work and toward which Javanese society was also gradually steered. This system will be described more fully after I attempt to establish some features of Javanese life upon which it was imposed. For the moment suffice it to note that this system did not succeed in making Java profitable during the time of Raffles, 1811 to 1815. Had it been otherwise the British might have been less favorably disposed to returning the island to the Dutch in 1816.

Java had long been a source of export commodities which had entered the world markets. At the beginning of the nineteenth century coffee and pepper were regarded as the most significant of these products, though indigo, cotton, sugar and rice had at times seemed to have export potential. In any event these products all involved the use of Java's lands and labor; all involved an agricultural cycle terminating in harvesting, processing, and delivery of the product. The work in this production process fell to the lot of the Javanese peasantry – I use the word 'Javanese' here in the residential sense, not in an ethnographic one. Long before there were Europeans in Java to affect in any way the internal housekeeping of that island, the Javanese peasant was applying his labor to the soil of Java to produce agricultural surpluses for local use and for export. This production and subsequent movement of agricultural products was economically and politically organized in the patterns of a civilization that had molded the thought patterns, social mores, and expectations of its members. As a civilization, it seems to have been extremely satisfying to its members. Historically we know more about the vicissitudes and changes of its elite than about any alteration in status of its peasantry. The early reports of the Europeans tend to emphasize the subordination and submissiveness of the peasantry to higher authority. This view of the peasantry may reflect the conditions of a given time since the Europeans had little occasion to have close contact with the peasantry and only entered the interior of the island in the late seventeenth and eighteenth centuries. By that time the principal Javanese state of Mataram was reaching a condition of disarrangement which may have brought greater oppressiveness with it. The declining fortunes of Mataram in the eighteenth century produced also a decline in vitality and morale of Javanese society which continued into the nineteenth century.[5] The governance of Java's northern littoral had passed into the hands of the Dutch East Indies Company, but the Company involved itself mainly with the local chiefs, not the peasants, leaving the way open for growing demands and pressures upon the villages of this area too.

Early nineteenth-century system builders had no objective basis on which to determine whether the state of Javanese villages in their day was any different or any worse than it had been in earlier times. In fact, there was very little precise information about the bottom level of Javanese society and what little there was came principally through the word of higher Javanese authorities rather than through direct observation.[6] The tendency of the time was to assume that the Javanese village had declined from a primordial autonomy and self-regulation into its present condition of submission: it felt that the village was, or traditionally had been, the determinant institution of Javanese agrarian society. The reports of observers from various parts of Java made it evident that such was not always the case in the early nineteenth century. These reports tended to support the conviction that the prevailing conditions were the result of usurpation of fundamental village rights by higher authority. The lack of close, detailed observation and the immense variety which seemed to exist in village institutions from place to place in Java, made it almost impossible to formulate a paradigm of *the* Javanese village. However, the central function of the village in the production process of Java made it necessary for every system to develop a conception of what the village had ideally been and what it might possibly become again. As a consequence an idealized notion of the Javanese village and its position in Javanese society emerged at this time as an essential aspect of European policy planning.[7]

---

[5]   While such matters as declining vitality and morale are difficult to document, I have been much influenced in my thinking by M.C. Ricklefs, *Modern Javanese historical tradition* (London, 1978).

[6]   Many Europeans, mostly Hollanders, were writing all sorts of things about what they had seen or heard about Java. It is interesting to note, however, that in the first half of the nineteenth century the two English writers, Crawfurd and Raffles, were most frequently quoted and regarded as the leading authorities. However great our admiration and indebtedness to these two observers, their information about village life in Java leaves many questions unanswered. See: John Crawfurd, *History of the Indian Archipelago*, 3 vols (Edinburgh, 1820), and Thomas Stamford Raffles, *The history of Java*, 2 vols (London, 1817).

[7]   My thinking about the position of the Javanese villages in the nineteenth century has been influenced by Jan Breman, 'Het dorp op Java en de vroeg-koloniale staat,' *Symposium* 1 (1979), pp. 187-215. The doctoral dissertation of Onghokham, 'The Residency of Madiun;

The conception of the physical aspects of the Javanese village was derived more from a passing observation than from an intimate, internal observation. That villages existed is quite clear from early nineteenth-century accounts, but how they looked and how they were put together is less clear. What was evident is that the village was made up of one or more residential clusters nestled in the midst of cultivated fields, woodlands, and meadows. What was also noted was that in Java the villages and their lands occupied only a small portion of the land surface – about one-eighth was a common estimate. This observation was the source of optimistic predictions about the potential profitability of the island if a proper system could expand the cultivated area. Most villages in Java could be reached only by paths which necessitated travel on foot or on horseback. Few Europeans visited them and when they did, it was generally for an overnight stop on the way to climbing one of Java's many mountains. The main highway or post road which Daendels had had constructed to link the island together was too costly for most travellers, so coastal ships remained the principal means of getting from one city to another. Anyway, the post road linked towns and cities; there were virtually no side roads into the rural countryside. This remoteness of most villages from normal European contact probably reinforced the notion of isolated independence and autonomy in both a physical and social sense.

The idealized village had control over its lands and controlled the manner in which they were divided among its inhabitants. Only residents of the village had a right to use the land; land use was regarded as a privilege. The actual relationship between the individual peasant and the piece of land he cultivated varied from village to village and from time to time. Some villages knew a right of individual possession. The European observers throughout the nineteenth century generally wanted to believe that this was the primordial pattern. Most villages in central and eastern Java seemed, however, to have communal landholding with either permanent or rotating shares for the members of the community. Not all persons in a village shared equally in the land. Influential families had substantial shares of land and participated in village affairs; some families had rights only to their house with its surrounding yard, while yet others lived on someone else's land in rather total dependency. These status levels, interrelated with landholding prerogatives, were locked into patron-client relationships which extended throughout the society. This latter arrangement was by preference overlooked by nineteenth-century system

---

Pryayi and peasant in the nineteenth century,' Yale University, 1975, also contains interesting views on this subject. What I have expressed in this paper is my own view which does not exactly coincide with that of either of the two scholars mentioned here.

builders in the belief that supravillage control over village land and labor was an abuse of earlier conditions. It should be noted that in the main the villagers' rights were limited to usufruct rather than ownership of the land, though here again there were conflicting bits of evidence, especially from West Java.

The work arrangements within a village were diverse and complex but were, it was felt, regulated by the village itself. Land was generally worked by the person who held it, but village officials and better situated villagers might have their lands worked by others under sharecropping or tenant arrangements. Such arrangements might involve more than field work and frequently blurred into dependency relationships. In addition to work on the land, the village also regulated other work services. These were divided into village services and corvée. Within the village, duties such as maintenance of paths and bridges, cleaning and upkeep of irrigation ditches, and guard duty were shared by all members of the community. For the supravillage authorities the villagers performed corvée. These chores seemed to be part of the obligation that attended being a member of the village community.

The production of the village, whether from lands or handicrafts, was in the first instance used for its own subsistence or exchanged in rotating markets for essentials produced elsewhere. While money was not unknown in Java prior to the nineteenth century it rarely seems to have circulated in the villages. A portion of the village's production was passed on to higher authority. There was great variation in the size of this portion ranging from zero for villages which had special obligations for the maintenance of a religious shrine or special services for a particular prince or chief, to as much as fifty percent for villages under the close control of a courtier's agent. The upward movement of goods took the form of tribute. For this tribute and the corvée, the village was supposed to have been free to regulate its own internal life style; this did not correspond to the reality of early nineteenth-century life in Java and led consequently to the abolition of both these devices in some of the systems, especially the one devised by Raffles. The Dutch East Indies Company, on the other hand, had made full use of both tribute and corvée in gaining control of products and labor. It felt this to be part of its sovereign rights which were taken over from the princes it had supplanted. The Javanese reaction to all this is difficult to determine. Since these institutions were a long-standing aspect of their civilization there is no reason to assume that they thought much about them at all so long as they remained within manageable limits.

The Javanese village usually, but not always, arranged its own internal governance and administration – at least this is what was generally assumed in the early nineteenth century. A village headman was selected by the leading villagers from among themselves. They would also select, or the headman would appoint, one or more secretaries and assistants, a police officer, and various other functionaries. The village would also have one or more Moslem religious representatives who would provide religious ceremonies for various occasions and look after the rudimentary education which was available to villagers. None of these persons performed work services, and all of them were rewarded in various allotments of land which were worked for them by others. The village headman represented the village to higher authority; he was supposed to be the controller of the village's internal affairs. If his control were just and in accordance with the village's customs, and if he provided the required tribute and corvée, the village could be expected to live in peace with itself and with the world around it. There may have been parts of Java where things worked in this way, but there were also many where it did not. It was this generalized conception, however, that served as the basis of system building from the time of Raffles forward. The result, given the fluid nature of many aspects of Javanese life, was that reality gradually moved in the direction of the ideal so that by the end of the century observers could ascertain deviations from a norm that had been little more at one time than a paper creation.

The higher authorities, or supravillage sphere, alluded to earlier, lived in the towns or court center, not usually in the villages. Ideally emanating from a single center of power in a descending hierarchy of prestige and authority stretching from a sultan or emperor at the top to collectors and supervisors who were in touch with the villages, this elite in the eighteenth and nineteenth centuries was scattered and divided. Loyalties were dispersed and patronage lines unclear. Not a large part of the population, the supravillage sphere had extensive family connections and service relationships which may have made them a substantial burden on the productive portion of the society.[8] This group sustained itself from the products and labor delivered by the peasantry, and at the beginning of nineteenth century was in many places asserting de facto authority in village affairs. Some members of this group may have derived an income from trading in the products passed on to them, but normally such

---

[8] It is not easy to obtain an estimate for the size of the supravillage group in the nineteenth century. An 1874 report on Kedu Residency estimates the actual authorities at 0.18% of the total population. However, when village administrators, religious officials, and others who were regarded as socially above the peasant masses were added to this the total comes to 15%. *De Residentie Kadoe naar de uitkomsten der statistieke opname en andere officiele bescheiden [...]* (Batavia, 1871), pp. 72-3. Information gathered in Cirebon in 1859 puts the supravillage elite, both active and retired, at 0.55% of the total male population. This source estimates the village administration and religious functionaries (i.e., persons free of work obligation) at about 2% of the adult male population. Netherlands State Archives (ARA), Ministerie van Koloniën, Verbaal 18-12-1861, Nr 52.

commerce was conducted by farming out the tribute and corvée rights to non-indigenous merchants who resided in towns and port cities.

The sultan or emperor was supposed to be the owner of all the land. This was a theory that fitted in well with European notions about sovereignty and was taken over by the system builders. The sultan or emperor could parcel out land and people to his retainers and favorites, who in turn could subdivide or turn over the appanage to others. Since land was plentiful, the grants were usually couched in terms of working men or households. Supposedly it made no difference to the village who was the recipient of its tribute and labor; in practice it probably made quite a bit of difference since the control through various agents and family members was often more delimiting of the village's prerogatives than should have been the case. Raffles noticed this and disapproved strongly. It would appear that his early intention was to remove this entire supravillage sphere from its position of power over villages and also abolish tribute and corvée. In fact this never happened, but he did push forward the notion of the autonomous, self-regulating village.

Returning to the European devised systems now, it seems best to begin with the system introduced by the English Lieutenant Governor T.S. Raffles in the years from 1811 to 1815. I have already touched upon this system, usually called the Landrent System, while describing the condition of Javanese society. I would now like to add a few details and discuss its effects upon the export cultivations.[9] Since the Dutch, after 1816, continued to apply most of the main lines of Raffles's system to the governance of Java, the impact of this system upon policies in Java was nothing short of revolutionary.

Raffles arrived in Java in 1811 determined to change the system of tribute deliveries which had prevailed under the Company. He was an advocate of the liberal ideas of economic freedom and individual liberty and justice, and he sought to apply these ideas to Java. He hoped to do away with the tribute deliveries by introducing an equitably assessed and honestly applied landrent which, if not immediately, was eventually to be paid in money. The model from which this idea was derived was the *zamindari* and *ryotwari* systems introduced earlier into India. Raffles was much opposed to the supravillage Javanese whom he regarded as despotic, tyrannical, arbitrary, and corrupt. The basis of his landrent settlement was with the village, thereby eliminating the intermediate layer of officialdom between the government and the village. Most of these officials were retained in

---

[9]   J. Bastin, *Raffles' ideas on the land rent system in Java and the work of the Mackenzie land tenure commission* ('s-Gravenhage, 1954), and *The native policies of Sir Stamford Raffles in Java and Sumatra* (London, 1957).

salaried positions in police and administrative capacities, but they were deprived of their ancient privileges, especially the right to unpaid services in the form of corvée from the population. Raffles firmly asserted the government's rights to all the lands of Java except for those retained in the hands of the Javanese princes of Central Java. The government's lands were to be essentially of two kinds, private estates and generality lands. Private estates were patches of land which had been sold to private persons starting in the eighteenth century and continued by Raffles. These lands were mostly situated around Batavia, though some were as far east as Pasuruan. The owners of these estates were expected to pay an annual tax to the government, set at about three-fourths of one percent of the purchase price. For the rest they had rights to the deliveries and services of the people residing on these lands much as had the appanage holders of the Javanese system. These estate owners were free to apply whatever pressures they wished and to grow whatever crops they wished – with a restriction on coffee growing in some areas since this remained a government monopoly – but they faced the possibility that too heavy a hand would depopulate their estates and make them consequently valueless.

The generality lands were all the rest of the government lands, which thus consisted of the cultivated lands of the Javanese villages as well as unused lands. The lands used by the villages were regarded as rented to them and they were expected to pay a rent to the government for the use of these lands. This landrent was assessed on the main crop, usually rice, and amounted to about forty percent on the average of this crop. The idea behind this was that the government would now derive its revenues from the landrent and from the various duties which it might impose. Unlike the system of the Dutch Company, the government was not to be both ruler and merchant. Both the Javanese villages and the private estate owners were now to function in a free, self-regulating market economy in which they would produce whatever commodity was most marketable and consequently most profitable. That this arrangement was different in almost every respect from the traditional Javanese political-economic system is obvious.

If the landrent system had worked as planned it would have led to a total change in the Javanese housekeeping; Raffles and his closest advisers (many of whom were Hollanders) knew this, intended this, and expected this. They were modernizers par excellence. The system did not, however, work as planned. Partly this was because the English were not granted sufficient time and partly because the years in which they were in Java were years of disrupted trade and commerce which made both the production and the export of marketable commodities difficult. In largest part, however, the system was not working because of inherent incompatibilities with the

Javanese socio-economic structure. Unfortunately for the Dutch, who took over the system in slightly revised form, this failing only became evident at the end of a short burst of prosperity in tropical export commodities following the restoration of peace in Europe. After 1820 the Netherlands East Indies (NEI) government was in deep and persistent financial difficulties, as were many of the merchant houses of Batavia and other port cities.

The problems which beset the NEI government after 1820 were manifold; the system was not working as it was supposed to. One of the clearest though by no means the only indication of this was the drop in value, quantity, and quality of the cultivations for export. The market value of these products was a function of the free world market and therefore not easily influenced by the NEI government. However, the quantity and quality of the products for export might have been subject to influence were it not that the prevailing system, as interpreted by the European administration of that time, seemed to make the government powerless. The statistical evidence for this period is admittedly uncertain, though what there is, as recently assembled and published in *Changing Economy in Indonesia*, tends to bear out the point I am making here.[10] More convincing by far are the contemporary accounts by observers and government reports which describe in some detail the overall problem: the Javanese peasant and village community were not turning freely to the cultivation of export commodities; the cultivations (especially coffee lands) which had been returned to indigenous control during the English period had been allowed to deteriorate; and entrepreneurs working on leasehold lands were unable to procure the necessary labor to further their enterprises because of lack of contractual certainty. The failures in the export sector were made more noticeable by a high level of governmental expenditure for infrastructure development and pacification operations.

These problems of the 1820s are central to the theme of this paper. I wish to examine them in slightly more detail, for there was clearly a crisis involving the mobilization of indigenous land and labor for the cultivation of export products. Proponents of the landrent system had expected the freedom to cultivate the land in the best interests of a free market economy, on the one hand, and the obligation to pay a landrent (or tax) in money, on the other, to force the Javanese peasant into greater productivity in his own self-interest. That this did not happen was the cause of much soul-searching by European administrators and the usual attributions of laziness and

[10]   P. Creutzberg (ed.), *Changing economy in Indonesia; A selection of statistical source material from the early 19th century up to 1940*, 3 vols (The Hague, 1975-77). See also, 'Tableaux comparatifs des principaux articles du commerce de Java et Madura, 1825 à 1844,' *Le Moniteur des Indes-Orientales et Occidentales* I, 1 (1846-47), pp. 116-7.

indifference directed toward the Javanese. What actually happened was diverse and complex.

Many villages, having no knowledge of monetary or administrative arrangements and finding it difficult to raise the required landrent, simply placed themselves in the hands of a European, or Chinese, or most frequently a Javanese notable who paid their landrent. In return, the village obligated itself to give this person a portion of its crop (often set as high as fifty percent) and to make its labor service, corvée, available to this person. There is little doubt that such arrangements were often heavier than they should have been under the planned landrent scheme. The Chinese and Europeans generally used the land and labor of the villages which came under their control in this manner to produce export commodities, either on the lands of the village or on leased lands in the vicinity. It is ironic that most of the export of agricultural products from Java during the 1820s resulted either from such arrangements; or from the production on private estates; or from forced cultivation and delivery of coffee to the government under the Preanger (West Java) System which had not been replaced by the new landrent arrangement; or from privately leased appanages in the Princely Lands by which arrangement the leasor gained control over the traditional tribute and corvée of the villagers. All of these arrangements worked with forced, labor, that is to say, labor which worked under patterns of traditional obligation, rather than free labor which, in the definition of the time, worked for a money wage. These arrangements thus were not in harmony with the basic principles of the prevailing system. The efforts of the government to restrict the application of these various devices seemed to worsen rather than improve the situation.

The Javanese notables who paid the landrent *for* some of the villages were generally the same local authorities who had previously drawn tribute and services *from* these villages. In return for their now paying the landrent, they continued to extract those goods and services which they regarded as an essential supplement to the salaries which their bureaucratic functions, in which the government had continued them after 1816, provided them. The goods and services were used to elevate their personal status and luster, which had always marked their social standing. To the European administrators throughout the century this status display was always viewed as a useless and distasteful aspect of Javanese authority which, in the early period, they often sought to counter by behaving in unpleasant ways toward these persons.[11] It was a well-understood reality in

[11]   Governor General Van der Capellen commented on this in 1820, urging better treatment of the Regents. In 1827 the Commissioner General Du Bus again had to remind the European administrators of this. S. van Deventer, *Bijdragen tot de kennis van het landelijk stelsel op Java*, 3 vols (Zalt-Bommel, 1865-66), Vol. 2, pp. 55 and 67.

the Javanese housekeeping that goods and services were a more malleable, and consequently more valuable, form of income than a salary. Some of the courtiers in the Princely Lands who had leased their appanages for money to European entrepreneurs had had this lesson brought painfully home to them. When in 1832 the government permitted a portion of the salaries of Javanese Regents (*Bupati*) to be paid in non-taxable appanage holdings, the Regents of the north and west-central parts of Java who had had the closest contact with the monetary landrent arrangements were the ones to take greatest advantage of this. It should be pointed out that during the 1820s the government did not sanction the practice of gaining control of the goods and services of a village through the device of paying the landrent. In practice, however, it was difficult to control. The government did allow contracts with villages for the use of their land or with individuals for the supplying of their labor; it was a very fine line between this and simply gaining control of the entire village by paying the landrent.[12]

Some villages sought to pay their own landrent under the new freedoms granted them. This was invariably done by turning to rice cultivation and selling the surplus on the open market. Where such was well managed – it rarely was because the Javanese villager had little sense of the marketplace and tended to be guided by immediate needs and wants – a village could certainly raise the money needed for landrent and more. The rice prices of the 1820s, especially in the vicinity of the major cities, were favorable. There is little doubt that this cultivation was important in meeting a social and nutritional need even though it did not contribute to the export balance of Java. From the point of view of export cultivations, the problem was not that some villages produced rice, but rather that they were interested *only* in producing rice. Villages in this happy position – or rather the peasants within these villages – were disinclined to seek additional work for added income. Leisure to them was more valuable than additional money. Small wonder that one finds periodic schemes to import labor into Java from Bali, Bengal, and China. In parts of Java where rice grew well it was also possible to grow export crops well, but precisely in such areas it seemed difficult to attract the needed labor at this time.

The effect of this problem on the export of sugar, for example, was quite clear. Sugar production at this time was concentrated mainly in the areas around Batavia where, already in the time of the Company, it maintained itself only through government price supports. Labor for these mills had been drawn from Krawang, Cirebon, and parts of the Preanger Regencies.

---

[12]   On the partial payment of official salaries in land see: *Nota over het ambtelijk landbezit van Inlandsche ambtenaren [...]* (Batavia, 1904). The Fundamental Law of 1818, article III, allowed for free agreements for hiring labor and renting land; such agreements had to be registered with the government.

Under the landrent system such labor became unavailable or too expensive so that most of the mills were abandoned and the fields deserted. Efforts to grow sugar along the north coast had thrived briefly after 1816 but had succumbed to difficulties in labor recruitment. Resident Vos of Pekalongan noted in 1823 that the local sugar mill was operating at less than a third of capacity while sugar had been imported from Siam and China for the past three or four years.[13]

The situation in coffee, still the most valuable export commodity from Java, was similar. In some of the upland areas of the north coast of Java the British had leased coffee lands to private Europeans or had given them to nearby villages. The Europeans had difficulty in recruiting labor, and, where it could be found, the plucking was done carelessly by stripping the trees and thereby reducing the value of the product. The villages neglected the trees and generally cut down the coffee gardens in order to convert the land to rice production. It was not that coffee was any less profitable at this time than rice, but simply a matter of preference. Production had fallen away to such a degree along the north coast that after 1822 measures were taken to re-introduce the forced planting and tending of coffee trees by villagers on behalf of the government.

Private entrepreneurs, European and Chinese, also discovered that the free contracts for land and labor which they were permitted to make with Javanese villages and individuals were frequently not fulfilled, resulting in the loss of a money advance as well as the crop which had been planted. Recourse to the courts in such instances might produce a decision in their favor but nothing more. The Dutch after 1816 had retained the judicial reforms of the British with modifications, but had made village lands inalienable and not subject to forfeiture for debt. Such court decisions, therefore, had a hollow ring to the persons who had suffered the loss. In practice it came to be recognized that the administration, European and Javanese, was the only body able to assure fulfillment of labor obligations by the villagers. Only those entrepreneurs who knew how to grease the machinery or who could gain government support were able to function. In the practical economic relationships needed to produce export cultivations the free market economy existed in name only; it was not producing such export cultivations in any great quantity in Java at this time.

Nor, for that matter, was it doing much to preserve or improve the indigenous socio-economic order. The various schemes described above had the effect of making the peasant subject to greater pressures and higher exactions by headmen and supravillage authorities. The former had in

---

[13] *Algemeen verslag over de Residentie Pekalongang 1823*, pp. 19-20. ARA, Collectie Schneither Nr 90.

many instances learned to use the intermediate role granted them by the powers inherent in the landrent assessments and assignments, while the latter found ways to use their bureaucratic authority to exert more impersonal economic pressures. Both these groups were now drawn more clearly into the colonial monetary and administrative system, but the peasant in the village remained outside this, confined to his traditional patterns, and unaware that he was suffering a relative loss of protection.

King William I and his Ministers of Colonies did not become cognizant of the lack of financial success in Java until 1823; reportage was not only slow, but financial statements of the time reflected more wishful thinking than economic reality. From out of the Netherlands schemes were now advanced to amend the existing system. The Treaty of London of 1824, which confirmed the British control of Singapore, attempted to give some advantage to Dutch shippers by recognizing tariff preferences. In the same year the government-supported Netherlands Trading Company (NHM) was launched in an effort to stiffen the Dutch commercial endeavor. But these measures were not terribly successful in wresting the mercantile activities from the British merchants who had come to dominate shipping and foreign trade in and out of Java. The advantages of home manufactures and outbound cargoes which the British had were not outweighed by the NHM which was over-capitalized and too bureaucratically cumbersome to drive British commerce from the seas of the archipelago. It is a fact that many trading houses in Batavia were driven into bankruptcy during the late 1820s and early 1830s, but more because of a liquidity crisis, which trapped them with their funds tied up in advances to export producers, than through any particular action by the Dutch or NEI governments. The general shortage of silver, with which to pay international obligations, at this time also severely affected British Agency Houses in India. The collapse of Palmer & Co. in 1830, once so powerful in both India and Java, illustrates the inter-relationship of the phenomenon.[14]

There was little capital accumulation in Java at this time other than the money tied up in private estates, and this was generally not interested in, or capable of, expansion beyond those limits. Later, after 1830, when the system was changed, copper coinage designed to circulate at the village level was introduced in great quantities, as were government loans to individuals, who undertook to develop processing plants or factories. Together these devices laid the basis for new capital growth. This was done, however, in opposition to the then current monetary concepts. The Java Bank was forced to issue copper-bearing paper currency which, along with the rather

[14] K.N. Chaudhuri, *The economic development of India under the East India Company 1814-58* (Cambridge, 1971), p. 22-3.

precarious investment and dividend policies of the Bank, led to a financial crisis in the early 1840s. The accursed flood of copper coins, as later financial experts called it, had the immediate effect, in my opinion, of laying the groundwork for a monetization of the village economy. This monetization made possible, in the last third of the century, a different economic atmosphere in which the cultivations for export could thrive.

When these remedies of the mid-1820s did not heal the financial situation and when the matter became increasingly desperate with the mounting costs of the Java War, the King, in 1826, sent out a new Commissioner General, Viscount Du Bus, who was empowered to take drastic economic measures. The economization measures which he instituted made him extremely unpopular and dismantled many developmental plans which had been started. More important, however, was his decision in 1827 to move away from the concept of economic freedom for the Javanese village and peasant. A 'colonization' scheme envisioned a larger role for private European planters and entrepreneurs who would be assisted by the government in gaining access to land and labor for the production of export cultivations. Before these plans had progressed very far, however, the King was persuaded in 1828 to try a totally new system which promised to obtain export crops from Java without European middlemen or private European capital, neither of which seemed available.

This new scheme was proposed by Johannes van den Bosch, whom the King designated Governor General for the East Indies in 1828, and who arrived in Java at the beginning of 1830 to put his plan into operation. This new plan was unofficially dubbed the Cultivation System (Kultuurstelsel in Dutch). Before he ever reached Java, Van den Bosch had to ward off accusations that his plans called for a return to forced labor and compulsory deliveries. He side-stepped these issues by claiming it to be his intention to apply the traditional concepts of Javanese housekeeping to the production of export crops and by contending that he was not opposed to freedom but would have to see, once in Java, what could be done. These answers, naturally, did not satisfy the proponents of the earlier liberal system who were strongly entrenched in the government at home and in Java, but the King was desperate for profit from the colony and stood behind Van den Bosch. In those days the King's word was law.

When Van den Bosch arrived in Java he issued general guidelines to the administration which clearly indicated a desire to restore the Javanese supravillage authorities to positions of prominence and to use them to promote the cultivation of exportable crops by the Javanese villages. The guidelines made only general suggestions as to how this was to be done, leaving the exact measures to local circumstances. Thus at the local level, the system became more a patchwork of accommodations to particular customs and practices than the uniform application of a single set of concepts.[15] At first there was talk of contracts made with the villages but this rather quickly gave way to arrangements based on the use of authority. Initially there were statements about the remission of landrent which were later to cause much confusion when critics noted that the landrent was not only being collected but was actually constantly increasing. In actual fact the remission of landrent occurred only in Madiun and Kediri, two areas taken over from the Princely Lands at the end of the Java War and hardly typical of the government lands on which the new system was applied. From the first, the landrent arrangement as assessed upon the value of the primary crop on the land remained in force.[16] What the new system would do was to provide a means whereby that landrent could be paid by the village with resources at its disposal. To the opponents of the System it was viewed as a return to the tribute and mercantile system of the Company. In a superficial way it was, but the comparison is misleading because it is too simple; the Cultivation System involved a greater European involvement in the Javanese economic structure and also developed, over time, a more complex pattern of control arrangements.

Let us now examine how the System operated in practice. To obtain crops for export and sale, the Cultivation System set about having the village communities in Java plant a portion of their lands with a crop designated by the government. Supposedly this was to be one-fifth of the village's lands, but the portion ranged from zero in many areas to almost one-half in others, depending upon the success of a particular cultivation in a particular area. In the government lands in Java about five percent on the average of the cultivated land was used for government cultivations, but this figure does not include the area under coffee since this crop was not grown on previously-cultivated village land.[17] At any rate, this government crop was to be tended to maturity by the villagers and then harvested, and delivered to the local processing plant or warehouse by them. The village was to receive a monetary payment for this in relation to the value of the product either as assessed while standing in the field in the case of sugar, or in terms of per pound of finished product in the case of indigo, or in a fixed payment per picul delivered to the warehouse for coffee. This monetary payment should have been sufficient, according to Van den Bosch's calculations, to

---

[15]   For the best descriptive survey of the System using the newest interpretations see: C. Fasseur, *Kultuurstelsel en koloniale baten; De Nederlandse exploitatie van Java, 1840-1860* (Leiden, 1975).

[16]   R. Van Niel, 'The function of landrent under the Cultivation System in Java,' *Journal of Asian Studies* 23 (1964), pp. 357-75.

[17]   R. Van Niel, 'Measurement of change under the Cultivation System in Java, 1837-1851,' *Indonesia* 14 (October 1972), pp. 89-109.

cover the landrent owed by the village on the full extent of its lands, i.e., those planted with its own crops as well as those planted for the government with its crop. In this way, ideally, the villagers, by devoting one-fifth of their land and one-fifth of their labor (calculated at 66 days per year) to producing a crop for their government would be better off than under the previous system. It should be noted here that if the value of the government crop was more than the assessed landrent the village would be paid the balance, while conversely, if the value of the crop fell below the amount of the landrent the village was expected to make up the difference. Crop failures beyond the fault of the village were not taxed, but not compensated either. The crop grown on the remaining four-fifths of the village's lands remained the village's to dispose of as it thought best.

The village community was to regulate its own internal arrangement for the assigning of land and labor for the government crops but under the watchful eye of the traditional Javanese supravillage authorities. The top levels of this elite received their orders and 'suggestions' from the Dutch colonial administration; these suggestions were then passed downward to the village headman who received them as requests from the traditional Javanese authorities. In order to interest the elite in cooperating in this new arrangement, they were, in appearance at least, restored to positions of prestige and power, in some respects even greater than they had ever had. This elite continued to be salaried by the NEI government as they had been since the beginning of the century, but they were now granted rights to portions of land with people in lieu of part of their salary. They were also allowed to have special guard units, enlarged personal entourages, and were clearly and openly more honored by the European administration than had been the case during the past two decades. They received assurance of hereditary succession to their positions, and, after 1832, were paid percentages of the value of the export cultivations produced in their territories. In very important ways the Javanese elite in the government lands was well off.

From the point of view of the village community the suggestions which it received from its traditional chiefs were regarded as the normal pattern of indigenous hierarchical arrangements; or at least that is what it was meant to be. The incentive for growing the government crops, which were frequently new crops as far as the village was concerned, was the fulfillment of the wishes and orders of the supravillage authorities. This should be what the village wanted to do out of respect for its superiors, and if the 'wanting' was not strong enough, there was available to the elite a subtle but effective range of compulsions which could persuade a village that carrying out the suggested plantings would be the wisest thing to do.[18] No longer was the Javanese peasant being expected to be a free and independent cultivator who would heed only the call of the open marketplace in determining what he would produce on his land. He was now expected to heed the wishes of his traditional chiefs who were, often unbeknownst to him, heeding the wishes of the European colonial administrator. Moreover, the same suggestions might now also extend to some of the private leasehold areas which the Cultivation System, far from removing from the scene, now wanted to see improved, albeit not expanded.[19] So it was that while equality before the law and justice to all were not removed from the books, the practical approach to Javanese internal conditions was to restore traditional authority which was now charged with the making, the execution, and the interpretation of the law.

Within the village community the power position of the headman, which had grown under the previous system through his role in determining the internal distribution of the landrent assessment, grew even more. In the first place the landrent continued to serve as the basis for assessing the village's contribution, though now it was in the form of a particular crop. In this arrangement the village headman continued to receive a percentage of the landrent collection as well as the right to an enlarged share in the village's cultivated lands. Secondly, the power to determine which villager's land would be used for the new government crop and to receive and distribute the cultivation payments made by the government for the delivery of the designated crop, added to the power of the village headman.

Over the time of the System's operation – from the early 1830s to the middle of the 1860s – the Javanese village headman and administration gained in both political and economic power. I would be inclined to see in this new power group the emergence of a class which became the intermediary between the traditional supravillage elite and the village masses. In any event, the village headmen were now subject to new and increasing pressures for the involvement of their lands and their people in the new System, and they in turn had to pass along this pressure to their

---

[18]   For interesting concepts about the methods and devices used by the Javanese elite see: W.F. Wertheim, *Indonesië van vorstenrijk tot neo-kolonie* (Amsterdam, 1978), pp. 42-51; Heather Sutherland, 'Between conflict and accommodation: History, colonialism, politics and Southeast Asia,' *Review of Indonesia and Malayan affairs* XII, 1 (June 1978), pp. 1-25.

[19]   Without changing the provisions of the Fundamental Law which allowed rental of land, the government (Indisch Besluit 25 Feb. 1840 Nr 2) forbade rentals which could operate to the disadvantage of the government's sugar cultivations. This greatly restricted new leaseholds until after 1855 (Indisch Besluit 8 Sept. 1855 Nr 2) when villages were allowed to rent up to one-fifth of their lands for free sugar plantings. In 1856 (Stbl. Nr 64) the rental of unused lands was again freely permitted.

fellow-villagers. It was, as earlier indicated, not totally new to the Javanese political-economic structure that the village community received suggestions from the supravillage sphere as to what sorts of produce or what types of labor it should deliver, but under the Cultivation System such arrangements became more explicit, more demanding, and, of course, more directed to the sector of the colonial export cultivations.

The function of village headman demanded increasingly shrewder bargaining, more clever obfuscation, and less-popular decisions. During the 1830s it was necessary for the colonial administration to exert physical pressure to gain the cooperation of some villages; public canings were meted out to make examples of headmen who allowed their villagers to neglect the government plantings or who resisted suggestions to make their fields available. By the 1840s such overt pressure seems no longer to have been necessary; the point had apparently been made and the villages and the headmen had in the main made the adjustment.

Also in the 1840s certain excesses in the application of the System had become evident. Too much time spent on government cultivations, often the most unremunerative ones – of which indigo was the worst – resulted in neglect of the rice crop which, when combined with a one or two year failure of the harvest, resulted in famines, epidemics, and migrations to other areas. The literature about the system leaves no doubt that these things did happen all too frequently, but not to the overall extent that the critics of the System made it appear.[20]

In practice, local arrangements were eventually made by the peasants and village leaders, generally resulting in more work than their traditional patterns of leisure would dictate, but not so hard as to cause the collapse of the Javanese housekeeping arrangements. Both the elite and the villages adopted various devices for cushioning the more excessive demands. One of the more commonly used devices was regular underreporting of the number of families in the village and the area of land under cultivation. The government from its side, fully aware of what was happening, turned a blind eye to this practice, and for years resisted the urgings of enthusiastic information gatherers who saw, or thought they saw, great advantages coming out of an accurate cadastral survey and a systematic population count. Various other local adjustments included such devices as new modes of land division, the inclusion of non-landholders in the performance of cultivation services, specialization of work services to keep some persons in particular jobs for longer periods of time, combination arrangements with nearby villages for land and labor exchanges, and the village's own

---

[20] The best critical account in English of the System is C. Day, *The policy and administration of the Dutch in Java* (New York, 1904).

distribution of cultivation payments after the European administration had made careful individualized payments. These adjustments and others made the System bearable.

Also during the time of the System, new tracts of land were brought under cultivation. The clearing of brush and forest lands for coffee gardens was one of the more usual ways for this process to have its beginning. Older coffee gardens would be cleared to be the lands used for new rice fields; beginning as dry rice fields they would in time be irrigated. New villages would spring up or small settlements would grow. More of Java was being brought into cultivation, and the population expanded into these new areas where they again clustered in villages. I do not really think that the population increased to occupy newly opened areas. The opposite, I suspect, is closer to the truth. The pressure to more regular and consistent work, and thereby the gradual loss of leisure, led to the begetting of larger families in order to have more hands to share in the labor burdens. This increased population required more land for food production and made practicable the labor involved in the conversion of old coffee gardens into rice lands. Not to be ignored in this process of population growth are other factors; smallpox vaccinations since the 1820s had reduced the deaths by this illness, the Pax Neerlandica after 1830 reduced the pestilential effects of war which had been more damaging to the population than actual battle casualties, and improved communications brought more regularized settlement patterns and marketing arrangements to many of the upland areas in Java. The settled village pattern of Javanese civilization was extending to areas where it had not previously existed. Raffles had estimated the population of Java in 1815 to be about 4.5 million which, I suspect, might have been almost a million under the mark. In the middle of the century the population of Java was somewhere around 12 million and, while still occupying only a fraction of the land surface of the island, had spread into many previously unsettled areas.

One frequently reported aspect of change in the colonial relationships in Java was the increased face-to-face contact between ordinary Javanese and Europeans. Before 1830 the rather small Dutch colonial administration had dealt only with the upper elite of Java, and for the first years of the Cultivation System this had continued. The Dutch administrators were not agriculturists so they turned for advice to their Javanese counterparts, who were not agriculturists either. The result was that many of the government crops, new to a particular district or village, were simply left to the best instincts of the peasantry. Small wonder that the failure rate was initially high in some areas; indifference and ignorance combined to make the results of the System during the 1830s not terribly impressive. But this began to change as the Office of Cultivations (established in 1833) brought in experts and sent around inspectors who were able to make suggestions for improvements in planting methods, crop varieties, work arrangements, etc.[21] There was also a numerical expansion in the lower ranks of the European civil administration; the *Contrôleur*, whose function had been designed to keep a finger on the pulse of the lower levels of Javanese society, became increasingly versed in agricultural matters. As might be expected, this development changed the locus of many cultivation decisions down to the sub-district and village level. After about 1837 the activities of the Office of Cultivations and the upper ranks of the Javanese and European civil administration are increasingly taken up in gathering statistics, survey reporting, and broad policy and executive responsibilities. The decisions about how the cultivations were to be handled were being made by the lower ranks of both administrative corps and the village leaders. The training which young Europeans received at the Javanese language school set up in Surakarta in 1832, and later at the Delft Academy (started in 1842) which combined indology and engineering skills, served to increase the tendency to work directly at the source rather than through the cumbersomely formalistic administrative arrangements of the higher levels. To be sure, the *Bupati* and the Residents remained important figures whose sanction and general supervision remained important, just as the NEI government remained a powerfully centralized, authoritative structure which kept sending reports some two to three years out of date to the Ministry in The Hague where ultimate decisions were made. It was simply that the production of export cultivations in Java did not run on ultimate decisions, but on immediate and practical decisions.

In providing financial profits to the motherland the system successfully met the expectations of its founder, but the hoped-for moment at which something might be done to benefit Java and the Javanese never seemed to arrive. The profits which flowed to the Netherlands only seemed to increase the appetite for more. The finances of the Netherlands became worse rather than better, mainly due to the policy of perseverance in Belgium, so that by the early 1840s the country was on the verge of bankruptcy with serious doubts in high places about its national viability. Baud, the Minister of Colonies at the time, could allow no indulgence of material improvements in Java, for financially 'the bowstring was always tightly drawn.'[22] Java was expected not only to supply the motherland with profits, but it also had to

---

[21] C.F.E. Praetorius, 'Gedachten omtrent noodzakelijk gewordene verbeteringen in het stelsel van Kultuur op Java,' *De Indische Bij*, I (1843), pp. 82-3.

[22] Whatever one may think of Baud's politics and personality, there is no doubt that he was extremely intelligent and a master at frank characterization of the realities of Dutch colonial affairs of his day. The often quoted statement about 'Java being the cork on which the Netherlands floats' is also his.

pay for its own internal administration and for its defenses against a never-clearly-defined enemy from without.

The landrent was the greatest single source of internal revenue at the time. It shows a steady rise over the years, proving, as the administrators never tired of pointing out, the constantly increasing production of rice and export crops on ever larger areas of cultivated land. So long as the rice price stayed generally level, the increased landrent was considered a normal factor of increased prosperity. More bothersome to both critics and proponents of the System, however, was the steady increase in these years of other sources of government revenue, specifically the opium farm, the tax on markets, the salt monopoly, and various other farms and monopolies. The actual revenue received by the government for these tax farms doubled, trebled, and quadrupled over the years, rising proportionately much faster than the landrent or the cultivation payments. When one keeps in mind that the farmer, invariably a Chinese, to whom the farm was auctioned, extracted even more than he had paid the government for it, one can easily share the mounting concern of many government officials. There seemed little they could do, however, for the government in Europe demanded profits and these had to be drawn out of the Javanese peasant. In Java an increasing need for money led to an increasing necessity to work; it was necessary to run ever faster in order to stand still.

It is tempting to go on about the effects of the Cultivation System upon the Javanese economic structure. As conceived, the System was supposed to work in and with the traditional pattern; obviously it did not. The Javanese was being brought quite forcibly into a market economy in which he had little voice. Some new forms of Javanese enterprise did arise at this time which show adaptability to the economic realities. Private transportation arrangements for the movement of cultivation products to factories and ports were a growing source of income; factory and warehouse workers became more consistent wage earners; manufacturing of local food, clothing and metal items expanded in some areas as increased communication widened the market area; and handicrafts such as shipbuilding and furniture-making (though often under European or Chinese supervision) grew apace – all these Javanese activities developed outside the village economy or forced labor. These activities, however much they may have been promoted by the impact of the colonial economy, remained either local or peripheral to the colonial export economy. The emphasis of the NEI government on preserving the Javanese life style and the Javanese tendency toward social stasis combined to keep the vast majority of the Javanese at the level of coolie labor, with or without a money wage. Entrepreneurship and capital accumulation did not occur in Javanese society in any really large scale or adaptive fashion. The groups described above are little more than petty businessmen, and where they proved to be anything more they were invariably Chinese, Arab, or European. Rising groups such as village headmen and administrators tended to use their wealth to gain greater control of agricultural land and labor. This in turn provided them with either products for the local market or with money by making available to European leaseholders the land and labor under their control. The supravillage elite, like the European civil administration, was restricted in its economic possibilities, but family members could have moved into the higher economic sphere if there had been any inclination to do so. The rewards in administration, money-lending, and other positions within the traditional Javanese sphere seemed generally greater, however, and what emerges is a sort of segmented economy divided on ethnic lines.

Turning now to the European view of the successes of the Cultivation System, there is no doubt that it was successful in producing profits. Even most of the original critics were amazed. Some, like Pieter Merkus, made their peace with the new arrangements and rose to high office within it; others remained critical but sought to reform the System rather than remove it. Only in the late 1850s and 1860s did this urge for reform change to total removal of the System and replacement with a new system. Few Hollanders, however, would have been inclined to lavish praise on the System as did the Calcutta barrister James Money, who holidayed in Java with his wife in 1858. For his English compatriots in India, still shocked by the events of 1857, he produced two volumes telling them how to flavor a colonial administration with hollandaise sauce.[23] He was impressed by the differences in welfare, contentment, and general orderliness between what he saw in Java and what he knew of India. His favorable impression was not shared by all Englishmen, however, for the Singapore merchant community voiced continuous liberal aversion toward a government that also functioned in the economic realm.

The details of the working of the Cultivation System from the side of the European-controlled export economy are more clearly understood than the workings of the System within Java. The crops produced by the Javanese villagers were brought to factories or warehouses. The factories or mills, principally for the manufacture of sugar, were owned and operated by European and Chinese entrepreneurs who had built them with interest-free government loans.[24] The entrepreneur paid the government for the sugar

---

[23] J.W.B. Money, *Java; or, How to manage a colony; Showing a practical solution to the questions now affecting British India*, 2 vols (London, 1861).
[24] *Staat der verleende voorschotten aan de suiker fabrijkanten en hetgeen daarop onder ultimo December 1833 nog aantezuiveren bleef*, ARA, Ministerie van Koloniën Nr 3203 shows that advances had been made in the early years of the System to Javanese villages in Jepara and Javanese individuals in Surabaya. A report by the Director of Cultivations, B.J. Elias,

cane which it had the villagers grow for his factory. This payment to the government as well as the repayment of the original loan and any other advances from the government were made in refined sugar at a price predetermined by the contract between the government and the entrepreneur. What had in the early 1830s been regarded as very risky contracts had by the end of the decade proved to be immensely profitable business ventures; more so in some parts of Java than in others, it should be added. Production often exceeded the amount required to repay the government, so the entrepreneur was left with a surplus which he could sell privately. As these enterprises became profitable, capital began to develop in Java – some of this returned to Europe and some was invested in other cultivation enterprises. Some private venture-capital now also began to come to Java to buy up contracts or to seek new ones. By the early 1840s there was a brisk competition for contracts which, as was the custom at this time, were frequently awarded on the basis of personal favoritism.

The products which the government obtained from the cultivations were moved out of Java and sold on the world markets by the Netherlands Trading Company (NHM), which found a new lease on life under the System despite the financial crisis it underwent in 1839 because of over-extended credit to the home government. The NHM paid for the Java export cultivations by advances to the government in Holland, not through purchases or payments in Java. The private sector in Java also expanded and did rather better than it had under the earlier system even though its portion of the market was generally smaller than the government sector. In 1840, for instance, the private merchants in Java handled about ten percent of the coffee export, about twenty-five percent of the sugar export, about sixty percent of the tin export, about ninety percent of the pepper export, and virtually one hundred percent of the rice and tobacco export. Indigo, nutmeg, and cinnamon exports were totally in the hands of the NHM.[25] Over the next thirty years, the remaining life of the Cultivation System, these percentages underwent noticeable change in favor of the private sector. Coffee remained more completely in government and NHM hands than most products; by 1850 the private share had risen to about fifteen percent of the total export, and by 1870 to about twenty percent. Sugar, however, presents a totally different picture. By 1850 about thirty-five

---

Aantooning der op Java gevestigde suiker etablissementen ten gevolge van gesloten contracten met het Gouvernement, dd. Buitenzorg 11 Sept. 1834, continues to show some small Javanese operators. These Javanese names vanish from the later lists of sugar contractors.
[25]   A letter from Van der Vinne to Baud, dd. 21 April 1841, indicates that from the mid-1830s to the early 1840s more than two-thirds of the import of goods and specie into Java was in private hands and less than one-third in the hands of the NHM. ARA, Ministerie van Koloniën Nr 3204.

percent of all Java sugar was exported by private merchants, by 1860 this had reached slightly more than fifty percent, and by 1870 was over sixty percent. Tea production, which needed government subsidies to survive, remained totally in government hands until 1860. Then the cultivation was opened to private entrepreneurs and by 1864 the total export was in private hands. Indigo remained mainly in government hands during this period, but this product declined in overall importance. The trade within the archipelago, which was increasing in size and importance, was totally in private hands. In summary, there is no doubt that the private mercantile sector increased its share of the export market during the time of the Cultivation System.[26]

The demise of the Cultivation System had its origins and causes in European society both in Java and in Holland; the new liberal attitudes typified by the political changes of 1848 created a feeling of distaste toward the personalism, favoritism, and autocracy of the colonial system in Java.[27] Javanese society, whatever pressures and changes it may have undergone, had little influence on this matter. From the very first there had been an undercurrent of private entrepreneurial interest in Java; requests for leases of unused land continued but were resisted by the NEI government. By the 1840s the success of the sugar contracts had induced the government to cut back on its advances, thereby allowing private capital a greater role. Cultivations such as tobacco and cochineal were promoted by private capital from the first. This private sector came out of the European society in Java in largest part. Persons who had a foothold in Java were in a better position to know how matters worked and what was possible. There was in Java an intricate network of colonial families with links into the administration, into private leasehold and government contract cultivations, into private business houses, and into the government in the Netherlands. Out of these family alliances much of the energy and capital for the expansion of the export cultivations was derived.[28] With the expanding wealth there was also an expanding interest in participating in European learning, culture and freer exchange of ideas. To the extent that the centralized autocratic NEI government held back such changes, largely, I suspect, out of fear for change within indigenous society, there was a growing movement within the European society in Java for liberalization and greater freedoms.

Without necessarily wanting to overturn the System, the private sector in Java, which now included many government contractors who felt that their enterprises represented mainly their private capital, began to seek greater profits for themselves. Such ideas grew naturally out of the qualitative

---

[26] *Changing economy in Indonesia*, Vol. I, Table 4.
[27] This point is nicely developed in C. Fasseur, 'Some remarks on the Cultivation System in Java,' *Acta Historiae Neerlandicae* X, pp. 143-59.
[28] *Changing economy in Indonesia*, Vol. I, p. 21.

improvements of the cultivations, especially sugar. Starting in 1840 the government was able to write quality provisions into its sugar contracts, and in that year instituted a numerical grading system which established and maintained higher standards of sugar refinement. Technological improvements made this possible. New machines, many of them developed for the beet sugar industry in France and Belgium, were imported. Steam power began to replace water power. The vacuum process of refinement was introduced. Not only did these changes lead to better quality sugar, but also led to more sugar being produced from the same land area planted in cane. This resulted in added productivity above the amounts needed to repay the government so that larger amounts went into the private sector. Figures show that the amount of sugar which the NHM brought onto the auction markets of Europe from 1840 to 1870 remained relatively constant, but the average quality of the auctioned lots improved over the years with a resultant rise in price.[29] On the other hand, it was fully realized by these sugar contractors that the government continued to play an important role in arranging for land and labor with the villages. They were, in the final analysis, sugar contractors, not sugar planters. The government remained the planter, along with the Javanese villagers, of course. Yet, as might be expected, many of these contractors began to feel that they could manage better with free labor instead of with the government's forced labor. Their experiences at the local level, working with the lower ranks of the European and Javanese administrations had produced such notions. Their factories had for some time been operating rather well with free labor, and it was becoming ever more evident during the 1850s that village headmen and even individual villagers could be manipulated by money. No one of good sense would have wanted to abandon the government's role in the process, but it did seem that this could be cut back.

The growing use of 'free' or wage labor became a central issue in the 1850s and 1860s. European entrepreneurs working in the Java export cultivations began increasingly to extol the cost efficiency of free labor over the forced labor supplied by the government (for which they also had to pay). Creutzberg has recently raised some interesting considerations on this phenomenon based on data which, while still provisional, seems to indicate the nature of the forces at work. First the large-scale introduction of money into the lower levels of Javanese society and the development of a road network created new economic activities for Javanese and made possible the movement of villagers into monetized activities. Second the escalating growth of population in the nineteenth century resulted in the opening of

---

[29]   I.J. and A. Seijlmans, *Suiker-veilingen der Nederlandsche Handel-Maatschappij 1840-1869*, ARA, Ministerie van Koloniën Nr 3208.

new lands and the creation of more villages to which much of the population moved. However, when faced with the prospect of opening waste areas for cultivation within the village context, increasing numbers of Javanese opted for wage labor in the export cultivations as a means of livelihood. The growth of private plantations after 1850, especially in highland areas, provided the possibility of both resettlement and a monetary income for growing numbers of Javanese. These factors of monetization and population pressure assumed greater significance as the century went on.[30]

The changes in the government in Holland after 1848 also contributed to the changes in Java. The Netherlands had found a new élan in the liberal changes that affected the governmental structure of the country.[31] Everyone knew that Java contributed heavily to the national finances and most persons were not anxious for this to cease suddenly. It did not, for in the period from 1851 to 1870 the net profits from the East Indies averaged about ƒ 24,000,000 per year.[32] However, there were liberal voices, increasingly strident, which were urging governmental change in Java. These liberals were not only in favor of reforming the Cultivation System to allow for greater private participation and free labor, but they also wanted freedom of the press, improved education for both Europeans and Javanese, and an extension of democratic rights to the Europeans in Java and humanitarian principles to the Javanese. Starting about 1850 there were some supposedly softening measures taken as typified by the appointment of less-autocratic governors-general. The overall impact of this might be hard to ascertain, however, especially if one drew his image of Javanese realities in the 1850s from reading Multatuli's *Max Havelaar*, which appeared at the end of the decade.[33]

As a result of these various influences, the colonial administration began to attract young men of high ideals and good education from Europe who were inspired by the Multatulian spirit of working in the interests of the Javanese population. They hoped to assist the ordinary Javanese on the road toward a freer, materially improved life. They felt that the government and the Javanese elite had conspired to keep the little man in traditional darkness. Such ideas were tempered by a realistic awareness on the part of the government with the economic realities of the colonial relationship. The government of the NEI was not opposed to economic growth whether

[30] P. Creutzberg, 'Paradoxical developments of a colonial system,' *Papers of the Dutch-Indonesian Historical Conference [...] 1976* (Leiden/Jakarta, 1978), pp. 119-29.

[31] J.C. Boogman, *Rondom 1848; De politieke ontwikkeling van Nederland 1840-1858* (Bussum, 1978).

[32] H. Baudet and C. Fasseur, 'Koloniale bedrijvigheid,' in: *De economische geschiedenis van Nederland* (Groningen, 1977), p. 322.

[33] E. Douwes Dekker (Multatuli), *Max Havelaar, of de koffijveilingen der Nederlandsche Handel-Maatschappij* (Amsterdam, 1860).

that growth was to be in government hands or private hands. It was in practice essential that the colonial administrator understood both sides of the equation. How, on the one hand, to protect the Javanese peasant against the rapaciousness of the economically and politically more powerful persons in both the European and the Javanese parts of the society in Java, while, on the other hand, making it possible for the export cultivations to obtain the needed land and labor to function profitably, was the sort of dilemma that weighed heavily on the conscience of many a young European civil administrator in Java. This is a recurrent theme in the Indisch novels which began to appear in greater number after the middle of the century.

The period in the NEI after 1870 is frequently referred to as a Liberal period, similar in name to the period from 1816 to 1830, but in practice seeing the fulfillment of many aims which were unrealizable in the earlier period. We could, I think, continue our use of the word 'system' in describing the Dutch colonial policy of this last third of the nineteenth century and refer to this as the 'Free Enterprise System.' This designation would certainly be appropriate for the export cultivations, but it is doubtful if the Europeans of the time would have been very taken with the use of the word 'system.' The word had come to denote a more exploitative arrangement than they cared to consider themselves involved in. Moreover, the term would not have harmonized with their self-image of rather freewheeling individualists. In effect, however, the mode of colonial operation after 1870 was more systematic in its application than could in many ways be claimed for earlier systems, reflecting higher levels of bureaucratization, legalism, and communication.

The year 1870 is used to delimit the new system, for that is the year in which the Netherlands parliament passed the Agrarian Law and the Sugar Law. The debate preceding the passage of a law which would make possible the transfer of government cultivations to private enterprise and which would set limits and rules for private economic endeavors in Java had been in progress since 1861 when Governor General Pahud had asked the Minister for further instructions about guidelines for the rental of land and the contracting for labor. In both Holland and the NEI the decade of the 1860s was a period of transition in colonial policy. The laws of 1870 resolved the matter in a broad sense but left the details to be worked out in the NEI. The ownership of land was left in the hands of the government and the Javanese people, but leaseholds were made possible for cultivation enterprises. The government was to remove itself from its role as planter in the sugar cultivations and to turn this over to private enterprise; this was to be done over several years.[34]

The remainder of the century saw the practical application of these laws with much wrestling between the civil administrators and the private entrepreneurs in the process. The Javanese village community – especially its land and labor – was at the center of the matter, but more as an observer than as a participant. How the indigenous housekeeping was to relate to the new leasing arrangements for land and to the contractual regulations for labor, resulted in many investigations and numerous reports. Fundamental to a determination in these matters was an understanding of exactly which village community one was making rules for, the ideal original village community or the existing one? Investigations such as those of the Umbgrove Commission of the 1850s, looking into the operations of the sugar industry,[35] and the Bergsma Commission of the 1860s, looking into the rights of the Javanese to the land,[36] had left the impression that the Cultivation System had forced communalization of landholding patterns upon the villages in many parts of Java and had almost destroyed the ideal autonomous village. Whatever the correctness of this contention, the practical effect was to cause many persons to feel that the new leasing arrangements should be made with the pure or unaffected village community. This community was now defined as having individual rather than communal land control, and it would, therefore, be in the natural interests of both the Javanese peasantry and the European entrepreneurs to return to the pattern of individual landholding. In the 1860s the government sought to prohibit leasing arrangements with village headmen in an effort to make leasing contracts only with individual peasants, but this could work only where individual landholding was recognized, which was not the case in most of the areas where sugar could be produced. To resolve this matter the government made it possible for communal landholding arrangements to be converted to individual land possessions, but left the matter to the villages to settle as they felt best. The result was that most villages with communal landholding arrangements chose to retain them, but generally with fixed rather than changing shares in the land by the

---

[34] *Nota over de verhuring van grond door Inlanders aan niet-Inlanders op Java en Madoera* (Batavia, 1895), pp. 6-19.

[35] *Stukken betreffende het onderzoek der [...] benoemde Commissie voor de opname der verschillende suikerfabrieken op Java* (Batavia, 1857). The supportive materials are in ARA, Ministerie van Koloniën Nr 1174, Exh. 24 April 1862, Nr 40.

[36] *Eindresumé van het bij Gouvernements besluit van 10 Juni 1867 No. 2 bevolen onderzoek naar de rechten van den Inlander op den grond op Java en Madoera*, 3 vols (Batavia, 1876-96). After the appearance of the first volume, Bergsma tried to point out, rather lamely, that he had not tried to show that the Cultivation System had had a communalizing effect upon landholding. W. B. Bergsma, *De conversie van communaal in erfelijk individueel bezit op Midden Java, getoetst aan het inlandsch grondrecht* (Leiden, 1881).

individual villagers.[37]

Since the practical application of land leasing and labor hiring continued to have to deal with communal rights, especially in the sugar growing areas, it was necessary to make the leasing and hiring arrangements on a village rather than on an individual basis. Such leasings of village lands were set on a short-term basis, never more than five years, as contrasted to the longer term leases of unused lands which applied to the cultivation of other crops. Thus it was principally the sugar industry that brought the private entrepreneur and the village headman together to determine the leasing arrangements. But, as stated earlier, it was actually the European civil administration that came to represent the weaker party in this contract, namely the Javanese village. The sugar entrepreneur was legally and economically the more sophisticated and better informed of the two parties to the contract, but he was generally also quite aware that he needed the goodwill of the administration in order to function.[38] Through the registration of contracts, which made them legally binding, the civil administration had the power to see that the rules were followed by both sides. In practice this meant that the entrepreneur had followed all the regulations and that the village understood what it was binding itself to do. Not infrequently the village, after some lapse of time, had to be reminded of its obligations. The role of the civil administration in such situations is clearly illustrated by a series of hearings held in 1898 throughout Java in which the government representatives met with private entrepreneurs to discuss the application of the rules. The civil administration of the government is walking a narrow line between strict legality on the one side, and flexible compassion on the other.[39]

From the point of view of the colonial economy and the private capitalist sector, the period from 1870 to 1900 witnessed the growth of production, the expansion of area under cultivation, and an increase in exports.[40] It was not totally a time of light and laughter, however. The first half of the period (1870-1885) was the heyday of the private entrepreneur. The world-wide depression of prices of tropical crops forced many of these persons into bankruptcy in the 1880s. The second half of the period (1885-1900) saw the

[37] *Nota over de conversie van communaal in erfelijk individueel grondbezit op Java en Madoera* (Batavia, 1902).

[38] J.W. Ramaer, *Nota over grondverhuur op Java* (Den Haag, 1908).

[39] *Verslagen van het verhandelde op de met ambtenaren en belanghebbenden bij de suiker-, indigo- en tabaksindustrie in de Gouvernementslanden op Java gehouden bijeenkomsten*, 2 vols (Batavia, 1898-99).

[40] From 1870 to 1900 sugar exports rose from 172,000 to 744,000 metric tons, tobacco from 12,500 to 78,000 metric tons, and tea from 1,540 to 6,640 metric tons. Only coffee, which was still under government control, declined from 90,000 to 54,000 metric tons, but this was due to the coffee blight of the 1880s.

growing domination of the economy by cultivation banks and corporate management. It also saw the extension of export cultivations to areas outside Java, especially Sumatra, and the growing importance of non-agricultural exports. According to liberal theory the costs of government would now be covered by new tariffs, especially import and export duties, which would replace the former profits which the government had obtained from the forced cultivations. This did not happen, however. The profits from Java to the government ended in 1875; from then until the end of the century there were as many years of deficit as of gain.[41] Tariffs on coffee and sugar had to be kept low in order to remain competitive on world markets, and the government found itself facing unexpected expenditures of which the cost of the Aceh War was the greatest.

Liberal theory had also suggested that free labor and private enterprise would bring about an improvement in the condition of the Javanese population. This did not seem to happen either, though the evidence is difficult to interpret.[42] The population of Java had risen to about 28 million by the end of the century – just keeping the level of prosperity constant would have required a substantial rise in goods and services. Using such standards as per capita rice production, average family income, and amount of livestock, it seems evident that the conditions in Java did not get better, and in the livestock category became worse.

The reasons for this stagnation and decline in the level of indigenous prosperity at the end of the nineteenth century are also difficult to determine. It is not particularly clear that the export cultivations were totally to blame, though they were certainly one of the more obvious meeting points of the colonial and indigenous economies and, therefore, rather easily singled out for criticism. When in the early twentieth century the NEI government took measures to improve the conditions of the Javanese, it seemed that the improvement in export cultivations brought about by conditions of the world market had already alleviated the problem. With so many uncontrollable and weakly-analyzed forces at work it is easy to bring forth sweeping notions of colonial exploitation, destruction of the Javanese village, and involution which may have some basis in reality. These are difficult to substantiate, however, and the subject is still awaiting much careful historical research.

---

[41] N.P. van den Berg, *The financial and economical condition of Netherlands India since 1870 and the effect of the present currency system*. Third edition (The Hague, 1895), pp. 2-4.

[42] The massive 'Diminishing Prosperity' investigation reports contain vast amount of raw information which awaits careful historical analysis. By the time the printed reports appeared conditions had generally improved so the data contained in the reports were never acted upon. *Onderzoek naar de mindere welvaart der Inlandsche bevolking op Java en Madoera*, 10 vols (Batavia, 1905-14). See esp. *De volkswelvaart op Java en Madoera; Eindverhandeling*, Xa, Pt. I (1914), pp. 552ff.

Within the pattern of the notions advanced in this paper, a number of summarizing considerations might be raised. Certain trends carry on throughout the century. A money economy increasingly dominates the Javanese economic structure, putting the less-calculating Javanese at a disadvantage to the shrewder and more market-conscious European and Chinese. The maintenance of a traditional social order did little to prepare the Javanese for the growing emphasis upon contractual arrangements with legal enforcements. This was especially felt among villagers who were often not aware of what they had agreed to or what had been agreed to on their behalf. A growing and insurmountable indebtedness often forced the Javanese into arrangements that were little to their liking. Increasing population often made wage labor the only solution to personal economic problems, but this brought with it a separation from the traditional community which led to social dislocation without providing a new basis of support. The supravillage authorities seemed increasingly unable to protect the Javanese peasant against the impact of the social and economic problems he was facing. The European civil administration did not and could not replace this group. The village headmen and leaders grew more powerful within the indigenous economic structure, but like the supravillage authorities, they did not adjust into the colonial economic pattern but instead extended their control of the local economy. Whatever oppor–tunities may have been present for involvement by the Javanese in the economic sector which was focused on production for export in the 1820s and early 1830s, the fact is that these were not utilized at the time. Later the chance had passed, for production for the market had passed to Europeans and Chinese who developed their capital basis upon it and upon other exactions which were premised on an economically weak and defenseless Javanese community. Using the argument that the Javanese was best served by the maintenance of his traditional life style, the NEI found it convenient and profitable to leave the Javanese peasant in a weak economic position and to allow the Javanese village to make its own internal adjustments to the pressures for land and labor which were put upon it. But for the Javanese this was a no-win situation, for in the short run they did not gain materially in proportion to the value of their productivity, while in the long run they were led in to a cul-de-sac where their traditional social values became increasingly anachronistic.

CHAPTER VIII

Rights to Land in Java

This paper appeared in print in its present form in early 1988 as a contribution to a Festschrift for Professor Sartono Kartodirdjo of Gadjah Mada University. (See *Dari Babad dan Hikayat Sampai Sejarah Kritis*, edited by T. Ibrahim Alfian, et. al. Yogyakarta, 1987.) However the question of landholding rights in Java was a topic on which I had been working since about 1980, and this paper had been the theme of seminar and conference presentations since that date; therefore I am placing this paper in the sequence of development at this point in the volume rather than later. The Sartono Festschrift has not been widely disseminated so this paper will be a new contribution for many readers.

In this paper my growing concern with the nature of Javanese society before the introduction of the Cultivation System becomes manifest, for in assessing the impact of the System on Javanese life I felt a need to establish what had gone before. For the Javanese peasantry the story of what happened had in the earlier literature been closely tied to the control over land, so in this piece and others it became necessary for me to come to grips with this literature about landholding. This was primarily legal and anthropological literature and was especially closely associated with the name of Professor C. van Vollenhoven, with whom I came to have some differences of opinion. In this paper and others that follow I have moved away almost totally from the early statistical approach. With the appearance of the *Changing Economy of Indonesia* series that my friend Dr P. Creutzberg had started, I came to be ever more convinced that the statistical information available to me would serve only to bolster broad generalizations and would not provide insights into the grassroots functioning of the system. I came to feel that I was getting closer to this level of analysis by interpreting texts based on anthropological and administrative reporting of observed conditions.

This paper represents a change of perspective on the Cultivation System from earlier papers; this change will be carried forward in greater detail and in other respects in the following two papers. This change of perspective after about 1980 was at the root of my growing conviction that I would not be writing a book about the System as a separate project, for I had drifted into a rather different level of involvement and would not feel comfortable moving back into my earlier level of activity.

The debate over about a century and one-half about the rights to land in Java reveals a number of approaches as well as a number of differing opinions, the latter frequently determined by the former. The debate, or better said, the opening of the inquiry began in the late eighteenth century. Since disciplines as we know and understand them today did not exist at that time, it is a bit difficult to categorize the approaches to the subject with terminology familiar to us now. In retrospect, however, it is possible to discern in these approaches such separate disciplines as political administration, political economy, civil law, and customary law cum ethnology. In each of these an historical past was deemed essential to the truth as it was perceived. There were, however, no historians per se involved in this debate, for modern historians in colonial Indonesia were almost an unknown breed.[1] I think it is interesting to consider this debate in terms of the various approaches to land rights in order to provide an example of how the historian, the user par excellence of interdisciplinary approaches, might serve to resolve some of the confusion. The debate is academic, for both the Netherlands East Indies Government and the Government of the Republic of Indonesia without deviation have pursued a policy of domain rights. The subject, however, gains significance because it provides one of the sharpest insights into the inner dynamism of Javanese society, both past and present.

Java, as used throughout this paper, refers to the present-day provinces of Central Java and East Java; literally, the lands of the Javanese. In the late eighteenth century this area was governed in two distinct fashions. A north coastal strip east of Cirebon had come to be governed by the Dutch East Indies Company (VOC) under a series of treaties with the Javanese rulers of Mataram, the one-time rulers of all Java. In return for the VOC's help in retaining their throne, the Emperors of Mataram had transferred sovereignty over pieces of the coast to the VOC. When, however, by 1755 the Company was no longer able to suppress all the claimants to the throne of Mataram, it was forced to recognize two, later three, and ultimately four princes as autonomous rulers. What was left of Mataram came to be known in the late eighteenth century as the Princely Lands (*Vorstenlanden* or the Uplands (*Bovenlanden*). The coastal strip which the VOC had acquired was known as Java's Northeast Coast (*Java's Noordoost Kust*), or frequently just

---

1   What passed for modern history during the nineteenth and twentieth centuries was mainly a recounting of colonial exploits and conquests, or an account of current administrative practices and abuses, or a detailed concern with some local happening. It is not surprising that when J.S. Furnivall's book *Netherlands India; A study of plural economy* appeared in the late 1930s it found a warm reception among Dutch readers, for it provided an historical perspective and interpretative overview of events in both colonial and native society that had been lacking.

as Java. Java was a sharp contrast to the major bastion of Company control; namely, Batavia, its surrounding lands, and the Preanger, all in West Java.

It is the matter of rights to the land in Java and in the Princely Lands with which this paper will be concerned. In the entire area certain basic principles prevailed with regard to land. This was not always clearly understood, for the Princely Lands were autonomously governed and there seemed to be variations on land rights here that did not exist in the Northeast Coast area, but underlying the entire area was a single principle. However, since the Europeans were the ones who became interested in the question of rights to land and actually waged the debate on the issue, much of the information used in this paper will be drawn from the Northeast Coast area.

The gist of the debate about rights to land in Java that developed over time was whether ownership of the land resided in the Sovereign (the State), or in a body of proprietors who collected revenue and determined land use, or in a corporate body such as a hamlet or village, or with the individual peasant cultivator. Additionally there were peripheral issues such as whether Javanese landholding was individual or communal, and whether landholding was related or not to obligatory labor, corvée. While all of these are interesting issues about which much can be said, the main thrust of this paper will be on the issue of rights to the land, i.e., who had what rights, how can these best be described, how was control exercised, and how were these rights applied in practice. The approach to this issue will be through the growing awareness on the part of the Europeans, for they were the ones who raised the questions. From time to time it will be necessary to consider information about Java before the arrival of the Europeans, for while the Javanese did not raise the same problems as the Europeans they were certainly not unconscious of their land, its uses, and its regulation.

Round about 1790 the Europeans in Java began to raise a number of questions concerning the political economy of the Javanese – or to turn a phrase of the time, the internal housekeeping of Javanese society. The VOC had had contacts with the island of Java for almost two hundred years, and its servants were certainly not without some knowledge of the island and its inhabitants. But in the late eighteenth century there appeared a more intimate concern with the internal workings of native society, especially for Java's Northeast Coast, which had only two score years before fallen under the unquestioned hegemony of the Company. More to the point, however, was that the VOC had in 1786 publicly proclaimed its virtual bankruptcy. The Fourth Anglo-Dutch War (1780-84) had decimated Dutch shipping, including the East Indies fleet, and the long festering financial decay of the VOC now became manifest.[2] The Board of Directors, in accepting limitations

2   *Staat der Generale Nederlandsche Oost-Indische Compagnie [...] 14 July 1791*, vol. 2

on their trading monopoly, hoped to regain their profitability by turning
Java into a producer of valuable export products. A Commission was sent to
inspect and reform the Company's factories. By the time the Commission
reached Java in 1793 the Dutch Republic was at war with the French
revolutionary armies, which in 1795 succeeded in ending the existence of
the Dutch Republic. It was in that same year that the Commission issued its
report with suggestions for improving the Company's affairs.[3] In 1795 the
Dutch Stadholder (chief executive) fled to England and issued orders (Kew
Decrees) to all Dutch overseas holdings to surrender themselves to the
English. Java did not comply. Since the Batavian Republic (as the
Netherlands was now called) was at war with England, and since England
ruled the seas, the Dutch in Java found themselves cut off from their
normal communication channels. This relative isolation of the Company in
Java – relative because there was some contact with private neutral
merchants, especially those of the newly independent United States of
America – made it difficult to implement the suggestions of the Commissioners. In these circumstances the Company personnel in Java – now
supplemented by Hollanders from Ceylon and Malacca which had given
themselves over to the English – became almost totally dependent on the
resources of the island, not only for their daily sustenance but for the
intended expansion of export productivity as well. All these reasons
provoked a greater need than ever to acquire knowledge about the
functioning of Javanese society, right down to the rice roots, so to speak.

The situation described above lasted in various degrees until the end of
the Napoleonic Wars and the restoration of Java to the newly created
Kingdom of the Netherlands in 1816. Though these years were not a period
of easy or profitable colonial administration, they were a seminal period for
acquiring knowledge and formulating ideas about how to manage the
political economy of Java. It is with this period (1790-1816) that we begin our
inquiry into the matter of rights to the land in Java, which was of such
immediate concern to the Europeans.

The VOC regarded itself as having assumed full sovereign rights to the
strip of land it knew as Java's Northeast Coast from the rulers of Mataram.
The VOC now assumed the same sole ownership as the Mataram rulers had
held, and set about to draw resources from its lands in the same way that the
rulers of Mataram had drawn their income from their lands and people.
The Europeans generally referred to the Javanese system as 'feudal' – a

---

(Amsterdam 1792), pp. 97-130.
3   [S.C. Nederburgh, S.H. Frykenius, W.A. Alting Siberg] 'Rapport van Commissarissen
Generaal aan de Bewindhebbers, houdende voorstellen omtrent den toekomstigen staat der
Compagnie in Indie,' dd. Batavia, 4 July 1795, in J.K.J. de Jonge (ed.), *De opkomst van het
Nederlandsch gezag in Oost-Indië*, vol. 12 (1884), pp. 335-58.

commonly used term from the eighteenth century to the present day – and set out to make use of it for their own ends. The VOC was not a reforming organization; it was a business seeking to turn a profit.

The major source of income of the Mataram rulers and their retainers had come from cultivated land. Briefly stated, the rulers as owners of all the land drew from it both produce and labor.[4] Land in the vicinity of the Mataram court (Negaragung) and the people on it, they kept for their own use. Stewards who managed these estates made arrangements for labor and produce with the villages. The villages in turn made arrangements with the individual peasant household. Grants of land to family members and retainers were made in an area outside the Negaragung known as the Mancanegara. These grants of land or appanages were meant to provide income and support for these persons who actually lived at the court but who had stewards to manage their holdings. Usually the rulers bestowed cultivated lands on their family members and retainers, but on occasion might assign uncultivated land with instructions to make it bloom. These appanage holders were also expected to provide some produce and labor for the ruler as tokens of submission and support. Such appanage holdings reverted to the ruler upon the death (or defection) of the holder, but while they were in the hands of the appanage holder they were his sovereign domain – he could do almost anything that he wanted with them.

Outside the Mancanegara lay the coastal areas (Pasisir) and other terrain that was either undeveloped or no longer under Mataram's control. It is the Pasisir that comprised what we have been calling Java's Northeast Coast. The ruler of Mataram (before transferring this area to the VOC) had two *wedana* who were the chief stewards of this coastal area, one for the eastern sector and one for the west.[5] The actual administration of the territory was divided into districts headed by a *patih* of varying rank who was frequently drawn from families long established on the coast and not infrequently connected through a marital tie with the court. These *patih*, later called *bupatih*, as governors of their districts were charged with delivering a certain amount of produce and labor to the ruler. Beyond this they were free to regulate their areas of control as they saw fit. As these *patih* and districts fell under VOC control they transferred their ultimate loyalty and deliveries to the VOC.[6] The Europeans came to call them Regents, a title of the

---

[4]   F.H. Van Naerssen and R.C. De Iongh, *The economic and administrative history of early Indonesia* (Leiden/Köln, 1977), p. 51, traces the ruler's right to produce and labor back before the eighth century.

[5]   'Aanstelling door den Soesoehoenan Hamengkoe Rat II van twee wadana's [...] over de zeehavens van Java op 13 November 1677,' KITLV H696b, No. 31, pp. 154-5.

[6]   'Reis van den Gouverneur-Generaal van Imhoff, over Java, in het jaar 1746,' BKI 1 (1853), p. 353, comments upon the key role of the Regents in opening new lands to cultivation, planning irrigation works, and promoting new crops.

powerholders in the major cities of the Dutch Republic.

The VOC administered the Northeast Coast from two centers, Samarang and Surabaya, and made contractual arrangements for the delivery of products and labor with the Regents. These contracts were for a kind of revenue farming in each district. Where there were two Regents, as occurred in the larger districts, the population and the revenue requirements were divided between them. The Regent would agree to deliver to a designated place on the coast a fixed amount of produce – rice, indigo, cotton yarn, timber, etc.; supply the VOC with a certain number of coolies each day; and also pay a certain amount of money which was usually calculated in Spanish Real or *Rijksdaalders*. Some of the produce was delivered at no cost to the VOC as a sort of tax or tribute called contingents (*contingenten*), but most of it was delivered at a fixed price below the market value called forced deliveries (*verpligte leverancien*). Should corvée labor be needed in areas away from the home base the workers often were supplied with minimal food rations. Beyond these obligations the Regent was free to collect whatever additional amounts he could. As long as he maintained order he could count on VOC support to maintain his position and to ensure his succession with an heir. Up until about 1790 the Company contact with the Javanese population was mainly limited to the Regents and their immediate subordinates. Common Javanese were encountered only as coolies or as military recruits. VOC personnel were after all merchants rather than administrators, who were looking out for their own financial interests next to those of the Company. These personal financial interests were of sorts allowed by the VOC – such as overweights, spillages, service fees, etc., and also of sorts not sanctioned by the VOC – such as money lending, extortion for favors, renting of villages, and accepting bribes for favored treatment. As salaries were almost non-existent it became standard practice for VOC personnel to look out for themselves. The Company servants in looking at Javanese life from the top down had come to see it as a society governed by unlimited corruption and totally arbitrary regulations. They, or at least some of them, came to behave in like fashion. It was commonly understood that the common man – the peasant, the coolie, the unattached wanderer – had no rights and little material goods to call his own. Europeans, then and throughout most of the nineteenth century, did not hold the Javanese elite in high regard, seeing them as parasites, brutalizers, opium addicts, and tyrannizers. This did not, however, stop them from using this elite to gain as much as they could for themselves at the expense of the common man.

The VOC servants began to realize that the Regents were in many instances beginning to have difficulty in meeting their quotas of contingents and forced deliveries.[7] Shortfalls became larger and more frequent. Was this due to too heavy an assessment? Or was it a matter of corruption by both Europeans and Javanese? Or did the Europeans not comprehend how the previous system worked? During the 1790s the Europeans became gradually aware of how the established assessment base in Mataram worked. This assessment base was revealed to be rooted in cultivated land and was also related to the rights to the land. Here was yet another reason for gaining more insight into the internal arrangements regarding land and taxation in Javanese society. In this fashion the Europeans came face to face with the *cacah* system. This became for many years with considerable justification a source of much confusion and misunderstanding for Europeans. It also became an instrument used to grasp the relationship between power and land in Java.

In the Javanese political economy the measurement of what should be given in produce and labor at the various levels of society was calculated in terms of *cacah*. The word *cacah* is a counting term and must be combined with another word to indicate what is being counted. In the earliest *cacah* list that I have found (dating from about 1640 AD) it is land (*cacah sima*) that is being counted – in this instance, only cultivated sawah fields.[8] The *cacah* was a unit of land. But how large was this unit? It was large enough for a household to maintain itself and to supply produce and labor for higher authority. This definition leaves the exact size imprecise. However, in most parts of Java, since some measurements had been recorded there was some basis for an areal measurement. Unfortunately, these measurements did not have the degree of exactitude that Europeans desired. Some lands had been measured in lance lengths and others in umbrella lengths. Such variable lengths not only differed from each other but were not categorically uniform. Moreover, the number of these units (of whatever length) to determine the size of a unit of land – known generally as a *jonk* – varied according to the nature of the soil and in proportion to the distance of the land from major towns or villages. The poorer the soil and the farther from major population centers, the larger the *jonk*. Finally, there was no common agreement on the number of *cacah* contained in each *jonk*. In general it can be said that each *jonk* in the Vorstenlanden contained four *cacah*, and in the coastal area two *cacah*, but one encounters variations. In

---

[7]   As an example see: 'Memorie van de Producten [...] ultimo Augustus 1796,' in J.K.J. de Jonge (ed.), *De opkomst van het Nederlandsch gezag in Oost-Indië*, vol. 12 (1884), p. 416.
[8]   'Aantal tjatjah's onder Sultan Agoeng van Be 1560 volgens de Babad Sangkala of Babad Mamana.' KITLV H696h, No. 4, pp. 63-5. The Kiahi Adipati of Demak claimed in 1812 that the 'cacah system was established in Majapahit times.' Notices of the arrangement of the native administration [...] August 1812, India Office, London, Mackenzie Collection, Private No. 13, 13, p. 496.

the eighteenth century a *jonk* in the Vorstenlanden was divided into five
equal parts. The fifth part went to the support of local authorities, while four
units gave half their produce to the ruler and retained the other half for
their own sustenance.[9] I do not find examples of this practice in Java's
Northeast Coast, however, which is where the Europeans were attempting
to make a judgment on this matter.

The *cacah* was the unit for assessing the value (or one could say, the
strength) of a particular area and was also used to designate the value of an
appanage or income yielding grant. In this respect it was more than just a
piece of land. It was a piece of cultivated land with a household on it. There
was plenty of land in Java but not enough labor. It is not to be wondered at,
therefore, that in time the household and the labor that it provided (both in
working the land and in services to higher authority) came to be regarded as
more important than the land per se. Now one finds reference to *cacah kerja*
(work units). The *cacah* had become what might best be described as a
production unit, in which a household worked a particular area of land,
passed on a portion of the produce (usually 50%) to higher authority, and
performed services as called upon. The term 'household' needed clarification. The European gradually became aware that a 'household' could not
be construed as a nuclear family of four or five persons. The household that
worked a *cacah* might in rare instances be that small, but more often
contained ten to twenty persons, and sometimes as many as forty or fifty.
These could indeed be substantial production units. Since Europeans in the
late eighteenth and early nineteenth century on occasion would equate the
cacah with a family as they understood that word, and then base their
population estimates on the number of *cacah*, it is no surprise to find that
numbers of people in some areas were grossly underestimated.

Each district in Java was designated as containing a certain number of
cacah. Thus some districts, like Demak, had many *cacah* whereas other
districts, like Jepan, had only a few. Should a district with many *cacah* have
a large population the Regent in such a district would obviously be more
powerful than a Regent in a small district. The number of *cacah* determined
how much tax – produce, labor, and increasingly money – would be channeled upward to the sovereign power, but also determined the potential
wealth of the Regent. A successful Regent attracted people to his district and
thereby increased his wealth. The *cacah* served as the basis for compensation
of all officials and hangers-on in each district. The chart made by
F.J. Rothenbühler in Pekalongan in 1798 of the way in which various
functionaries of the Regent were compensated in *jonk* of land (which

9   G.P. Rouffaer, 'Vorstenlanden,' *Encyclopaedie van Nederlandsch-Indië*, First edition
(1905) edited by P.A. van der Lith, et. al., vol. 4, pp. 587-653.

translated into *cacah*) must have been a real eye-opener for the Europeans on how Javanese society functioned, for the chart was reproduced many times and as late as the 1860s. [See Appendix A pp. 180-181 for a portion of this chart.] It will be seen that the Regent kept a large share of the land for himself and divided the remainder in descending amounts among his officials from his *patih* to individual soldiers, scribes, and laborers. Each was expected to support himself by the produce and labor of his assigned number of *cacah*. As an individual's *cacah*, coincidentally, were not always clustered together, persons with several *cacah* frequently needed additional personnel to collect their due.

Each *cacah* holder was expected to hand over a specified amount of tax (paid increasingly in money) to the Regent and was, of course, expected to serve the Regent in whatever his capacity. Observing this, the VOC included *cacah* money as one of its regular cash assessments upon the Regents under its control. In the early nineteenth century this came to be viewed as a household tax, and later was transformed into a head tax.[10] The *cacah* holder was a dependent or client of the Regent, or other high official. Any shortcoming on his part, or his demise, meant that the *cacah* would be given to someone else. The *cacah* holder or his agent was expected to use the labor and collect produce from his assigned *cacah*. Here thus is management's contact point with what is the actual production unit: the peasant on the land. The functioning of this nexus could vary greatly depending upon who the *cacah* holder was, or upon the location, size, or strength of the production unit. In some instances, the *cacah* holder could be the head of the production unit household, i.e., a well-to-do peasant. In this function, which was tied into higher authority, he was a patron to those within the production unit and a client to higher authority. In other instances, the *cacah* holder might be an outsider who had bid to win control of the *cacah* and who would now seek to extract as much as possible from it. In this case, he would not deal with the peasant cultivating the soil but rather with a single individual in the hamlet or desa who would organize the production unit. The villager, chosen from the nuclear group, who was in charge of distributing lands to the actual cultivators was seen as the headman. Such village headmen held power through their capacity to determine the way the land would be divided – in some villages an annual event – and who would perform corvée services. A group of nuclear villagers were in a sense patrons of a production unit since it was they who controlled those who actually worked the land. Settlements were frequently very small, some constituting only a fraction of a *cacah*, but there were also villages of several hundred persons which might account for two or three

10 Ibid., p. 618.

cacah.[11] The heads of these production units (whatever their titles) were caught up in a set of relationships with the *cacah* holders. Just as the heads of production units would try to minimize the amount of produce and labor exacted from them, so would the *cacah* holder just as naturally try to maximize his income.

The servants of the VOC were aware that the *cacah* system had a number of shortcomings but hesitated to rectify them. The Company held to its old time-tested practice of keeping out of local housekeeping matters as long as it obtained the coveted products and services. Toward the end of the eighteenth century, however, the VOC officials began to feel that they and the Company were not getting their just due.[12] What led to this feeling? The population in Java's Northeast Coast was growing noticeably larger, especially in and around the major ports and residency towns. The area of cultivated land was also expanding. Yet the assigned number of *cacah* for each district remained fixed in tradition. No one seemed to know when it was last revised, for no-one's memory reached back that far. Whether or not the Regents were aware of this discrepancy and were collecting more revenue than was reported is not known, but it is likely that they were cognizant. Another source of unease was that the Regents were falling ever further in arrears in the delivery of products. Their growing need for money to support an enhanced lifestyle had induced them to rent entire villages to Chinese for immediate cash payments. Once these villages had become totally dedicated to the needs and wants of a Chinese landlord they no longer delivered their quota of products for the contingents. The products required by the VOC had to be drawn from an ever smaller number of villages (or *cacah*) with a resultant increased burden on these villages. Following the Regent's practice other officials obtained money in lieu of produce from their *cacah*; this gave them more flexibility in fulfilling their needs. Default in produce delivery increasingly put the Regents and other *cacah* holders in the position of having to buy the products that had to be delivered to the Company on the open market, a market that was increasingly controlled by the Chinese.[13] Around the end of the eighteenth

11   As examples see 1. the population statistics of the Jepara district for 1812 found in the Raffles collection of the India office records, Vol. 7, MSS Eur. F32; and 2. the 'Generaale opneem over de gansche prefecture Japara,' Arsip Nasional RI, Surabaya No. 4, 1809, pp. 565-91; and 3. for a broader overview the 'Generale te zamentrekking van het getal negorijen, verhuurde dessas [...] tjatjas, jonken rystvelden [...] dd. Samarang ultimo Junij 1796,' ARA, Collectie Nederburgh, No. 387.

12   'Verslag van W.H. van IJsseldyk over de gesteldheid van Java's Oosthoek, dd. Sourabaya, 15 Juny 1799,' in J.K.J. de Jonge (ed.), *De opkomst van het Nederlandsch gezag over Oost-Indië*, vol. 12 (1884), pp. 480-3. Van IJsseldyk figures that Surabaya had 23,000 households instead of the traditional number of 6,000 used for the *cacah* count.

13   N. Engelhard, Governor of Java's Northeast Coast, to the High Indies Government in Batavia, dd. Samarang 30 June 1804. ARA, Collectie Van Alphen/Engelhard 1900 No. 210,

century, so many of the Northeast Coast Regents found themselves caught up in growing personal indebtedness; diminished control over the human resources needed to sustain their economic and social position; and a vortex of shortfalls in deliveries to the Company, that they were ripe for plans to bail themselves out.

The VOC servants, especially at the higher levels, became increasingly interested around 1790 in expanding the economic base of Java's Northeast Coast. Examples abound, but one of the most expansionist ideas must certainly have come from P.G. van Overstraten, Governor of Java's Northeast Coast (1792-96) and Governor General (1796-1801). His report to his successor of 1796 is filled with ideas for introducing the cultivation of indigo, coffee, and sugar.[14] Meanwhile, the man who was to succeed him as Governor in his earlier post as Resident at the Court of the Susuhunan, was involved in expanding pepper cultivation in the Pacitan area under a land rental arrangement.[15] A third entrepreneur, best known because of his later radical ideas, was Dirk van Hogendorp, who as the postholder in Jepara started a sugar mill that was a modern wonder of its day. This type of entrepreneurship was encouraged by the VOC which retained control over the products while allowing its servants to profit personally. The new trend toward economic expansion reached full flight in the ideas of Commissioner General S.C. Nederburgh as he made his way across Java. His report of 1798 conveys a high-level development policy that reads almost like the plans of J. van den Bosch some thirty years later.[16] But Nederburgh also had a scheme for strengthening the financial position of the VOC by reforming the administration and by imposing *ambtsgeld* (an assessment on income) on the Company servants. This highly unpopular move brought him into such direct personal conflict with Dirk van Hogendorp that it resulted in the well-known polemic on free market economy vs. government control in Java.

This expansionist spirit required a lot of fundamental information about how relationships in Java actually functioned: land was only one of the

---

Par. 63. 'since the rice crop in Jepara is insufficient, the Regents are continually obliged to buy their contingent in other places such as Grobogan or Demak [...].'
[14]   'Memorie met derzelver bijlagen tot naricht voor den Heer Johan Fredrik Baron van Reede tot de Parkeler, aankomend Gouverneur en Directeur van Java's Noord Oost Kust ingericht en overgegeven door Mr Pieter Gerardus van Overstraten [...] Anno 1796', ARA, Collectie Hoge Regeering van Batavia, No. 993.
[15]   'Orders en instructien omtrent de cultivereing en bereiding der onderscheide op Java vallende producten,' [Inspektie reis door Patjitan en Bagelen in Mei 1793], pp. 125-275, ARA, Collectie Nederburgh, No. 878.
[16]   Commissioner General S.C. Nederburgh to Johan Fredrik Baron van Reede tot de Parkelar, Governor of Java's Northeast Coast, dd. Samarang, 6 September 1798, ARA, Collectie Van Alphen/Engelhard 1900, No. 180.

investigations, but it is land on which we are concentrating here. The method of obtaining this information was through questionnaires, a method employed throughout the period to 1816, when the investigative report and the proclamation of a 'System' built on theoretical socio-economic concepts became more common.[17]

This mode of information gathering showed that the top administrative levels had an immediate need of information in order to determine how best to adapt the Javanese system to the Company requirements for labor and exportable commodities. Someone at the top of the Company hierarchy – the Governor General, or the Governor of the Northeast Coast, or a Commissioner General – would compose a list of questions, (grouped under topics) for distribution to his officials. The list would be translated into Javanese and/or Malay and then be sent to the Javanese officials. Written responses, assembled into a report, would be returned to the source of the original inquiry. While some responses were perfunctory, others were substantial treatises that shed light on many aspects of Javanese life.[18] A number of the original responses which are still extant in archives are found to provide more specific regional information than the final report.[19] Obviously this source, though providing a view from the top of the administration, gives us more detail than we can obtain in any other way. Although grey areas remain – for neither VOC servants nor Javanese officials spent much time examining how peasant life actually did function – one learns to look beyond these limitations to uncover some facts about the lifestyle at all levels of Javanese society.

All of these reports are consistent in recognizing the sovereign as owner of the land. The officials and *cacah* holders are seen as proprietors of the moment who are free to make whatever arrangements they wish with their lands (including renting them to third parties), but the lands were not theirs to sell outright. The peasant, who was the actual cultivator of the soil, had a right to use the land. He had for his own disposition the product he drew from his work after payment of taxes and labor. He might in some localities receive compensation for improvements he had made, should the land be

---

[17]   The most extensive set of questions were those of Raffles to the Mackenzie Land Tenure Commission, dd. 14 January 1812, ARA, Collectie J.C. Baud, No. 1002.

[18]   Most voluminous of these reports were two reports to Raffles in 1812. 1. *Rapport van J. Knops en Van Lawick van Pabst aan Raffles over de mogelykheid om het tegenwoordig op Java bestaande stelsel van alleenhandel, verplichte leveranties en contingenten te vervangen door een van vrijen handel en vrije cultures*, 29 July 1812, ARA, Collectie Engelhard 1916, No. 136. The same is in India Office, London, Mackenzie Collection, Private No. 56. 2. F.J. Rothenbühler, 'Rapport van den staat en gesteldheid van het Landschap Sourabaija [...].' (31 December 1812), *Verhandelingen van het Bataviaasch Genootschap* 41 (1881), pp. 1-70.

[19]   See for example the extensive response (almost 60 pages), dated 1813, by the Regent of Pati in response to Raffles' questionnaire, Arsip Nasional RI, Jepara, No. 11, 5.

transferred to another, but this was by no means a sale of the land. *Cacah* holders and nuclear villagers held actual possession, rather than ownership, of most of the cultivated land, which was worked for them by their clients whose rights were virtually non-existent. If a new piece of land were opened to cultivation, the cultivator was freed from taxation for a period of time (usually three years), after which the land would become part of the village's landholdings and then treated like all other village lands. Such lands were normally worked by the same peasant and his family; but where there was insufficient land for the number of people, the plots were rotated annually. Control over land, or possession of a piece of land, generally entailed an obligation to perform corvée service for higher authority. Over and beyond the delivery of produce and labor, both landholders and non-landholders were subject to innumerable taxes and exactions.

The VOC had every reason to think of itself as the owner of the land of Java. Having stepped into the sovereign rights of the rulers of Mataram, there was little reason for the Company not to use land as it thought in its best interests. Its use of land took two basic directions. First, the VOC encouraged arrangements to grow export products such as coffee, sugar, indigo, pepper, and cotton, and if necessary they would rent out entire villages to people who could raise these commodities.[20] Such people were usually either Chinese or European. In a couple of early instances Javanese Regents assumed such functions, but they seemed less skilled at overseeing quality control than the Chinese or Europeans. The VOC's second gambit was to sell land outright to private persons, again usually Chinese or European, though there is one instance of a private Arab landowner. With the increased isolation of Java it was ever more difficult for the VOC to meet its local obligations. Land sales were primarily directed at bringing money into the treasury. Direct land sales, though known around Batavia, were now extended to Java proper and occurred mainly around the major cities of Java's Northeast Coast.[21] Both Daendels and Raffles sold lands to meet immediate cash needs. Such private estates frequently contained peasants and cultivated lands within their boundaries. The peasants were not to be disturbed in their lifestyle, but were now obliged to render tribute and tax to their new private owners, while their corvée obligation continued to be owed to the Government. In both the renting and the sale of lands the

---

[20] 'Copie-instructie van den Gouv. van Java's NOK, N. Engelhard voor de Europeese opzigter van de regentschappen [...],' 1803 April 27, ARA, Collectie J.P. van Braam, No. 202, contains detailed information on what export crops were to be grown, processed, and delivered, but also warns against any interference in the internal affairs of the Regencies.
[21] Another long report from Rothenbühler to Raffles, dd. 6 August 1812, speaks in great detail of the way in which lands should be sold to private persons, ARA, Collectie J.C. Baud, No. 1002.

Government was beginning to take a more involved posture toward the rights to land in Java.

The English administration under Lieutenant Governor T.S. Raffles which took over control of Java in 1811 viewed land rights in quite a different manner. Much influenced by the land settlement in India since the time of Lord Cornwallis, Raffles was a firm believer in sovereign rights to land ownership as well as in the principle of a fixed land tax (or rent) as a major source of Government revenue. Reports of the Mackenzie Land Tenure Commission, which Raffles had charged with finding an arrangement that would afford security of tenure in place of the monopolistic system of the VOC, bore out the fact that in Java the sovereign was considered owner of the land. Only in West Java, specifically Bantam, did proprietorship of the land seem to reside in individuals. Probolingo in East Java seemed also to have private possession, but it turned out that this area had been farmed to a Chinese who had introduced a system of fixed tenures that worked so well that it came to be seen as custom (*adat*). If land was to become the basis of Government revenue through a tax or rent, then some determination had to be made of where within the socio-economic hierarchy this tax was to be settled, i.e., who was to be regarded as the proprietor responsible for the payment of the rent. Within a three year span (1812-1814), Raffles made three different determinations of this matter. He first thought that the supra-village heads were the proprietors; then he decided that the village, specifically the headman, should be the one to pay the rent to the Government; and finally he decided that the settlement should be made upon the individual cultivator.[22] Changing the location of proprietary rights to the land – that is the implicit right to say, 'this piece of land is mine to use as I see fit' – opened the door to changes in Javanese society. The former appanage holders, renters of villages, and *cacah* holders who had previously held this right were essentially the people that Raffles had in first instance thought of as the proprietors. Some of the *cacah* holders had been members of the nuclear village group so that even Raffles' second choice of settling the rent on the village headman was not totally revolutionary. But his third and final decision to settle the landrent on the individual cultivator of the soil was totally outside the Javanese order of things.

---

[22]   F.J. Rothenbühler, 'Rapport van den staat en gesteldheid van het Landschap Sourabaija [...] (1812),' *Verhandelingen van het Bataviaasch Genootschap* 41 (1881), p. 16. In this Report, prepared for Raffles, Rothenbühler makes the point about the election of village heads. By the Revenue Instructions of February 11, 1814 (viz. J. Bastin, *The development of Raffles' ideas on the land rent system in Java and the work of the Mackenzie land tenure commission* ('s-Gravenhage 1954), pp. 161ff.), Raffles was claiming that land ownership resided with the individual cultivator.

In practice, Raffles' ideas concerning rights to land were too rapidly introduced to have a full and immediate impact. Great confusion resulted. Were it not for the conscious decision of the restored Dutch administration in 1816 to adhere to Raffles' plans – with some modifications – the long-range and decisive influence of Raffles' concepts might never have taken place. As it was, the Netherlands East Indies Government decided to retain the landrent and to place the settlement on the village. In the long run this came to mean that the village and the village headman assumed an administrative role that was markedly different from what had been the case earlier.[23] In the years to come it would be assumed that the village was an autonomous entity that had always been free to regulate its own affairs and had always had control over its lands. There is no evidence of this, however, either in the pre-Raffles period or in the initial years of the restored Dutch administration. It is frequently said that Raffles 'discovered' the Javanese village. This does not mean that villages did not exist before the time of Raffles, but rather that Raffles and now the restored NEI Government devised a new administrative role for the village.[24] Out of this would eventually grow new socio-economic factors that would realign the village into the nexus of colonial economic control in Java. But I run ahead of the story.

The changes that Raffles introduced were not based on any new information about the nature of Javanese society. Nor were they based on any revised system of collecting data about land rights.[25] In fact, most of his information came from resident Hollanders such as Muntinghe, Rothen-bühler, Knops, and Van Lawick van Pabst, who had tendered their services to the British administration. His ideas came mostly from liberal economic theory and British policies in Bengal; he disliked the VOC mercantile system. He believed in liberal, free-trade, laissez-faire economic theory, whereas the Company had operated a monopolistic, mercantilistic economic

---

[23] 'Rapport over de Residentie Sourabaya gediend aan hunne Excellentien de heeren Commissarissen Generaal over Nederlandsch Indie door den provisioneele fungerende Resident P.H. van Lawick van Pabst op den 15 Mey 1817,' ARA, Collectie J.C. Baud, No. 27, pp. 143-5. Van Lawick makes very precise comments about the changing role of the villages heads in Surabaya where Rothenbühler in 1812 had spoken of election of the village heads by peers in the village, now in 1817 the same area and office had come to be keenly contested because of the salary and other perquisites that now went with it.

[24] The 'discovery' of the Javanese village is generally attributed to Raffles. However, D.H. Burger, 'Structuurveranderingen in de Javaanse samenleving,' *Indonesië* 2 (1948-49), p. 390, dates the 'discovery' in 1807, and Van Vollenhoven, *Javaansch adatrecht* (Leiden, 1923), p. 9, attributes it to Muntinghe.

[25] C. van Vollenhoven, *Javaansch adatrecht*, pp. 47-8, expresses amazement that the scholars of his day thought that the regularized collection of rent as introduced by Raffles was the hallmark of change and Westernization, while the *pajeg* that had been collected under Javanese rule was essentially the same thing.

arrangement. It was these liberal economic ideas that were taken over by the restored NEI Government. In fact, these ideas were very much part of the intellectual baggage of the time. Many of the VOC servants had believed in them also but were not in a position to do much with them. To these people as to Raffles, the Javanese Regents and *cacah* holders were parasites upon the fundamental productive base of the country, namely the laborers and peasants. If these overlords could be eliminated and the government brought closer to the actual production base of the society (which now had been given tenure rights to the land it worked), there would ensue an upsurge or market-directed prosperity. The Javanese cultivator-cum-laborer would see that his best economic interest lay in producing the exportable commodities. Growth in exports from Java would ensure a great source of wealth to the country that controlled it.

In the years after 1816 this economic dream did not materialize. The price of tropical export commodities fell after 1820. English shipping and money were overriding competition for the Dutch, who were discovering that the Javanese cultivator preferred to harvest rice rather than coffee, indigo, or other crops for the export market.[26] At the local level in Java, the Dutch found that some villages were less prepared to deal with their new function than others. *Cacah* holders who had been either part of the village structure or closely bound into its patron system might be able to convert to the landrent arrangement easily. But most villages and hamlets were unable to respond to landrent. The *cacah* holder of old (of whatever rank) and the omnipresent Chinese were quite prepared to take over landrent payments and to collect tribute in the forms of produce and labor as had always been done previously. Technically this was not supposed to happen, but government administrators regularly exposed such practices by as late as the 1830s and 40s. Thereafter we hear less about it because the village headmen themselves had come to assume a more direct negotiating function with the Government. Also the moneylending syndrome had become more firmly entrenched so that control over land and labor could be more indirectly managed. In this regard, it should be pointed out that the Javanese supra-village elite never really passed from the scene as Raffles had proposed they should. Raffles had quickly discovered that matters could not move without them. In a sort of bureaucratic arrangement, Daendels had paid the Javanese elite salaries as recompense for allowing the Government to take over revenue collection. Raffles' step in removing them from proprietorship in the land did not, therefore, meet with such strong resistance as had long been feared. Also, the Regents were given tracts of lands with villages in

[26]   Robert Van Niel, 'The effect of export cultivations in nineteenth-century Java,' *Modern Asian Studies* 15 (1981), pp. 25-58.

addition to a money income. The new arrangements relieved many financial problems for them. Assigning them functions as police or revenue officers allowed the Regents to maintain their honored stations.

The restored NEI Government intended to pursue liberal economic policies after 1816. It sought to promote economic involvement by the Javanese in export production. This policy failed. The outbreak of the Java War (1825) not only put a strain on the budget but led to a change of policy. The so-called 'Colonization Report'[27] of 1827 now looked to European and Chinese entrepreneurship on leased lands to promote the growing of exportable commodities. Before this could be made operational, however, a 'better,' i e., more immediately profitable, scheme was proposed by J. van den Bosch. King William I seized upon this new plan and the author was sent to Java as Governor General (and Commissioner General) in 1830. This scheme became known as the Cultivation System (*Kultuurstelsel*).

The Cultivation System was an application of old principles in a new fashion. In so far as rights to land were concerned, it continued to apply the principle that the sovereign owned all the land but now pursued this principle more actively. It also continued to recognize the settlement of landrent within the village, but now proceeded to contract with the village for the cultivation of exportable commodities on lands under village control. These contracts, supposedly voluntary, were actually coerced through enlisting the supra-village elite in the process of persuasion. This elite had never really disappeared, and now could be reinstated into their old power position but with government support.[28] Hence the System is often referred to as the 'Forced' Cultivation System. Whatever specific pressures the System put upon the Javanese village their total effect was to bring the village into a more direct relationship with the world-oriented export economy. The System reinforced the notion that the village was the fundamental productive force in Java. During the life of the System the European civil servants began to deal more directly with the village (bypassing the elite). This in turn spread the notion that the village was an autonomous entity. The greatest pressure upon the village – as I have indicated elsewhere – was upon the aggregation of labor.[29] When the Cultivation System began in 1830 the term *cacah* was still used to refer to the tribute in produce and labor that the Government expected, but by the late

---

[27]   The 'Colonization Report' of 1827 is to be found in D.C. Steijn Parvé, *Het koloniaal monopoliestelsel getoetst aan geschiedenis en staatshuishoudkunde* (Zalt-Bommel 1851).
[28]   H.I. Domis to GG Van den Bosch, dd. Pasuruan, 23 February 1831, Confidential La A, ARA Archief Van den Bosch No. 314, notes the continued attachment of the *cacah* to the Regents and other Heads, who made whatever arrangements they saw fit.
[29]   R. Van Niel, 'The labor component in the forced Cultivation System in Java, 1830-1855,' *30th International Congress of Human Sciences in Asia & North Africa 1976, Southeast Asia 1* (Mexico City, 1982), pp. 99-111

1830s the term has fallen from use. The reason for this undoubtedly lies in the System's need to tap more labor than the large production units of a *cacah* allowed. Now the household in the sense of the nuclear family became the unit of measurement. Labor was demanded of everyone, whether or not he had control of a piece of land. The village headman and nuclear village administration, meanwhile, obtained new perquisites, one of which was exemption from corvée.

During the 1830s and 40s the pressure on villages that were involved in Government cultivations had brought about a greater participation by peasants in control over a piece of land. This was done (often under orders from European administrators) in order to broaden the labor base. This later came to be seen as communalization and as a breakdown of individual proprietorship, but what usually occurred was not a transfer of ultimate control but rather a redivision of user rights. As liberal economic sentiments began to gain ground in The Netherlands the demands for the dismemberment of Government cultivations grew. In 1848 when the absolute power of the King of the Netherlands was broken, a parliament came into being which now had control of the colony. In the new fundamental regulation (*Regeerings Reglement*) of 1854 the colony was firmly placed under the legal control of the parliament. Land controls would have to be based on native customs and rights. This term was now interpreted to mean that the cultivated land would fall under the control of the village, which now for the first time was officially referred to as an autonomous entity.[30] We see thus, by mid-century, the fruition of the seed that Raffles had planted much earlier.

With the application of law to the colony, devising the kinds of 'systems' that were based upon principles or theories of political economy ended. No longer were the reports of administrators who were compelled to work within the 'system' merely accountings of annual progress. Now the NEI Government, in order to make the laws, required background studies and research by teams of highly trained and experienced administrators. Such administrative reports came to replace the old questionnaire style of information gathering and the reports of individual inspectors of the cultivations. These government sponsored reports are treasure troves of information for Java and increasingly, to the end of Dutch colonial rule, for the rest of Indonesia. Because of their erudition and greater professionalism they make easier reading than earlier reports. Because they were often critical of Government policy there is a tendency to accept their findings and conclusions as more reliable. Actually, they suffer from the same limitations as the earlier reports.

---

[30] *Regeerings Reglement* 1854, Art. 62.

In so far as rights to land are concerned, the Final Report (*Eindresumé*) of an investigation into land rights in Java and Madura that was launched in 1867, is the report of central concern to the subject of this paper.[31] Undertaken to establish individual rights to the land in Java, the Final Report fulfilled this purpose by recognizing that sovereign ownership did exist throughout Java. At the same time it proclaimed that the traditional pattern of individual ownership had been destroyed by the pressures of the Cultivation System. Although the individual cultivator was now seen to have freer disposition rights within the village context, it was claimed that in most villages of Java it was the village community that exercised control over the land and its use. This sort of conclusion was necessary in order to confirm the liberal economic tendency of the 1860s, which saw again the need to lease lands to European (less said now about Chinese) entrepreneurs. Where the Government would withdraw from the cultivation of export products, the new entrepreneurs would step in. Unused lands – by the Agrarian Law of 1870 – could be leased on a long term arrangement while cultivated village lands could be rented for short periods of up to three years from the village (or from the individual cultivator depending on the type of tenure).[32] The village, especially the village headman, thereby strengthened in control, became an even more vital link in the colonial economy. The law (common law and administrative law) now became the determining factor in the use and control over land. The individual cultivator, however, found himself to be what he always had been, powerless in the face of forces beyond his control. Only now these forces were closer to him than they had been in the past.

A careful analysis of the Final Report reveals that the accumulated evidence hardly supports its conclusions. Memories of the villagers who were interviewed are noticeably short and are limited to their immediate experience. Conclusions about the rights to land are flawed through a couple of semantic fallacies, one in Dutch and one in Javanese. First, the Dutch word *bezit*, which is used extensively to describe the right to land, can mean 'possession,' or 'ownership,' or even 'tenure.' With these variant meanings it was quite possible, given the nature of Dutch statute law, to prove almost anything that one wanted, or nothing at all. Second, in the Final Report the Javanese term *jasa*, a term applied to the cultivator's rights on newly opened lands, is translated as ownership of land. Whereas, in fact, the term refers only to improvements made upon land for which some compensation might be given, but it does not refer to ownership which in

---

[31] [W.B. Bergsma], *Eindresumé van het bij Goevernements besluit van 10 Juni 1867 No. 2 bevolen onderzoek naar de rechten van den Inlander op den grond op Java en Madoera*, 3 vols (Batavia: 1876, 1880, 1896).
[32] *Ind. Stbl.* 1870 Nos. 55, 118.

the Javanese sense belongs to the sovereign.

The explication of rights to land in the late nineteenth century had been imprecise to say the least; Van den Berg pointed this out at the end of the century.[33] Some indication of the problems associated with land rights may be gleaned from an important omission. Rouffaer's report on the legal aspects of agrarian rights of the native population in Java and Madura was excluded from Mr C.Th. van Deventer's survey of the economic condition of Netherlands East Indies, that appeared in 1904.[34] Rouffaer's report was not issued as a separate publication until 1918. By that time it received a cold counterblast – literally an 'Anti-Rouffaer' – from the highly respected professor of international law Mr C. van Vollenhoven.[35] What had Rouffaer done to deserve such a sharp rejoinder? In one respect he had done nothing more than piece together a report that tried to please everyone by condemning past policies and recounting the current state of confusion on the matter of land rights.

The debate about the rights to land in Java underwent one further twist in the early twentieth century when the concept of *adat* (customary) law rose to prominence as the brainchild of Van Vollenhoven. He professed a rather new view of land rights which he most clearly explained in his publication of 1919 entitled 'The Indonesian and His Land'.[36] His concept was based on his research of customs and traditions throughout the East Indian archipelago. The root of his concept lay in ethnological investigation, which had produced masses of information about indigenous practices that he now sought to consolidate into some form of statutory taxonomy. This classification of custom would foster a respect for traditions, whereby native peoples would be better understood – and more wisely governed. What an interesting idea! It was from the first methodologically flawed, because it sought to crystallize what was in essence polymorphous and changing.

Van Vollenhoven's view of rights to land was based on an evolutionary notion. Throughout the archipelago, clans, tribes, and villages possessed native disposition right, *beschikkingsrecht*, a coined legal term.[37] The disposition right of the village is manifested in the rights of members of the village to use village land and to limit the right of outsiders to its use. The

---

[33] L.W.C. van den Berg, 'Het eigendomsrecht van den staat op den grond op Java en Madoera,' *BKI* 40 (1891), pp. 1-26.

[34] *Koloniaal-economische bijdragen*, 4 vols ('s-Gravenhage, 1904).

[35] G.P. Rouffaer, 'De agrarische rechtstoestand der inlandsche bevolking op Java en Madoera,' *BKI* 74 (1918), pp. 305-98, and C. van Vollenhoven, 'Antirouffaer,' *BKI* 74 (1918), pp. 399-406.

[36] *De Indonesiër en zijn grond* (Leiden, 1919), especially pp. 3-28.

[37] J.M. Van Der Kroef, 'Land tenure and social structure in rural Java,' *Rural Sociology* 25 (1960), 415 ftnt., translates *beschikkingsrecht* as 'communal disposal rights.'

right, according to Van Vollenhoven, cannot be permanently alienated.[38] In Java this disposition right of the village had been abused by both the Javanese kingdoms and the European administration.[39] The abuse had taken the form of a violation of the land rights of the Javanese peasant in particular, and the autonomous, self-regulating rights of the village-community as a legal body. In parts of Indonesia where native kingdoms and European control did not have the intensity of impact which they had in Java, the village's disposition right had gradually faded into an 'oriental ownership right,' i.e., the right of a peasant and his family to possess and use a piece of land and to enjoy the benefits of participation in the village community. Oriental ownership right was not the same as Western owner-ship right. This view of land rights not only had an immediate appeal but still enjoys great popularity in some intellectual circles today.

Here one is confronted by a methodology and information base that are markedly different from methods previously used to examine rights to land in Java. Ethnological information is historicized in order to create an evolutionary, legal framework. The result is a radically different conclusion about the right to land in Java from earlier-held beliefs. While unable to dismiss outright the long established fact of the sovereign's ownership of the land, Van Vollenhoven was able to make it meaningless by dismissing all the historical evidence supporting it as part and parcel of the abuse of village rights by the Javanese kingdoms.[40] The autonomous self-regulating village in Java he saw as the law-making entity (*rechtsgemeenschap*) par excellence because of its disposition over land. There was no person or institution (other than the sovereign) that stood above or below the village in its power to make laws regarding land.[41] Historical evidence as well as information gained through questionnaires focused on existing conditions; political-economic theories and administrative and common law practices were all made invalid. To Van Vollenhoven the only appropriate basis for establishing right to land was the natural evolution of primordial rights, documented by investigations into customs and traditions – and the *Eindresumé* (which he used extensively).

Is this then the ultimate answer to the question about right to land in Java? I think not! Whether the concept of disposition right is valid or not with regard to the earliest land rights in the archipelago, to argue as Van Vollenhoven does is to ignore, whether consciously or unconsciously, the impact of high civilization over centuries of time in Java. This impact did not occur in other parts of the archipelago. Long before Islam entered

---

[38] Van Vollenhoven, *De Indonesiër en zijn grond* pp. 8-10.
[39] Ibid., p. 1.
[40] Van Vollenhoven, 'Antirouffaer,' pp. 399-400.
[41] Van Vollenhoven, *Javaansch adatrecht*, p. 8.

Indonesia the Javanese sovereign's rights to land and to tribute had been established, and the rights to land were perpetuated in this established pattern. In other parts of the archipelago the impact of Islam was more foundational and could even be instrumental in extending rights of the individual. In Java this simply was not the case, however, and it makes no sense to conjecture that this was an abuse of a preordained evolutionary pattern. No civilization suddenly undoes its established legal practices in order to restore primordial rights. Could Van Vollenhoven envisage that all Roman-derived law patterns in Europe be abandoned in order to resurrect early tribal rights? I think not. Actually, this was not his intent. In devising his theory his chief purpose was to challenge the domain rights of the Government and thereby to stop its leasing of unused lands. This was in and of itself not an ignoble purpose, even though his design failed to move the Government. The dialectic used to promote his theory was a very strange exercise of some intellectual disciplines which were at the time in the process of developing some solid methodological principles.

Not only is the methodology questionable, but one of Van Vollenhoven's accepted truisms is doubtful. I refer to his notion of the autonomous, self-regulating village in Java. In this paper I have pointed out how the village evolved. It is certainly true that practices within the boundaries of the village or hamlet, including the use of land, were regulated by the village leaders. But the village is not and probably has not for thousands of years been an automous, self-regulating entity as Van Vollenhoven construed it to be. From very early times the village in Java was embraced by the total civilization, and thereby was subject to regulation in various forms by higher authority.[42] Soetardjo has pointed out that the word 'autonomy' has no place with regard to the Javanese village.[43] It was not correct to magnify the position of the village within the Javanese context as Van Vollenhoven did. In this respect he allowed himself to be misled by his evidence.

In conclusion, I wish to return to the opening point of this paper, that is the question of intellectual disciplines and their interrelationships. A considerable amount of information, through a wide variety of methods and techniques, has been obtained over a century and one-half about rights to land in Java. Yet little has been resolved because each of the methodologies was linked to a particular set of circumstances composed of desires and preconceptions about what rights to land were present. The initial questionnaires of the period 1790 to 1816 probably elicited more basic information about rights to land in Java than the later preconceived notions

---

[42]   D.H. Burger, 'Structuurverandering in de Javaanse samenleving,' *Indonesië* 3 (1949-50), p. 230.
[43]   Soetardjo Kartohadikoesoemo, *Desa* (Bandung, 1965), p. 212.

about administrative law, socio-economic theory, and ethnologically created custom. What is totally absent in applying all these methodologies is the craft of the historian, which by its very nature cuts across and combines different approaches. One of history's key functions is to provide perspective to the problems of the world about us. History also deals with social realities in so far as they are recoverable. In the particular function of the historian, this paper has hopefully made a contribution by indicating how both the ideas and the realities about the right to land and the nature of the Javanese village both persevered and changed over time. It has also attempted to show how the desires and programs of higher authority in Java as seen from the top, tend to become the accepted reality. The ground level of the society underwent undetected social alteration while retaining an amazing constancy of human values. History will not answer all questions and it has no ironclad guarantees against error or incorrect interpretation. History does, however, tend to clear up confusions. By putting the results of the various modes of assembling information in an historical context, I trust that this paper has helped to clarify the Javanese view of rights to land and to show how this view has been altered during the colonial period.

APPENDIX A

Extract from a letter from F.J. Rothenbühler, resident of Pekalongan, to Mr S.C. Nederburgh, Commissioner General, dated 1798. [A manuscript copy of this letter is to be found in Arsip Nasional RI, Pekalongan No. 47, 1 (57 pages); an English translation is to be found in the India Office Records, Mackenzie Collection, Private No. 7, 3, pp. 55-105, a printed extract (including the portion given here) is to be found in *Eindresumé*, volume 2, Bijlage I I.]

In Pekalongan Regency there are 3693 *jonk* of rice fields (sawah) and 7499 *cacah*. These rice fields are divided among various servants and workers in the following manner.

The patih, mantri, and lesser heads

		jonk
1	Mas Patih	90
70	Mantri, jaksa, etc.	616
64	'Priests', one upper and 63 lesser	63
4	Kabayan	14
39	Umbul	117
75	Lurah	112

The people working in the fort

192	Laborers in the warehouses, etc.	125
126	Stevedores	36
12	Artisans	11
	Horses for sending letters, etc.	10
4	Prahu mayang	40

The people serving at the regency

46	Laborers on the passeban	42
60	Laborers for extra service	15
29	Horses	58
10	Laborers at Labuan	5
10	Laborers at the stocks	10
100	Laborers and 30 span cattle when timbers are being cut, but this is not happening now	–
4	Laborers at the transportation service	4
1	Chief of the transportation service	2
12	Men at the signal flags	12

People at the indigo manufactories

3	Demang	26
6	Umbul	18
20	Lurah	30
260	Laborers	90
5	Coppersmiths	5
60	Cattle carts	60

Military people

		jonk
50	Artillery men	25
150	Musketeers	143
120	Archers	120
60	Assegai men	18
170	Pikemen	168

People serving at Samarang

544	Laborers at Samarang	544
2	Mantri anom	27
8	Laborers attached to the mantri anom	8
4	Demang of the cruiser ships	34
88	Lascar	44

The Regent's personal servants

		4
4	Mantri	34
8	Palangkung or Lesser Chiefs	26
5	Kebayan	7
26	Lurah	40
80	Gardeners	35
71	Stable boys	65
34	Kitchen servants	31
30	House servants	25
36	Musicians	45
14	Wayang and topeng players	15
31	Scribes and artisans	51
20	Livestock keepers	18

This totals 3,134 *jonk* of rice fields. Since Pekalongan has a total of 3,693 *jonk* of rice fields, the Regent has 559 *jonk* at his personal disposal.

CHAPTER IX

Nineteenth-Century Java: Variations on the Theme of Rural Change

When in early 1983 I was asked by William Frederick of Ohio University to join a panel on 'Agricultural Involution Revisited' at a Conference of the Southeast Asia Summer Studies Institute (SEASSI) that year, it seemed like an excellent opportunity to cast some of my ideas into the perspective of a much discussed work about rural change in Java. Obviously the focal point of this panel was to be Clifford Geertz's book on *Agricultural Involution* which had appeared in 1963. I had read Geertz's book when it first came out and had discussed it at length with my friend Harry Benda. We had both been much impressed with it as well as with Geertz's other writings. By the early 1980s, however, much had changed in my thinking as well as in the thinking of many other Southeast Asian scholars.

My own questioning of Geertz's thesis began in 1968-69 when I was poking around many places in Java and was further reinforced by my two years in Malaysia where I again had the opportunity to have contact with Malay society from top to bottom. My research direction of the early 1980s, as typified by the previous paper (number 8) was, however, quite directly and specifically a questioning of Geertz's basic assumptions. Though I was not challenging Geertz directly – frankly it had never entered my mind to do so – when confronted with the challenge of the conference panel, I began to reread and rethink the whole *Agricultural Involution* thesis.

In the first few pages of this paper it will become evident that criticisms of the *Agricultural Involution* idea were quite prevalent in the late 70s and early 80s. Geertz later answered his critics in a 1984 article.[1] My approach to the questioning of *Agricultural Involution* is quite different from the other critics with quite different results. My questions arise out of my views concerning the Javanese village and what did or did not happen to it in the nineteenth century. My approach to the problem is historical and historiographic, and my argument focuses on the notions of 'shared poverty' and social 'homogenization,' which are essential elements in Geertz's thesis, and about which I have

---

[1] Clifford Geertz, 'Culture and social change: The Indonesian case,' *Man* 19-4 (December 1984), pp. 511-32.

certain doubts. What both Geertz and I are writing about is
directly involved with the Cultivation System, and for this reason
I have included this paper in this volume. This paper has not
been previously published.

In the past decade Clifford Geertz's book *Agricultural Involution* (1963)[2] has
been examined and subjected to criticism from many points of view. This
would not be happening if the book were not influential. It was well
received at the time of its publication, and, along with other of Geertz's
writings, has influenced research scholars and students during the past two
decades. Its brilliant conceptualization of the roots of Java's socio-economic
situation has provided many either with a believable ready-made pattern of
development or lack of same. Its very title has become an almost daily
expression for an irremediable downward economic syndrome. Its style and
its scholarly apparatus make it an appealing synthesis of what the well-
informed person should want to be thinking about Java. Its sympathies lie
with the undernourished, overcrowded Javanese peasant who has been the
unwitting and unwilling victim of Western capitalism. In short, the book
has much going for it: yet it is being challenged on a number of counts.

Clifford Geertz was first in Java from 1952 to 1954 with a team of social
scientists attached to Harvard and MIT universities. The team settled into
the town of Pare, which they called Modjokuto, in the Kediri district of East
Java, where they studied various aspects of the local Javanese society. In 1956
Geertz published a lengthy paper in ditto format entitled *The Development
of the Javanese Economy*,[3] which contained the nucleus of concepts later
more fully developed in *Agricultural Involution*, and in *The Religion of
Java* (1960) and in *Negara* (1980).[4] The earlier 1956 study, to which I will
return presently, contained somewhat more historical background and
somewhat less conceptualization than the published book on *Agricultural
Involution*. I make note of it here to stress the fact that Geertz's observations
were made in the mid-1950s, a fact which Geertz himself stresses in various
of his writings. From an agricultural point of view the period from 1950 to
1965 in Java has recently been characterized as one of rural stagnation when
landless laborers and marginal farmers were competing for employment
and land.[5] In *Agricultural Involution*, this time factor, namely the mid-

2   Clifford Geertz, *Agricultural involution; The process of ecological change in Indonesia.*
Berkeley and Los Angeles: University of California Press, 1963.
3   Clifford Geertz, *The development of the Javanese economy; A socio-cultural approach.*
Cambridge, Mass.: MIT Center for International Studies, 1956.
4   Clifford Geertz, *The religion of Java.* Glencoe, Ill.: The Free Press, 1960. Clifford Geertz,
Negara; The theatre state in nineteenth century Bali. Princeton, N.J.: Princeton University
Press, 1980.
5   W. L. Collier, et. al., 'Acceleration of rural development in Java,' *Bulletin of Indonesian*

1950s, does not serve as a limitation any more than the physical location of the town. Rather, the fundamental theory of the book, which stresses an interaction peculiar to Java between capital-intensive commercial agriculture in European hands and labor-intensive subsistence agriculture in Javanese hands, is stated in timeless terms and for all Java. The limiting case on which this theory is built is described in another of Geertz's books, *The Social History of an Indonesian Town* (1965).[6] What emerges is that in order to obtain a fix on the historical assumptions and conceptualizations contained in the *Agricultural Involution* book, one must also examine the earlier 1956 paper and the later 1965 book. *Agricultural Involution* is the centerpiece of the three; it is the most theoretical and the most difficult to pin down.

It is precisely the timeless and all-Java aspects of *Agricultural Involution* that lie at the root of many of the criticisms which derive from recent observations by agricultural economists, rural sociologists, and other social scientists. The theory advanced in the book does not fit their current observations. If the book were seen as being fixed in time and place like *The Social History of an Indonesian Town*, it would have been largely ignored and almost without influence. Therefore, by raising the book out of the category of history which by its nature is time-bound and subjective, to the level of general social theory, Geertz has gained audience appeal but at the cost of vulnerability to contrary observations. Before examining the historical aspects of Geertz's theory, I will note some of the current criticisms which are based on contemporary observations or differing theoretical assumptions.

During the 1970s a series of agro-economic surveys were conducted in Java. William L. Collier, an agricultural economist, was involved in this activity and has written, alone and with others, a number of papers about the results.[7] In a 1977 paper he directly challenges Geertz on the following points: Geertz fails to account for off-farm labor of Javanese peasants; Geertz fails to take account of the socio-economic differences of villages; Geertz fails to take account of class divisions based on landownership in villages; and Geertz is wrong when he contends that involution has become institu-

---

Economic Studies 18-3 (1982), p. 85.

[6]   Clifford Geertz, *The social history of an Indonesian town*. Cambridge, Mass.: The MIT Press, 1965.

[7]   W.L. Collier, 'Agricultural evolution in Java: the decline of shared poverty and involution,' mimeographed (Bogor, 1977). W.L. Collier, Harjadi Hadikoesworo, and Suwardi Saropie, *Income, employment, and food systems in Javanese coastal villages*. Athens, Ohio: Papers in International Studies, Southeast Asia Series No. 44, 1977. W.L. Collier, 'Declining labour absorption (1878-1980) in Javanese rice production,' mimeographed (Bogor, 1979). W.L. Collier, 'Agricultural evolution in Java,' in G. Hansen (ed.), *Agricultural and rural development in Indonesia*. Boulder, Colorado: Westview Press, 1981, pp. 147-73.

tionalized in Javanese life. An Indonesian agricultural economist, Sajogyo, in the preface to the 1976 translation into Indonesian of *Agricultural Involution* raises a number of challenging criticisms, outstanding among which are the matter of compatibility of sugar cane growing with sawah agriculture and the concentration of population in sugar areas – which points are central to Geertz's theory, but which seem not to be borne out by the facts.[8] Similar points have been elaborated and further detailed by the Australian scholars J. and P. Alexander.[9] They and Benjamin White,[10] have also pointed to possible reasons for Javanese population growth which would not fit into the ideas advanced on this subject by Geertz. Hiroyoshi Kano has recently summarized many of these arguments and has raised the question that if 'agricultural involution' and 'shared poverty,' the two basic concepts of Geertz's theory, do not accurately reflect the present-day rural situation in Java, at what point in historical time can one discern Javanese types which do not fit Geertz's model?[11] Since Geertz's model is basically economic history, this is a fitting question, and one which we will try to answer.

It is immediately apparent to the reader of *Agricultural Involution* that the book's fundamental theory is supported by evidence drawn out of the historical past of Java, especially out of nineteenth-century Java. Since the author perceives a dual economy pattern arising between the capital-intensive Western enterprises and the labor-intensive Javanese rural sector, the historical information also tends to divide into these two streams, though they are, of course, interrelated. Let us briefly state the historical underpinnings of the theory. From the time of earliest Dutch contact with Java around 1600, the mercantile East Indies Company (VOC) sought to expand its economic involvement without involving the inhabitants in the capital markets which underlay its economic activity (*AI*, pp. 47-8). This VOC approach of using native society for its productive aspects without transforming it was continued into the nineteenth century after the VOC was ended and the government of The Netherlands took over in Java. This

---

8   Sajogyo in preface to *Involution pertanian; Proses perubahan ekologi di Indonesia.* Jakarta: Bhratara, 1976.
9   Jennifer and Paul Alexander, 'Sugar, rice and irrigation in colonial Java,' *Ethnohistory* 25 (1978), pp. 207-23. Jennifer and Paul Alexander, 'Labour demands and the "involution" of Javanese agriculture,' *Social Analysis* 3 (1979), pp. 22-44.
10   Benjamin White, 'Demand for labor and population growth in colonial Java,' *Human ecology* 1 (1973), pp. 217-36, followed by Geertz's comments. Benjamin White, 'The economic importance of children in a Javanese village,' in: Moni Nag (ed.), *Population and social organization.* The Hague: Mouton, 1975. Benjamin White, 'Population, involution and employment in rural Java,' *Development and Change* 7 (1976), pp. 267-90.
11   H. Kano, 'The economic history of Javanese rural society; A reinterpretation,' *Developing Economies* 18 (1980), pp. 20-1. While the question is a fitting one, my own reading of Javanese historical developments differs from that of Kano.

exploitation of the production of native society without modernizing it reached its full bloom in 1830 with the introduction of the Cultivation System (which earlier writers call the Culture System) (*AI*, p. 52). With the introduction of this agrarian production system the dual economy pattern was fully accentuated as the Javanese economy was prevented from participating in what might have been autochthonous agricultural modernization (*AI*, p. 53). From this point on the divergence between the two economies becomes even greater (*AI*, p. 62). Yet the continuing mutuality between the two economies forced the Javanese village to make adjustments to the impingements of high capitalism by land tenure arrangements in the form of 'communal ownership,' which allowed the village to retain its basic pattern of life while also allowing the Western enterprise to operate (*AI*, pp. 90-1). With the steady growth of population, the Javanese villagers subsisted, if not altogether evenly, at least relatively so, in a comparatively high degree of social and economic homogeneity (*AI*, p. 97). This then is the 'post-traditional' village with its involuted rights and obligations, and its shared poverty. On the European side the private plantation economy after 1870 continued to build and grow upon the pattern as earlier established.

While somewhat condensed, the above sketch touches upon the essentials of the historical backstopping for the theory. Yet, this historical background seems to be lacking information, not because I have left it out of the condensation, but because it is not present in *Agricultural Involution*. It would be desirable in judging this historical sketch to know something more about Javanese rural society before 1830, especially its class structure, landholding patterns, and relationships to supra-village authority. If Javanese society changed after 1830 it is essential that we know what it changed from. Is there evidence for a lack of autochthonous moderniz-ation? If social and economic homogeneity occurred, there must have been something else beforehand, but what was this? To test Geertz's theory of 'agricultural involution' and 'shared poverty' one would want to have some insight into these and related matters. Yet these matters are not detailed in any satisfactory way in *Agricultural Involution*. It is small wonder that most critiques of the nineteenth-century backgrounds of the book have been prefaced with the words 'by implication,' for very little detail is provided.

To gain a fuller view of what conceptions reside behind Geertz's portrayal of nineteenth-century rural change in Java and of the nature of pre-1830 Javanese society, I shall follow two paths. First I shall examine the most frequently used sources which are cited in *Agricultural Involution* regarding nineteenth-century change; and second, I shall look into Geertz's 1956 paper (*Development*), and his 1965 book (*Social History*), for additional details of his perception of nineteenth-century change and what preceded it. Beginning with the changes in the nineteenth century and by looking at the footnotes in *Agricultural Involution*, we find that Geertz has used most of the major sources that any reputable scholar working in the 1950s would have referred to in order to reconstruct the history of the nineteenth century – especially after 1830. Central to these sources, in part because it is an economic history, and in part because it is compatible with the perception of the changing nature of rural society under the impact of Western capitalism, is the standard work of J.S. Furnivall *Netherlands India* (1939).[12] Geertz has, however, moderated Furnivall's view somewhat – as I shall show in a moment – by using the sociological views of D.H. Burger (1939), especially as these have been incorporated into an account of the Cultivation System by R. Reinsma (1955).[13] The underlying assumptions by all three of these writers will be discussed further along in this paper, but first let me briefly reconstruct Furnivall's conception of nineteenth-century change in Java for you.

In discussing the Cultivation System, Furnivall, in *Netherlands India*, indicates that Van den Bosch's 'policy was to strengthen the regents and leave the village, "the little republics," under their own heads with as little interference as possible' (*NI*, p. 139). 'The headmen [under the Cultivation System] were in the same position as before, but instead of standing on their own feet, they were hanging on to the Dutch Government; it was not from the consent of the people but from the authority of Government that they derived their power, and they used it for Government, and for their own advantage' (*NI*, p. 140). 'So great were the demands on landholders that land-holding was no longer a privilege but a burden which occupants tried to share with others; also officials encouraged or enforced communal occupation, so as to facilitate the allocation of large areas for sugar plantations and to have greater freedom in controlling irrigation' (*NI*, pp. 140-1). 'This encouraged communal possession and obliterated hereditary social distinctions' (*NI*, p. 141). [Since classes in Java were based on land-holding] 'the wide extension of land-holding with a view to increasing the number liable to compulsory service cut at the root of the customary social order' (*NI*, p. 141). 'But a still more serious reaction of the system from an economic standpoint was that it cut the people off from economic life; they "gained no trading experience... and were deprived of the stimulus to increased production which comes from a knowledge of the market."

---

[12]   J.S. Furnivall, *Netherlands India; A study of plural economy*. Cambridge: Cambridge University Press, 1939. [My page citations, as well as Geertz's, are from the 1944 reprinting.]
[13]   D.H. Burger, *De ontsluiting van Java's binnenland voor het wereldverkeer*. Wageningen: Veenman, 1939. R. Reinsma, *Het verval van het cultuurstelsel*. 's-Gravenhage: Van Keulen, 1955.

[Citation from Van der Kolff here.] Not only was their social life perverted, but their economic sense destroyed' (*NI*, p. 141).

The perception of the Cultivation System provided by Furnivall was commonly held by scholars in the pre-World War II period and was based upon the best scholarly apparatus of the time. As already indicated, Geertz took off some of the sharp edges by using Burger and Reinsma, but the basic idea remains. Land tenure, as Geertz calls it, or land-holding as Furnivall calls it, for both stands at the center of the village picture. As the village was affected by pressures of obligatory labor and the need for land by Western enterprises, the social structure was changed. The trend was toward communalization with a resultant destruction of property in land and thereby a destruction of social differentiation. It seems simple and straightforward enough. Scholars and officials in Java in the nineteenth and early twentieth centuries were totally captivated by this entire landholding question. Right to landed property was a fundamental liberal tenet of the bourgeois West, and a great amount of energy and thought was bestowed upon the nature of Javanese landholding. In peasant society, however, property in land is more deceiving than illuminating, for it constantly changes with circumstances. In Java the *Final Report* (*Eindresumé*) of an investigation into native land rights in Java conducted in the late 1860s provided a wide variety of contradictory views on this subject and resolved very little.[14] The summary of this report stressed the basic individual rights of the cultivator. This was in turn used by Van Vollenhoven in preparing his great synthesis of the subject which held that colonial policies and native elites had destroyed the Javanese village by crushing its landholding patterns.[15] These ideas underlay the conception of both Furnivall and Geertz.

Having seen the basis of the view for the economic and social destruction of the Javanese village in the nineteenth century, we will now want to know something about Geertz's view of the pre-1830 Javanese village. The perception we are seeking is not found in *Agricultural Involution*, but rather in the 1956 paper (*Development*), specifically in Chapter III. I shall sketch this perception for you, taking the liberty of providing both Geertz's terms and my own in the process.

In early Java there was constant competition between state (*negara*) authority and village (*desa*) authority for political control over the use of labor. The *negara* were loose collections of *desa*, which were not totally sedentary and therefore flexible in their relationship to a higher authority which asserted a religious-like attraction (*D*, p. 42). The emphasis was not on

---

[14]   (W.B. Bergsma), *Eindresumé van het bij Goevernements Besluit van 10 juni 1867 No. 2 bevolen onderzoek naar de rechten van den inlander op den grond op Java en Madoera*. 3 vols. Batavia: Ernst and Landsdrukkerij, 1876, 1880, 1896.

[15]   C. van Vollenhoven, *De Indonesiër en zijn grond*. Leiden: Brill, 1919, p. 11.

territory but on the control of manpower; at the center this manpower consisted of nobles, priests, and soldiers, while at the periphery it consisted of peasant labor. When central power weakened, the peripheries could drift into an autonomous condition, only to be drawn to a new center when that arose, for the center was always stronger than the periphery. This loose and flexible pattern of villages was changed by intensification of agriculture, contact with the West, and population growth (*D*, p. 44). A sedentary settlement pattern emerged as irrigation systems and sawah were developed; villages grew in size due to administrative convenience (especially during the Cultivation System), and authority relations were increasingly expressed in terms of land rights so that land and labor came to be combined in a single system of social relationships. Political (social) status in these sedentary villages came to be defined in terms of land tenure; the nuclear villagers – that is descendants of the village founders – controlled the sawah in common, but as time passed (especially after the Cultivation System) they came to hold fixed plots which could be inherited but not sold (*D*, p. 45). If nuclear villager families died or left, other families could be co-opted into this group. The village head had additional land at his disposal as did other members of the village government; this put them at the top of the village class structure. Below the nuclear villagers were persons who held only dry fields, then persons with only a house and garden, and at the bottom those who owned no property and lived in with others. Labor obligations for both village and higher authority remained and were now tied to land rights; land was assigned in order to obtain labor rights over persons of lower status (*D*, p. 46). Since land and labor are not regulated by a free market system there has not been a growing concentration of landholding or sharpening of class antagonism. Landholders have not increased their returns vis-à-vis labor returns; consequently landholder and laborer need each other almost equally (*D*, p. 47). Economically the village absorbs ever more persons through intensification of agriculture and politically (socially) institutes an ever more gradually graded pattern of differentiation. What has happened is the replacement of a few broad distinctions by a multiplicity of smaller ones, avoiding thereby a two-class opposition between haves and have-nots.

The above perception of the dynamics of Javanese village life as taken from Geertz's 1956 paper (*Development*) relies principally on ideas drawn from Furnivall with some theoretical formulation derived from Max Weber. Though only loosely fit into a time frame, it claims that in early times the state, or central authority, and the village, or agricultural community, competed for the use of the labor power of the peasants. There was then a class distinction between the state and village leaders on the one hand, and the peasant/laborer on the other. At some time this begins to change in the direction of villages becoming more sedentary, less flexible, and with status based on land rights rather than claims to labor. This change is vaguely associated with the coming of the West. Quite clearly the sedentary village pattern predates the Cultivation System (1830). Less clear is whether the political (social) statuses based on land tenure emerged before, during, or after the Cultivation System. However, as the nineteenth century wore on these statuses grew more fixed and became tied more firmly to smaller plots of land. There was then so little difference between landholders and laborers that instead of class antagonisms there emerged instead a grading of socio-economic distinctions. This social homogeneity, found again in *Agricultural Involution*, seems to date from the end of the nineteenth century.

This perception of pre-1830 Javanese society, especially its rural aspects, is based on many of the same authorities as the nineteenth-century changes were based. It is a perception drawn principally from writers who were present in Java during the 1920s and 1930s and is based upon the writings of earlier authorities, especially Van Vollenhoven. It is clearly an advance over the writings of the nineteenth century. This advance stems chiefly from the introduction of a broader vision, which in turn was derived from the viewpoints of liberal and social theories and observations. In all of this the impact of the West plays a centrally destructive role, overwhelming the earlier Javanese socio-economic system, which is variously described as 'closed' or 'feudal,' by the imposition of Western capitalism. Furnivall and Burger, mentioned above, remain the key figures in formulating this perception; their writings were the best available sources in the 1950s, as witnessed by both Reinsma's and Geertz's use of them. The Java of the 1920s and 1930s seemed strongly to represent the destructive powers of the West, especially in its landed aspects as Van Vollenhoven had shown, for the economic malaise of that time seemed to have left a dispirited and disrupted society which had been torn from its traditional roots. Thus the perception showed what seemed like a socio-economic certainty; namely, that Java had once been a society of autonomous, self-sufficient, self-regulating villages with a closed economic system which owed labor and produce to higher authority in a type of feudal arrangement. This society was torn asunder by the West. It is to Geertz's credit that, while continuing to adhere to this destructive perception, he does not see the early Javanese village as closed and autonomous but instead adds some dynamism to the picture.

During the 1960s and 1970s a number of new historical interpretations of Java's past began to emerge from scholars increasingly interested in Java's developments before the twentieth century. This direction in historical research grew out of recognized shortcomings in the historiographical endeavors of the 1950s (and earlier) and sought to look at local and institutional developments and changes. At the same time the opening and ordering of new and existing archival materials made this research possible. But there was again, a certain time-bound aspect to this research, for studies of the 1960s and 1970s by anthropologists, sociologists, rural economists, and others were showing a very lively and flexible Javanese (Indonesian) society to be in existence. Also, visits to Java by all of these as well as historians led to a feeling that life in Java might be at a low economic level, but it was not destitute or devoid of hope and instead showed a great power of survival and a great dynamism. Thus the work of social scientists and their on-the-scene observations helped historians to sharpen the questions which they asked of their materials. One of the principal aspects of this new perception was premised on the notion that Javanese society, including its rural aspects, was tough, flexible, and enduring; and that it tended to handle outside forces on its own terms, not succumbing but adjusting and adapting, and turning the force of change to its own objectives. In short, Javanese society was more an agent of change rather than the victim of change.[16]

It is now time to convey this newer historical view of Java's past, first in broad terms showing the dynamic nature of early Javanese history, and then a somewhat more detailed account of change in the nineteenth century, especially under the Cultivation System. In what follows you will be able to see how close in some respects this perception remains to Geertz's view of a flexible Javanese village, and how in other ways there are significant differences. As this background perception is altered, the new historical evidence on nineteenth-century developments will result in a longer term view of change, which will not alter the fact that the West imposed new pressures but will shift the impetus of the change to Javanese society itself. Our knowledge of the origins of villages in Java or elsewhere is mostly based on speculation and theory. However, Van Naerssen and others, working with inscriptions recently found in Java, have developed a historical sequence which ties the settled agricultural community and its irrigated lands into the process of higher state development with its magical-religious sanctions needed to hold the order together.[17]

---

[16]   I would be remiss not to mention at this point that this notion has earlier been set forth by Margo L. Lyon, *Bases of conflict in rural Java*. Berkeley, California: Center for South and Southeast Asian Studies, 1970, pp. 8-14. In challenging Geertz's perception of present-day Java, Ms Lyon has taken a long view of historical change in questioning some of his historical assumptions.

[17]   F.H. Van Naerssen and R.C. De Iongh, *The economic and administrative history of early Indonesia*. Leiden/Köln: Brill, 1977. N.C. van Setten van der Meer, *Sawah cultivation in ancient Java*. Canberra: ANU Press, 1979. J. Wisseman, 'Markets and trade in Pre-Madjapahit Java,' in: Karl L. Hutterer (ed.) *Economic exchange and social interaction in Southeast Asia*. Ann Arbor, Michigan: CSSEAS, 1977. H. Kulke, 'Early state formation and ritual policy in East Java,' Paper presented to the Eighth Conference of International Association of Historians of Asia, Kuala Lumpur, August 1980.

The social distinctions between village and supra-village were vague. Family connections and client relationships placed the village leaders in close proximity with higher authority. The centers of authority (*negara*) drew upon labor and produce from the lower groups in society, but the relationships from top to bottom were loose and flexible. The distance between state and village was not always great. Political fortunes could change rapidly in the competitive power plays which centered on physical strength, ritualistic enhancement, and accumulation of wealth. The villages, especially those on irrigated land, might be frequently disrupted in such power plays. In addition to the peasants, whose labor and produce provided much of the material sustenance for the system, there were also merchants, who came from both inside and outside the society, who moved goods into and out of the society, and whose importance came increasingly to be recognized by the leaders of the *negara*. The total population under the control of the Javanese system might vary in size, as major disruptions might drive persons off the cultivated lands and into surrounding areas of swidden cultivation. When peace and authority were restored, these persons would return to the land and once again open it to settled cultivation. People lived clustered together on a relatively small amount of the land surface; there were vast tracts of jungle and much unused land. The line between settled and mobile agriculture was not always clear, but the security provided by the *negara* was always a magnet for some to return to a settled life. Village settlements were never separated or closed off from higher authority. The village might regulate its own internal affairs, but it was not autonomous since it was tied to supra-village authority by both personal and economic ties. Not surprisingly, individuals moved back and forth between negara and desa as their fortunes and the occasion warranted.[18]

By the time of the Mataram Empire (about 1600) a few more details become available on how the relationships between *negara* and *desa* were regulated, but one must be careful not to read these arrangements too far back into earlier times. Mataram in the seventeenth century became a powerful state with rather firm, almost bureaucratic-like controls; there is little to indicate that this had occurred to the same degree in earlier states. Well before the time of Mataram, Java had become increasingly involved in commercial relations with other parts of the world. It has often been thought that Mataram eschewed these commercial relations, but this is not true. It may have sought to control these relations centrally, but since the Dutch East Indies Company (VOC) began its activities at about the same time

---

[18]   Sartono Kartodirdjo, 'Agricultural radicalism in Java,' in C. Holt (ed.), *Culture and politics in Indonesia*. Ithaca, NY: Cornell University Press, 1972, pp. 83-4.

as Mataram became a power center, the Emperors of Mataram never gained
the total control they may have sought. Another commercial aspect of Java
seems to have been an increasing amount of bullion in circulation from the
sixteenth century on. All of this impacted only slowly on the Javanese
villages. There was an expansion in market-oriented production, which by
the eighteenth century had resulted in the monetization of the produce and
labor deliveries in Java into a sort of annual tax. In Mataram times, probably
as early as the seventeenth century, the emperor of Mataram rewarded his
family and retainers by assigning them units of produce and labor, known as
cacah. In turn the retainers and, in the coastal areas, the administrators,
further bestowed these service units upon their subordinates and clients.[19]
These units (*cacah*) were originally measured in land, namely, the amount
of land which an able-bodied man needed to support himself and his family.
Since unused land was plentiful, the real value of such a unit lay not in the
land per se, but in the peasant who worked it, and in the produce and labor
which he was able to deliver to his supra-village patron, whether this was
an individual or the state. Therefore in time, such a unit came to be thought
of as a man or, more appropriately, a household. The Dutch Company
servants always used the household designation, but as the produce came to
be monetized into an annual tax (*pajeg*), the designation used by the
Europeans was head tax, even though it was a tax basically imposed on a
piece of land. In this process of change the landed nature of the unit seemed
to be lost, but in fact it never ceased to be essential. In the coastal areas of
north Java – which particularly interest us because this is where the Dutch
control first developed and the later cultivation enterprises were for the
most part established – these service units (*cacah*) were scattered throughout
villages and hamlets in varying measure and with diverse sorts of
obligations. By the eighteenth century the VOC had become the government
in these coastal areas. Some of these units were assigned to them, while
others were assigned to the supra-village authorities through whom the
delivery of goods and performance of labor service were regulated. One
must not confuse the assignment of these service units – whether in
produce and labor or in money – with the manner in which the peasantry
organized its arrangements within the village. In the village or hamlet the
nuclear villagers were heads of households which consisted of many
retainers and hangers on. Such households formed the basic production
unit (*cacah*) which provided produce and labor for higher authority. These
households regulated these matters internally in various ways.

---

[19]   G.P. Rouffaer, 'Vorstenlanden,' in: *Encyclopaedie van Nederlandsch-Indië*, First edition
(1905) edited by P.A. van der Lith, et al., vol. 4, pp. 587-653 is the best source for these
arrangements. An English version of Mataram arrangements is Soemarsaid Moertono, *State
and statecraft in old Java*. Ithaca, New York: Cornell Modern Indonesia Project, 1968.

By the middle of the eighteenth century Java, or what today is Central and East Java, had been decimated by more than a century of fighting occasioned by the expansion of Islam into the interior, by the consolidation of Mataram's authority, by the rebellions against this government, and by the involvement of the VOC in supporting one or another pretender to the throne. When in 1755 a truce arrangement was worked out, whole areas had been depopulated and once-cultivated areas returned to jungle. On the other hand, other areas which had once been little used were now densely settled, especially areas in and around major coastal cities where protection against roving bands was greater. The number of service units (*cacah*) assigned to each area remained the same, having little or no relationship to the actual amount of land in cultivation or the size of the population. Efforts at reforming this system were neither successful nor sufficient, though the Dutch servants were quite aware before 1800 that the traditional measurement of service units had fallen behind the land in cultivation and the size of the population.

After 1800 the VOC became increasingly interested in the production of consumables, particularly rice, and in the use of obligatory labor (corvée) on roads and defenses. Java was now inaccessible from The Netherlands, and consequently the Europeans were thrown onto the local economy for their survival. The Company servants began to scrutinize the indigenous system of deliveries and labor obligations more closely. A number of more detailed reports were then written in an effort to shed some light on these matters.[20] While these reports are not always as clear as we would wish, they do provide a great deal more information than we have for earlier periods. Along the coast between 1800 and 1812, reports indicate that wage labor was being used in the cultivation of some fields; that village lands were rotated periodically among a large labor pool, that there was share-cropping of lands which were controlled by nuclear villagers; and that there were workers who in hiring themselves out to do corvée for others were almost constantly employed in this fashion. Yet in this period the service unit (*cacah*) continued to be a measure for forced delivery of produce and labor. In the densely populated areas a service unit might consist of six or eight or more families; whereas in the remote and thinly populated areas one household head might be on a tract of land larger than he could manage. There was a drift of population from the thinly settled areas to the more densely settled areas – however strange that may strike us today, for it was

[20]   Among others, 'Verslag W.H. van Ysseldyk [...] 1799,' in De Jonge, *De opkomst [...]*, vol. 12, pp. 480-83; H.W. Daendels, *Staat der Nederlandsche Oostindische bezittingen [...]*. 's-Gravenhage, 1814; N. Engelhard, *Overzigt van den staat [...]*.'s-Gravenhage, 1816; M. Waterloo, *Memorial [...] actual state of Cheribon*, 1811; J. Knops and P.H. Lawick van Pabst, *Java zo als het is en zo als het kan zijn*, 1812; F.J. Rothenbühler, *Rapport [...] Sourabaija*, 1812.

easier to share the obligation of delivery and labor than to have to face it alone. Also there was a continuous population movement out of the Princely Lands (*Vorstenlanden*) to the coast, for in the interior areas the practice of rack-renting by appanage holders and their agents had destroyed all claim which an individual family might have had to its plot of land. In the coastal areas the household head of a service unit (*cacah*) who had recognized rights to irrigated land might become a patron of added families who shared his obligations with him. They in turn were able to find security and a means of livelihood either through working areas of old land, or by opening new land adjacent to the old plots, or through involving themselves in the expanding economic life of the coastal urban areas. These local heads of the service units (*cacah*) worked out these arrangements for the residential areas, hamlets or villages, allowing land areas in cultivation to grow in a personalized, uncontrolled basis. The supra-village authorities knew about this practice and, to a certain degree, controlled this through sanctioning new settlements and new areas of cultivation. Nonetheless, it was all extremely flexible and with much variation from place to place. Among the peasantry rights to use of land were locally adjusted. Certain persons had control or possession over land, but the individual who worked the land had a claim to his portion of the produce, usually half, and would normally expect to have that same plot or some other plot for his use in the next year or in some future year. Ownership in property was unknown, but possession of rights to use of land was known and was then already very complex. In the densely populated areas the obligations that adhered to the head of the service unit could be divided in many ways and regulated in various fashions; these arrangements were handled internally within the hamlet or village. For the rest, however, the hamlet or village was tied politically (socially) and economically into the supra-village world of forced delivery, corvée, and markets.

In the early nineteenth century the expanding population and cultivated area along the coast began to have more pressure put on it without any change in the traditional number of service units. This was done in first instance by the VOC, as previously noted, because of its greater need for local products and for work on roads and fortifications. In second instance, however, this added pressure came from the supra-village hierarchy of Javanese officials who were now freed from control by the Javanese courts, and who now began to develop their own pretensions for a courtly life style. This involved larger houses, expanded retinues, more artisans and craftsmen, and imported goods. Such a life style had to be supported either directly out of the population under their control, or through products drawn from this population which were sold or exchanged on the markets, or with the VOC. In these years the price of basic commodities rose steadily, especially rice. There was expansion under the control of supra-village authorities of areas where coffee, indigo, and cotton were grown. The Company servants bought up and speculated in these items for their own account as well as for that of the Company, but the higher Javanese officials and their agents played a central role in this expanding economy. This was an economy that operated outside the reach of the heavily devalued paper currency of Batavia, which was not allowed to circulate here, and so was thrown upon bullion, which was ever in short supply. The result was a series of bookkeeping transactions which appeared on paper to be much further out of balance than they actually were.

In all of this, the peasant was, as in many societies, the economic stabilizer of last resort. Forced labor for higher authority, which had in the eighteenth century amounted to between one and two months per year for each service unit, now became as much as six months per year in the coastal areas. Javanese supra-village officials increased their demands in like measure. Yet there was a great deal of slack in the Javanese taxation system, and this now began to be drawn in; many people had less leisure than previously, but many more people were also living off the labor and produce of others. Expanding population in certain areas and expanding areas of land in cultivation allowed the villages to adjust to the growing demands; yet they retained their flexibility, fitting into the total economic growth of Java at this time. The introduction of the Landrent System in 1813 was the formal beginning of changes in the pattern of village taxation and arrangements to deliver produce and labor. The actual change was more gradual, much slower, and much less deep-seated than the proponents of this System had proposed. Also the impact was more varied, both in a locational and an applied sense, than was reported by the European administration throughout the nineteenth century. The impact of landrent on the village was not, as has all too often been said, a result of seeking to impose a tax or rent in the form of money or produce. As we have seen, such a tax was already in place. What the landrent did, however, was to change the basis for the collection of this tax. The service unit (*cacah*) arrangement was now supposed to be replaced by a direct collection from each village, as represented by its head, which was to be in the form of produce or money. The obligatory work service for higher authority (corvée) was abolished (on paper), and the supra-village authorities were (on paper) transformed into police and revenue officers. The tax or rent which the village head was to collect from his constituents was (on paper) to be based on three considerations: the quality of the land, the extent of the land, and the success of the major crop, rice. To accomplish this work in any comprehensible fashion would have required cadasteral surveys throughout Java and a well-trained group of administrators. Neither of these conditions existed, nor did they come to be until very late in the nineteenth century. Instead of assessing the tax as prescribed, the amount to be paid was negotiated by the village head with the Javanese and Dutch officials in what, after 1818, came to be called an accommodation system. So it came to pass that the landrent system existed in law but hardly in practice. To European observers throughout the nineteenth century it was the law of the land and was supposed to work as registered in the various ordinances and regulations. In fact, something resembling a rational landrent arrangement only emerged toward the end of the nineteenth century, when other sources of revenue had already begun to replace it as the chief source of financial support of the government.

What was the effect of the Landrent System on the arrangements in the Javanese villages? No single answer will suffice, for there was enormous variation. In general, however, there was more continuity than change, both within the village and with higher authority. The previously existing class structure within the village remained basically intact. The heads of service units had been the controllers of land and landed arrangements and now continued in this function under the new arrangement, in which the village was seen as an administrative and territorial unit. Gradually during the nineteenth century the power position of village heads was enhanced, as government regulations became more strictly enforced. They found that they could use their controlling position over land in new ways. Generally speaking, they continued to parcel out the lands to various lower social levels, while they themselves benefitted from their rights to special headman lands (which were worked for them) and in their right to retain a percentage of the landrent collection. They, along with the entire village administrative hierarchy, were also excused from obligatory labor service (corvée), which had been put back into place again before 1820. With the end of the Java War (1825-1830), the colonial government gained control over interior lands which had previously belonged to the Mataram princes. Since the war had devastated and largely depopulated this area, it was now possible for the expanding population to move into these lands and open them for cultivation. Geertz's Modjokuto is situated in one such area, which accounts for the fact that in his *Social History* (1965) he informs us on page one that the life of the town there dates from about 1850.

This brings us to the Cultivation System, which J. van den Bosch introduced into Java in 1830, and which, according to Geertz and his sources, resulted in the disruption of the socio-economic structure of the Javanese village. Reinsma already in 1955 presented new information on the Cultivation System which allows one to see how it produced economic stimulation at all levels of the economy, not only in the European sector. However, Reinsma retained the earlier conceptions of Furnivall and Burger (especially the latter whom he quotes extensively to build up his picture of change in the nineteenth century) about the feudal nature of the early Javanese village. If one starts with the assumption that the village in Java – right into the nineteenth century – was a closed, autonomous, self-sufficient entity which related to higher authority in a feudal-like manner, then the impact of the Landrent System and the Cultivation System appears indeed as an opening of Java's interior to world commerce (to paraphrase the title of Burger's book). But Geertz does not hold to this view of a closed, autonomous village, for as we have seen, he favors the more flexible view of the village rather similar to what I have been advancing. His argument is that the Cultivation System did *not* allow the Javanese village to change and to modernize in a socio-economic sense.

Since I have had a personal involvement in the research concerned with the Cultivation System over the past two decades, I shall attempt to show how the perception of the System changed during this time, and how this has gradually led to a shift in the entire notion of change in nineteenth-century Java. The final result is different from Geertz's perception because it starts from different assumptions and has more recent evidence, not because it disagrees with all of Geertz's evidence or conclusions. When my 1964 article on landrent under the Cultivation System appeared,[21] I was working with the same perception of the Javanese village as Burger and Reinsma. What this piece shows, was that the landrent arrangements of the pre-1830 period continued virtually unaltered into the Cultivation System. Van den Bosch always claimed to be restoring Javanese traditional patterns, thereby making it easier for the Javanese to pay their obligations without falling into the arbitrary power of supra-village heads or into the usurious hands of Chinese or Arab money lenders. Much more than many of his contemporaries, and even more than later scholars credit him with, Van den Bosch was quite aware of the fact that the service unit (*cacah*) arrangements were still essentially operative in Javanese villages. He had no desire to improve the accommodation system by which landrent was negotiated with village leaders; he was merely interested in a usable device for extracting labor and produce out of the village. The landrent proved useful in this regard. In the writing of this piece, I became aware how difficult it was, from the archival materials I was using, to get an insight into how the actual cultivations worked on the ground, so to speak. My materials provided new insights into the thinking at high governmental levels, but told nothing about lower level activities. It was clear that information had to be obtained at the local and institutional level.

[21]   R. Van Niel, 'The function of landrent under the Cultivation System in Java,' *Journal of Asian Studies* 23 (1964).

In 1966 I urged this priority upon Southeast Asian historians.[22] In 1968 and 1969 I made some tentative stabs in this direction with the materials available to me.[23] In looking into the introduction of sugar cultivation under government auspices after 1830, I noted two points which were to recur in later research: first, the Cultivation System was actually a series of local accommodations to local practices and arrangements, and second, the System was pumping more money into the village society than earlier realized, though it was not yet clear to me who within this society benefited or received this money. Much of the archival evidence, which I had had on hand for some years, was statistical: it was in the form of Cultivation Reports to which Reinsma had directed me in 1961. I was unable to conceptualize the meaning of these statistics until I prepared them for computer manipulation. Then a series of relationships became evident which I incorporated in a 1972 article.[24] This piece made more clear the diverse nature of the System and its varied impact in different areas, but it also tended to support a general growth in prosperity, on the one hand, and an enormous increase in forced labor demands, on the other. Whatever I had done up to this point was still very much within the existing perception of the Javanese village and its alteration through the impact of Western influences. Moreover, my research and finding had nothing to do, one way or another, with Geertz's notions of agricultural involution and shared poverty, though I could not help feeling that my evidence did not jibe totally with that theory.

In the 1970s historical researchers in other parts of the world began to probe the Cultivation System. A number of doctoral dissertations began to explore various aspects of nineteenth-century Indonesian history. The Cultivation System studies built upon and extended my concepts and probings by examining newly available evidence not available to me, and through the extension of my ideas about the positive economic impact of the System. Among these authors a more positive and direct stance in opposition to Geertz began to appear. In 1975 the doctoral dissertation of C. Fasseur appeared in The Netherlands.[25] It is a comprehensive study of the System, based on many of the newer ideas as well as some expert use of Dutch archives which yielded some highly interesting finds. Fasseur went

[22] R. Van Niel, 'Nineteenth century Java: an analysis of historical sources and method,' *Asian Studies* 4 (1966).
[23] R. Van Niel, 'The regulation of sugar production in Java, 1830-1840,' *Asian Studies at Hawaii* 2, 1968. R. Van Niel, 'The introduction of government sugar cultivation in Pasuruan, Java, 1830,' *Journal of Oriental Studies* 8 (1969).
[24] R. Van Niel, 'The measurement of change under the Cultivation System in Java, 1837-1851,' *Indonesia* 14 (1972).
[25] C. Fasseur, *Kultuurstelsel en koloniale baten; De Nederlandse exploitatie van Java 1840-1860*. Leiden: Universitaire Pers, 1975.

further than I in assessing the growing prosperity in Javanese life under the System, but we both continued to lay emphasis upon changes in land-holding patterns as an indication of the deterioration of village life under the System, a concept at the heart of the old perception. The Australian scholar, R.E. Elson, using many newly available archival materials dealing with local areas, moved our insights into what was happening under the System yet another step forward in a preliminary paper in 1978 and then in his doctoral dissertation in 1979.[26] He found that in the district of Pasuruan, a major sugar area, there was local entrepreneurship, individual initiative, and prosperity after 1830 among the Javanese villagers. What he found ran in every way counter to Geertz's propositions about the sugar industry and its effect upon Javanese village life. Pasuruan, it could be argued, however, was in Java's East Hook (actually 'hoek' in Dutch which should be translated as 'corner,' not 'hook'). In his 1956 paper (*Development*), Geertz had suggested that his involutional notion might not apply to the eastern and western ends of Java (*D*, p. 118, ftnt. 49). Were Elson's findings only an exception to the general rule which was still valid for the central section of Java? It seems not. Fasseur continued to turn up long forgotten reports in the Dutch archives; a 1981 paper detailed land arrangements in Jepara which shows the persistence of large landholders despite apparent redistributions of land.[27] In 1982 another dissertation from Monash University by the Sri Lankan scholar M.R. Fernando plumbed the local materials, only shortly before made available in the Indonesian National Archives, for Cirebon district.[28] His findings very clearly establish a growing prosperity among the villagers who controlled land, showing that they profited from the introduction of government cultivations in both sugar and indigo, and that the class differentiation between them and other villagers became greater, not less. Increasing communalization occurred mostly in areas where the Cultivation System was not operative. The socio-economic sharpening occasioned by the System continued right through the nineteenth century.

Meanwhile, I had examined the impact of export cultivations in Java and had concluded that the Javanese village was seemingly adjusting to the

[26]   R.E. Elson, 'The Cultivation System and "agricultural involution",' Monash University, Melbourne, Australia: Centre of Southeast Asian Studies, Working Paper No. 14, 1978. R.E. Elson, *Sugar and peasants; The social impact of the Western sugar industry on the peasantry of the Pasuruan area, East Java, from the Cultivation System to the great depression.* Unpublished doctoral dissertation, Monash University, December 1979.

[27]   C. Fasseur, 'The Cultivation System and its impact on the Dutch colonial economy and the indigenous society in nineteenth-century Java,' mimeographed (Leiden, 1981).

[28]   M.R. Fernando, *Peasants and plantation economy; The social impact of the European plantation economy in Cirebon residency from the Cultivation System to the end of the first decade of the twentieth century.* Unpublished doctoral dissertation, Monash University, October 1982.

changes brought about by its exposure to increased world commerce.[29] What troubled me was the landholding pattern which, by all nineteenth-century accounts as synthesized by Van Vollenhoven, was moving toward a communalization of land and away from individual holdings. In the old perception this was supposed to represent a destruction of traditional village rights and life styles under impact of Western colonial policies. In a paper prepared for a 1982 conference I showed that Van Vollenhoven's assumptions about landholding arrangements in Java were unwarranted and that communalization of land had occurred in peasant society in Java (and I would now contend elsewhere also) under circumstances which showed this to be a response designed to preserve the community.[30] Communalization was not destructive of the community, and, as the writings of Fasseur, Elson, and Fernando show, its presence does not mean that the nuclear villagers who had control of land are necessarily obliterated. Government policies, in any event, seem to have less influence and impact upon landholding matters than was thought to be the case in the nineteenth century. Most recently, G.R. Knight has published the results of his investigation into sugar and indigo cultivations in Pekalongan district and has found entrepreneurship, nascent capitalism, and rural social differentiation to exist both before and after 1830.[31]

This newer research does not, from an historian's viewpoint, call for the formulation of a new theory of socio-economic development in nineteenth-century Java. Nor do these findings contradict everything that Geertz has said, only certain parts of the involutional notion are questioned. No one would deny that changes occurred in Java in the nineteenth century which brought both economic and social pressures into Java, but such pressures were not new to the Javanese village and did not lead to a social levelling. Also nineteenth-century population in Java grew at a faster pace than the area of land in cultivation – and there was a greater crowding onto the available land – but this did not result in an homogenization of village society. A class of large landholders persisted. In fact, Geertz himself in his 1965 book (*Social History*) notes the presence of such in class in Modjokuto around 1920, but he does not seem to draw conclusions from it (*SH*, pp. 39-40).

In conclusion, I wish to point out that the newer perception would

---

[29] R. Van Niel, 'The effect of export cultivations in nineteenth century Java,' *Modern Asian Studies* 15-1 (1981).
[30] R. Van Niel, 'Landholding in Java,' Paper presented to the Eighth International Conference of Economic Historians, mimeographed. (Budapest, 1982). (This is an earlier version of the previous paper in this volume on rights to land in Java.)
[31] G.R. Knight, 'Capitalism and commodity production in Java,' in: Hamza Alavi, et. al., *Capitalism and colonial production*, London/Canberra: Croom Helm, 1982, pp. 119-58.

contend that the long term historical changes in the Javanese village would
see an adjustment to increased involvement in outside marketing,
commodity production, monetization, supra-village demands, and growing
pressure on cultivated land which extend over centuries of time. The
peasant community has made adjustments to these, retaining its social
distinctions and its basic peasant economy. Selo Soemardjan, observing
social relationships in Javanese villages in the 1960s, places emphasis upon
the continuance of the age old peasant qualities of hard work, individual
capacity, and flexible adjustment to change.[32] His observations do not
include social levelling or destruction of individual differences, whatever
sorts of communal arrangements might be made. Finally, to return to the
question posed by Kano as to when in historical time one can discern
Javanese types which do not fit Geertz's model, the answer seems to be that
as far back as we can see into Java's past there have always been Javanese
types which do not fit Geertz's model.

---

[32]   Selo Soemardjan, 'The influence of social structure on the Javanese peasant economy,' in:
Clifton R. Wharton, Jr (ed.), *Subsistence agriculture and economic development*. Chicago:
Aldine, 1969, p. 43.

CHAPTER X

The Legacy of the Cultivation System for Subsequent Economic Development

At the end of 1983 a conference on the economy of colonial Indonesia was held at the Australian National University in Canberra. I was asked to prepare a paper focusing on the title given above and I set about doing this for I saw it as an opportunity to pull together many of the ideas that I had been exploring over the previous couple of years. At the time that I was preparing this paper I was revising parts of the paper on labor (number 6) for another conference and had shortly before held a seminar in Europe on the landholding matter which is here presented as paper number 8. The legacy paper (number 10) grew out of this mindset. It is, therefore, quite appropriate that this paper is the final one in this volume for it draws together many of the ideas and views presented in previous papers. If one places this paper and the paper on export cultivations (number 7) together, one will have a pretty good summary of what I think about the Cultivation System.

I have no illusion about having answered all questions and settled all doubts about the Cultivation System. Quite to the contrary, I have at least in my own mind raised more questions than I have answered, and I sincerely hope that others will answer them or at least wrestle with them in the future. As for me, my interest in Indonesian history continues, but I have turned to other matters, most of which are related to the earlier period in Java before 1830 as I have previously stated. However, I am also returning to the early years of the twentieth century with some renewed interest. Renewed, I might add, through the reading of the three historical novels and the biographical study of Pramoedya Ananta Toer about the early nationalist Tirto Adhi Soerjo.

This paper (number 10) is in the process of being published in a collection of papers by the Yale University Southeast Asian Studies program and is here reproduced with their kind permission.

Would it have made any difference in the economic development of Java if the Cultivation System had never been introduced? If, instead of Van den Bosch's scheme being introduced in 1830, the government had simply carried on with the direction sketched by Du Bus in 1827? I cannot, of course, answer this question because it is purely suppositional, but simply asking the question causes me to reflect on long term as opposed to short term trends. When I do this, I tend to find all sorts of reasons for thinking that the Cultivation System made very little difference at all, and that things would have been much the same no matter what. These thoughts are not totally satisfying, however, for there certainly were changes that the System brought about. Actually, these were probably changes that in a general sense might have come to pass anyway but at a different pace. I would certainly not be the first to say that the Cultivation System used and built upon social and economic patterns already present in Javanese society. In a very real sense that is precisely what Van den Bosch said he was about. But then Van den Bosch said so many things. Truth be told, I think that he and other Hollanders had much less influence in affecting in any way the fundamentals of Javanese life throughout the nineteenth century than they thought they did.

In any event, I shall not beg the question. Instead I shall take three areas of change in which I think the Cultivation System did influence economic matters with important consequences. Nonetheless I am not prepared to argue the issue that the Cultivation System was exactly revolutionary in what it did. The three areas which I will expand upon are 1. capital formation, 2. cheap labor, and 3. village economy. Before I begin discussing these, I must devote some consideration to the manner in which writers have regarded the Cultivation System over the past century and a quarter. These earlier writings, of which there are many, reflect the feelings and attitudes of another day about the System. Though not uniform in their views, these writings form a body of received knowledge which has shaped our thinking on the Cultivation System and the entire course of change in nineteenth-century Java. A general perception of this earlier view must be conveyed in order to make more explicit the new views which have been emerging in recent years.

The historiography of the Cultivation System can, for my present purposes, be divided into three phases. The first of these dates from the later years of the System, that is from the 1850s and 60s, and extends up to the early 1920s. This is a longish period which witnessed diverse types of writings about the System, but I propose it as a single phase because it was imbued with an optimism about how much better things could and would be once the errors and terrors of the Cultivation System were out of the way and saner economic principles would be allowed to prevail. As with the other two phases, these writings may tell us more about their authors and the notions of their time than about the Cultivation System. Van Soest and S. van Deventer writing in the 1860s highlighted the abuses that the System visited on the Javanese people and sought a restoration of liberal economic principles; they also felt that they knew all there was to know about the System and that it was mostly bad (Van Soest 1869-71, S. van Deventer 1865-66). Some liberal writers such as Pierson and Cornets de Groot were less bitter and absolute in their condemnation but felt that the System went wrong in practice and that a more enlightened economic policy which promoted private enterprise would help matters (Pierson 1877, Cornets de Groot 1862). Clive Day's classic account is an English-language version of this kind of thinking and optimism (Day 1904). In the early twentieth century writers were more inclined to ignore the details of the Cultivation System labelling it merely exploitative, as a black page of the past which had now been turned over. C.J. Hasselman and J.E. Stokvis are examples of this kind of scholarship (Hasselman 1912, Stokvis 1922). In the area of archival publications the endeavors of M.L. van Deventer, De Roo, and Van der Kemp to extend the great documentary publication of De Jonge, never reached beyond the 1820s (De Jonge 1862-1888, M.L. van Deventer 1891, De Roo 1909, Van der Kemp 1890-1920). Transitional to the next phase is C. van Vollenhoven who condemned Netherlands' policy for the entire nineteenth century, especially in its impact on landholding rights of the Javanese village (Van Vollenhoven 1919). Van Vollenhoven provides much of the raw data and fundamental viewpoint of the second phase.

The second phase of writings about the Cultivation System dates from the 1920s and 30s up to the end of Dutch colonial rule. Not only had Van Vollenhoven's writings and polemics about land policy raised questions about all aspects of Dutch policy over the previous century, but De Kat Angelino's magnum opus, in the philosophical spirit of the time, displays a synthesization and aloofness which takes the sharp edges off the whole of the Dutch impact in Java thereby providing a blandness that is almost unreal (De Kat Angelino 1929-30). The striving for balance is best found in the classic work of J. S. Furnivall. While exposing how the Cultivation System diverted and undermined Javanese village life, he at the same time shows some of the positive changes which the System promoted (Furnivall 1939). At the same time, D.H. Burger in his sociological-historical studies attempted to detail how Western ideas and institutions had penetrated into the interior of Java resulting in a de-feudalization and opening of Javanese society (Burger 1939, 1949-50, 1975). Detailed historical studies of nineteenth-century Netherlands Indies history using archival source materials began to appear in the University of Utrecht dissertations directed by C. Gerretson. In Batavia the writings and statistical pamphlets of W.M.F. Mansvelt on nineteenth-century economic developments began to raise some questions about the impact of the system, for it became evident that some rather positive economic changes had occurred; these materials have been reissued and updated by Creutzberg (Creutzberg 1975–). A number of developments in the economic and political arena during the 1920s and 1930s tended to make people aware of the impacts of colonial policy and practices on Javanese society and also somewhat more conscious of the role of government in economic life. When combined with a growing interest in socio-historical theorizing, these developments tended to veer writers toward a mixed view of the Cultivation System. While recognizing the advances made by the System in the growth of the export-oriented sector, they became more severe in their criticism of the impact of the system on Javanese society and more theoretically consequential in their condemnation of European imperialism. No one of these writers, however, would have gone as far as C. Gerretson in trying to change the earlier view of the System when he wrote in 1938 that 'The Cultivation System was the greatest benefaction bestowed by the Netherlands on the Indies' (Gerretson 1938).

The third phase of historical writings begins after Indonesian independence and is still ongoing today. More than the earlier periods it represents a worldwide interest in Indonesian studies. During this phase new questions were being asked and new historical evidence became increasingly available. In both the Netherlands and Indonesia new archives were gradually opened and the new materials which they contained enabled historians to penetrate more deeply into the workings of the Cultivation System than had previously been possible. Pioneering of this phase of writings about the Cultivation System was the work of Reinsma which appeared in 1955 and which offered some startling revisionist ideas, especially as regards the general prosperity in Java during the time of the system (Reinsma 1955). In other respects, however, the work leaned heavily on ideas of the previous period, especially those of Van Vollenhoven and Burger. In 1960-61 while in the Netherlands I began my research into the early years of the Cultivation System. In the early 1970s Fasseur began to examine the economic effects of the System both in Java and the Netherlands (Fasseur 1975). Both of us were then still much influenced by the second-phase authors, but we had new materials with which to work and new questions to ask, so gradually we began to digress further and further from these earlier ideas (Fasseur 1977a, 1977b, 1978, 1981, Van Niel 1972, 1976, 1981, 1982). In the mid-1970s the study of nineteenth-century Indonesian history gained popularity especially in the Netherlands, where a group of young scholars began exploring anew their colonial past, and in Australia, where Indonesian studies and economic history were combined in a most fruitful way. These studies were able to gain access to historical evidence at a local level, closer to the actual operation of the System than had earlier been possible. This has resulted in a further advance along lines suggested in the 1950s and 60s as well as into channels not previously considered (Van Niel 1966). The overall effect of this third phase of historical writing has been to move us into the beginning stages of a robust revisionism of the first two phases of writings about the Cultivation System.

This brief historiographic sketch of writings on the Cultivation System has been undertaken to add a dimension to the three economic legacies of the System which were mentioned above, namely, 1. capital formation, 2. cheap labor, and 3. village economy. These three legacies have been differently viewed – or not viewed at all – in earlier writings about the System, while other legacies, which I will mention only in passing, were in earlier times considered more worthy of attention than I am now willing to accord them. As our knowledge of nineteenth-century events increases it becomes concomitantly more difficult to make broad generalizations for all of Java or even for those parts of Java where the Cultivation System was operative. From the very first the Cultivation System made local adaptations in order to get at its desired goal of exportable products which could compete on the world markets. The very word 'system' is misleading since it implies a higher level of coordination than existed. The phases of historiography move us through a spectrum of ideas about the System from severe condemnation to selective criticism to broader social perspective to discerning positive social changes to economic developments in Javanese society. No one is prepared to say that the System worked without hardships and ill-treatment being visited on the Javanese peasantry, but increasingly the historical view looks to larger socio-economic changes which must be understood for better or for worse if the current state of affairs is to be understood.

Capital formation

Already before the introduction of the Cultivation System in 1830 there were efforts by Europeans to break away from the system of forced deliveries and contingents which had characterized the operation of the Dutch East Indies Company (VOC). The potential producers of exportable agrarian commodities in the years before 1830 were: 1. Javanese villages which controlled lands on which they paid an assessed landrent, 2. private planters, chiefly European who used 'waste' land for which they paid the government a rent, 3. private planters, chiefly European, who contracted with Javanese princes for the use of their appanage holdings in the Princely Lands, and 4. owners of private estates, chiefly European, who had seigniorial-like rights over their lands and the people on them. Each of these forms of production had great difficulty in attracting capital with which to expand and improve its operations. European capital – the only capital available at the time – had had varied experiences with colonial agrarian enterprises and was not attracted to investment in Java at this time because of the high risks.

Among the four forms of production arrangements only the second one, the private planters working lands rented from the government and making individual labor arrangements with the local population, seemed to have any potential in the direction of attracting capital. The Javanese village was totally outside the realm of capital economic involvement and for that matter showed no interest on its own in the area of export cultivations. Left to its own devices it focused on its own subsistence, producing rice, cotton, indigo, and other products of daily use. Moreover, since the normal Western legal procedures had little application to village matters there was no protection for capital investment. Experience between 1815 and 1830 had shown that where export cultivations, such as coffee gardens, had been turned over to village control they were neglected or abandoned. Such export products as were obtained during this time came from either private planters on rented lands, or appanage holdings, or from areas where forced delivery arrangements remained in effect (Van Niel 1981). Private planters on lands rented from the government could not attract much capital because they did not have title to the land. What they could and did do, however, was to work with export-import houses in Java – these were mainly Dutch and British – and obtain money from them in return for the crops which they produced which could then be exported. Not only was this a precarious existence, but it provided only enough capital for ongoing operations, not for expansion or improvement. Private planters in the Princely Lands appeared at the beginning of the century to have the best potential for growth and expansion. For reasons not fully clear, this did not occur. Perhaps the limits of their expansion were restricted by the appanage arrangements and the manner in which they drew upon land and labor through traditional obligations. Or it may have been that they were satisfied with the level of operation which they had reached and had become part of the Javanese lifestyle which surrounded them. In any event, they continued on throughout the century at roughly the same size and profitability which they had had by 1830. Lastly, the owners of private estates seemed not to be much interested in export cultivations or in expanding their economic operations. Increasingly such estates became more symbols of prestige rather than economic items; their greatest economic value was as real estate. Also many of the owners had tied up most of their revenue in their estates and did not want to involve themselves with outside interests. A few of these lands, such as the P & T Lands in Krawang, did obtain outside financing and subsequently expanded and grew. This was an exception, however, and most of these private estates became increasingly anachronistic.

The Cultivation System was introduced in 1830 with the primary goal of stimulating the production and export of agricultural commodities salable on the world markets. The government from the first realized that any processing which these products would require had to be developed by inputs of capital which the government itself was prepared to supply. The government now loaned money to persons with whom it contracted for the construction of mills for processing the production of the villagers' fields. Such contractual arrangements were tried for various crops, but only in the area of sugar did they become a significant factor in the development of expansion capital. In coffee and indigo production, the two other profitable export crops, contractors were either not used at all or became superfluous because of the small scale of the production. In sugar processing, however, the government-sponsored system seemed to be just right. Government contractors received not only the capital needed to build their facilities, but also had the help of the government in obtaining the raw cane and the necessary labor. The government contractor was obliged to sell his processed sugar to the government in repayment of the loan made to him. Sugar in excess of the amount needed for loan repayment could be sold privately by the contractor for his own account. There was money to be made here; within a few years the resale value of these sugar contracts rose greatly in value.

The village lands which supplied contractors with their raw materials were in the same general areas as the former wastelands used by the private planters who had rented lands from the government before 1830. This is understandable, for being dependent on an adequate labor supply, both drew upon land tracts in the vicinity of population concentrations. The lands planted for the government cultivations were in close juxtaposition to those of the private planters. Over the years both did rather well and both expanded at about the same rate, the private planters maintaining a constant ratio of about one-fourth of the land area planted by the government. As contractors gained wealth they either expanded their operations as private planters or assisted family members in opening new cultivations in other crops. Government restrictions periodically limited private expansion into profitable cultivations such as coffee, sugar, and indigo, while less-profitable cultivations such as tea, tobacco, and nopal (cochenille) were turned over or left to private planters. This role of the private planter and the growth of capital has been amply expounded by Reinsma with further explanation and correction by Fasseur (Reinsma 1955, Fasseur 1975). Government contractors, private planters, import-export houses, and members of the Dutch civil service in Java came to be closely linked through family ties in the capital and political needs for this agricultural expansion. During the Cultivation System the capital base of the agro-economic export sector expanded many times over, largely through the rather cozy family ties of the

European families in Java (Van Niel 1964a). Much of the annoyance with the System expressed by Hollanders in Europe after the middle of the nineteenth century was directed against the nepotism and personal influence exercised in the awarding of contracts and land rights. Outsiders to the Java clique saw a good thing and wanted part of the action. The development that had occurred, however, was attributable to a capital buildup stimulated by forces internal to Java, not from outside.

The Cultivation System, through government injections of capital and through the expanding cultivation of products for the world market, had stimulated the formation of private capital, which in substantial amounts was invested in further expansion of the export agrarian sector. The very success of this process created problems. One has already been noted – annoyance with the special privilege accorded a group of intimates. Among Javanese planters, too, there was a growing feeling that they could expand even faster and operate more efficiently if the government would remove itself from the cultivations. Traditional wisdom in the first two historiographic phases regarded the Cultivation System as opposed to all private enterprise and restrictive of capital formation. It was long thought that private capital which suddenly flowed into Java from outside during the 1850s and 60s forced the dismantling of the System. This is not correct in any of its parts, as Reinsma has pointed out. Expansion was generated mostly in Java, and the amount of outside capital remained relatively small until the 1880s. The close alliance among government contractors, private planters, import-export houses, and government civil servants is at the heart of the matter. It is a subject that awaits a great deal of historical research; fortunately, much of the needed evidence is available. The formation of capital among Chinese planters and entrepreneurs was, I am quite certain, also occurring at the same time. I know much less about the available evidence here and am less certain of the prospects for historical investigation.

Cheap labor

A cost-effective and ample labor supply was a prime requisite to export-oriented cultivations. For the nineteenth century, control over labor was more crucial than control over land, for the latter seemed in oversupply, the former, if not in short supply, was difficult to manage and exploit. The Cultivation System addressed this problem by utilizing the traditional mode of Javanese labor exploitation through obligatory deliveries of produce and labor to higher authority in a new way. Since very early times the Javanese peasant had fulfilled societal obligations. He delivered a portion of his production to a higher authority and worked part of each year at tasks designated by his superiors (Van Naerssen 1977). He was not paid for this labor (corvée). His work instead was viewed within the context of social solidarity and the maintenance of a harmonious social order. By the early nineteenth century, before the Cultivation System, a tax on the produce of the land, known as landrent, had been substituted for the delivery of produce. The village had been designated as the unit for collecting this tax and also as the unit for supplying the cost-free obligatory labor service. From both an economic and a socio-political point of view, these changes were disruptive to Javanese society, for such matters had been handled differently in earlier times (Breman 1980). This will be discussed in greater detail in the following section.

The government of the Netherlands East Indies, as the VOC before it, viewed itself as the successor to the Javanese sovereigns and laid claim to all rights previously claimed by Javanese higher authorities. This included a right to labor service, which was used to develop an infrastructure of roads, fortifications, waterways, irrigation projects, and public buildings – all at a minimal cost to the government. Needless to say, the amount of such public works was greater than it had ever been. Obligatory labor service for the benefit of Javanese superiors and for village headmen now also seemed to grow greater, despite the professions of the government to check abuses. In fact, the Javanese headmen at the village and supra-village level were so essential for tapping the available labor supply and for collecting the taxes that the government could not have done without them, and was obliged, therefore, to leave restrictions on them unenforced. Everything was to remain as it always had been, or was thought to have been. The Javanese peasant was to work under the orders of his immediate headmen and superiors while regarding this work as his traditional tribute to the rights of higher authority. Even private planters who managed to hire labor for wages had to buy off the corvée value of that labor. Others obtained labor by paying the taxes of a village, and in this way obtained quasi-seigniorial rights to labor service.

Since obligatory labor was the substance of cultivating export crops, the Cultivation System now added some new wrinkles to the practice of forced labor. In the Fundamental Law (Regeerings Reglement) of 1830, Article 80, the practice of obligatory labor in the forests of Java, formerly imposed by the government for either a wage or for a remission of landrent, was extended, at the government's discretion, to use in areas other than forests. The System planned to use one-fifth of the village's land for the cultivation of export crops. The value of the produce grown on this land was supposed to be enough to pay the landrent (tax), which had earlier been assessed at two-fifths of the production of the chief crop. In this way the village was calculated to be better off under the new System. In practice, I hasten to add, things did not quite work in this way, but the relative point here is that the government set aside a proportional amount of the peasants' labor, that is one-fifth of the year or 66 days, for government use and designated this as *cultivation service*. This cultivation service was really a substitution for the amount of landrent (tax), which in turn had been a substitution for the obligatory delivery of produce. This cultivation service was not a substitution for corvée service, which the government had been imposing, but was added on to it. Since the peasant, or rather his village, was paid for the crops produced by the cultivation service – however inadequate that payment may have been – the cultivation service was always considered by the government to be quite separate from the corvée service. It was also separate from the personal services extended to village headmen and supra-village superiors (Van Niel 1976). The work on the government crops was, however, very much coerced by the government in the same manner as other obligatory services. To the Javanese peasant there was no distinction in the type of obligatory labor, there was only a marked increase in the amount.

The amount of forced labor required of the Javanese peasant during the time of the Cultivation System cannot be weighed or measured because no rule or consistency prevailed, even within a single village. Already before 1830 there are indications that within villages there were divisions of labor that had some people working much of the year on government corvée while others worked the land. After 1830 there were persons who worked consistently in government cultivations or in the nearby processing establishments. There had always been persons who worked as day laborers or tenants for other villagers. In all such circumstances, some form of monetary payment was usual, and there was thus some movement in the direction of specialization and a wage system. But wage-payment must not be overestimated, for wages were generally not adequate for survival. The individual or his family remained bound to the village and to the traditional obligations which had to be fulfilled. The Javanese peasant did not become accustomed to an open wage system and did not generally see wage labor as an exclusive means for satisfying wants and desires. Instead, he continued to view labor within the context of obligatory service to higher authority which had to be fulfilled. Increased demands for labor were accompanied by an increased use of coercion by officials tied into government service. With the growth of population and the pressure on land in areas of government cultivations, the extra money from wages became increasingly important and necessary for the survival of the poorer peasant. The first historiographic period makes much of the fact that planters and contractors, starting already in the 1840s, claimed that wage labor worked better and more efficiently than forced labor. This is undoubtedly true, given the tasks it was assigned. But, in the late 1850s efforts to introduce wage labor into areas normally covered by corvée labor had to be abandoned because no laborers were forthcoming for the kind of wages that the government was prepared to pay (Schoch 1891, p. 64). The masses of the Javanese peasantry had not learned to value work as a means toward an end, but continued to view their labor as a burden to be endured and suffered. Extending coerced labor in burdensome amounts throughout wider sections of the population, may have taught the peasant how to work in new cultivations. It did not, however, stimulate any personal interest in these export crops for it never managed to instill any change in the context in which labor was viewed.

When in the 1860s and 70s the private planters began to institute labor- and land-contracts with individuals and villages, it was evident that the Cultivation System had not done much to prepare the way for a free and voluntary labor market. Instead, it had attached a negative value to labor by keeping the compensations minimal through continued use of traditional authority patterns. It had also created a need for supplemental incomes for use in villages in those areas where export cultivations could flourish. For the private planters this had both advantages and disadvantages. The advantage lay in the fact that the prevailing wage level was low and they could thus continue to compete on world markets. The disadvantages, which for a while outweighed the advantages, arose from the problems in attracting and keeping laborers. In this period a number of devices were tried in an effort to overcome these disadvantages. These devices were all, in one way or another, a return to coercion and to the use of traditional authority figures as intermediaries in the process. Labor recruiters were used: often these were village headmen or other power figures. Advances of money were needed to attract labor, but frequently the laborer did not come to work as agreed. Here various pressures had to be applied. The regular courts were slow and inadequate. More effective was the use of strongarm men to coerce the laborer. Sometimes the planters could persuade administrative officials to assist in coercion, but there were limits to this. Eventually force of circumstances rather than any particular device solved the dilemma. By the 1880s the pressure of population growth was becoming evident in the amount of land available and in the limitations of basic food requirements: some people had to find greater sources of income outside village production. Also at this time diseases struck both the sugar and the coffee plants in Java, forcing a sharp reduction in sugar and coffee production. This resulted in less income from wages and crop payments, on which many persons had come to rely. At this very moment the sugar prices became depressed because of beet sugar competition. Planters had to cut down on the amount of wages they were prepared to offer and on the amount they were prepared to pay for land rental. These factors in combination resulted in a reduction of the amount of money available to Javanese society, which had to respond with a greater readiness to take on wage labor at prices, and under conditions not previously agreeable (Elson 1982). Current research into prosperity in Javanese villages tends to support the idea that there was more material wealth in Java during the Cultivation System than in the years following its demise.

Cheap labor was only partly a legacy of the Cultivation System. Powerful forces, beyond policy restrictions, were at work to keep the cost of labor down in Java. It is a fact, however, that population growth was more rapid in the Princely Lands and in areas under government cultivation, than in other parts of Java. Why this should be so has led to much discussion. Population was already densest in these areas before 1830 and the economic stimulus of the System led to a faster influx and increase than elsewhere. Over the years of the Cultivation System these areas became more accustomed to costs of traditional village activities being supplemented with outside injections of money. As will be pointed out in the next section, these were also the areas which witnessed the greatest socio-economic evolution: increased powers of the village elite and diminution in the power of the supra-village groups. Even if there was no stimulus to move out of the traditional context of labor, a climate developed for a concentration of available labor, which also provided mechanisms for aggregating that labor for use in export cultivations. Earlier historiographic accounts were certainly not unaware of the impact of forced labor on Javanese society. If anything they tended to underestimate the magnitude of the number of labor days coerced out of the population, for the government rarely exposed itself by lumping corvée and cultivation services into a single statistic. Truly the System was a tax in labor. Multatuli's famous condemnation of the administration for burdening the Javanese which appeared in 1860, laid the blame on the doorstep of maladministration (Multatuli 1860). His experience, ironically however, was in parts of Java not affected by government cultivations. In his later writings he clearly saw the failure of wages to attract labor in a free and open manner. J.H. Boeke, writing early in the twentieth century, saw a division between the village household economy of the Javanese and the export-oriented, capital-intensive economy of the government (Boeke 1910, *Indonesian economics 1961*). His observations, which, of course, involved cheap labor as part of the distinction, were astute and comprehensible. The reasons he assigned to this were quite unacceptable, however. The Javanese was not oblivious to personal advantages or gain, but the demands made upon him within the context of the arrangements in which he lived did not make it possible for him to react in ways that a liberal economic system would find appropriate.

Village economy

One of the aims of the Cultivation System was to use the traditional authority patterns of Javanese society to induce the peasantry in selected areas to work on the production of export crops. What was supposed to happen was that the village headmen and their supra-village superiors were to use their authority to induce persons to work in new ways, and to surrender the use of part of their land for government cultivations instead of rice production. This was supposed to keep Javanese society static. In fact this did not happen. The economic impact of the System induced changes and speeded up tendencies already present. The supra-village superiors had already at the beginning of the nineteenth century been disrupted out of their traditional ruling patterns; the Cultivation System could only restore these in an artificial way. Authority figures were placed under increasing pressure by the demands which the System made upon them. The European civil servants came in time to find them more a hindrance than a help and proceeded to bypass them while working to improve the cultivations. In the areas where the government cultivations were applied, the supra-village Javanese were forced to adjust to new circumstances which gradually eroded their prestige in the eyes of the population at large (Sutherland 1979, Van Niel 1981). This was such a slow process, varying from place to place, that one cannot really speak of a loss of power on the part of these groups until early in the twentieth century. However, there were changes both within the supra-village group and in its relationships to the villages.

More significant as a legacy of the Cultivation System, in my estimation, is the change which occurred where the System touched the Javanese villages. Earlier writings make the point that the Cultivation System destroyed the Javanese village. Such charges were made already during the first phase of writings about the System, but in the second phase they become a major theme. The Cultivation System was thought to have forced a communalization of landholding rights upon the villages and thereby destroyed older individual rights to the land. Landholding rights were of special interest to the private entrepreneurial groups intent on replacing the System with their own form of exploitation. The investigation into land rights launched in the 1860s was supposed to provide the raw data with which this argument would be supported (*Eindresumé* 1876-96). It was especially C. van Vollenhoven who brought this landholding issue into sharper focus by tracing the evolution of indigenous land rights and demonstrating how government policies had destroyed an evolutionary trend toward private user rights (Vollenhoven 1919, pp. 3-28). Writers of the 1920s and 30s used this to explain the economic and social disintegration of the village into a sort of gelatinized egalitarianism under the impact of

European imperialism. While Furnivall and Burger are eloquent spokesmen for this trend, the clearest unfolding of this argument in English is found in Clifford Geertz's study of agricultural involution (Geertz 1963). Drawing upon the conclusions and evidence of these earlier writers to explain the developments since the introduction of the Cultivation System he finds that a social homogenization has occurred in the Javanese village which has resulted in 'shared poverty.' In light of the observations at the time, namely the 1920s and 30s, these earlier writings probably made sense; but recent writings, reflecting more contemporary observations, tend to portray the Javanese village as a vital social unit with clearly defined and commonly understood social differentiations. It would seem that accounts of the disintegration and demise of the Javanese village were exaggerated. What then seems to have happened and how do current historical research and writing explain it?

Our knowledge of the origins of villages in Java or elsewhere is mostly based on speculation and theory. However, Van Naerssen and others, working with inscriptions recently found in Java, have developed a historical sequence which ties the settled agricultural community and its irrigated lands into the process of higher state development with its magical-religious sanctions needed to hold the order together (Van Naerssen 1977, Kulke 1980, Mulherin 1970-71, Setten van der Meer 1979, Wisseman 1977). The social distinctions between village and supra-village were vague with an uninterrupted hierarchy of family connections and client (or bondage) relationships from top to bottom. The centers of authority (*negara*) drew upon labor and produce from the lower groups, but the relationships were loose and flexible and could change rapidly in the struggles for power. The distance between state and village was not always great. Not surprisingly, individuals moved back and forth between *negara* and *desa* as their fortunes and the occasion warranted (Sartono 1972).

The village was in first instance a cluster of agrarian families with ties to the surrounding fields, but it also might serve as a residence of families tied into the supra-village power groups, and merchants from inside and outside the village, and craftsmen and artisans of various sorts. Such a village was not isolated from outside contacts and was autonomous only to the extent that it might regulate some internal functions such as rituals, land arrangements, etc. The actual tribute of produce and labor which the peasants were obligated to deliver was probably channeled through patrons rather than through the village per se. Family clusters or corporate households were headed by a patron who was in turn attached into higher authority. These patrons exercised influence over diverse socio-economic matters in addition to the tribute deliveries. For instance, they would arrange for opening new lands, introduction of new crops, movement of produce to market, and reassignment or relocation of some of his clients.

In Mataram times (1600–) a firmer bureaucratic control had fixed many of these relationships in a more rigid pattern. To judge from the development of the Javanese language, social distinctions become sharper and more formalized. Retainers of the *negara* were rewarded in units known as *cacah* which, while possibly a land measure in origin, had come by the eighteenth century to be corporate households or production units under a single head. These *cacah* were originally expected to deliver produce and labor in varying amounts and of different sorts. The higher retainers subdivided these *cacah* units among their subordinates or clients (Rouffaer 1906, Moertono 1968). Everyone was tied into this hierarchy except for 'free' villages which were attached to religious institutions or temples and thereby freed from service and delivery to the government. Such 'free' villages were, I suspect, far fewer in number since Islam gained control in Java. By the late eighteenth century the obligations of *cacah* had been converted to a monetary equivalent in the interior Mataram areas; thus they paid a sort of tax known as *pajeg*.

This monetization in the interior seems to have resulted from an increasing amount of bullion in circulation after the sixteenth century, from a growth in European and Chinese mercantile activity, from an increasing amount of imported luxury goods which affected the lifestyle of the upper classes, and, above all, from the loss of Mataram lands to the VOC. The VOC government in the coastal areas continued to collect produce and labor officially, but private dealings were often in money. As the Java wars from 1679 to 1755 decimated the interior areas there was a migration of population to the coastal areas under VOC control. This population shift continued into the early nineteenth century resulting in heavy concentrations of people in and around some coastal cities and the abandonment of some interior areas considered unsafe.

In the coastal areas it was evident to many European administrators at the end of the eighteenth century that the traditional *cacah* system of assessing deliveries of produce and labor was no longer an accurate appraisal of the human resources of the area. As the wars of the French Revolution and Napoleon cut off Java from the Netherlands (1795-1816), the VOC servants were thrown onto the local economy for consumables, particularly rice, and corvée labor for roads and defenses. This produced a sudden concern with how Javanese society functioned and this led to a number of reports which detailed arrangements at the grass roots level in a way that had not previously been done (Ysseldyk 1799, Rothenbühler 1798, 1812a, 1812b. Waterloo 1806, 1811, Salis 1809, Daendels 1814, Engelhard 1816, Knops 1812). While these reports were not always as clear as we would wish, they do provide more information than is available for earlier periods. Along the coast between 1800 and 1812, wage labor was being used in the cultivation of some fields; village lands were rotated periodically among a large labor pool; lands were share-cropped under the control of *cacah* heads; and some landless persons who hired themselves out to do corvée for others were almost constantly employed in this fashion.

Thus well before the introduction of either the Landrent System or the Cultivation System, the Javanese peasantry was making flexible adjustments to the needs of the locality in which they found themselves. These qualities of hard work, individual capacity, and flexible adjustment to change are much the same as Selo Soemardjan noted in the 1960s (Selo Soemardjan 1968). The supra-village authorities knew of all this and worked out the details with their *cacah*, whom, interestingly enough, Hoadley, examining the Cirebon and Priangan regions, sees as bondsmen of these higher authorities (Hoadley 1983). This allowed these supra-village persons to meet the government requirements for produce and labor while also meeting their own expanding needs for labor and for more cultivated land. Under their direction the use of available land was regulated and adjustments were made. Possession rights or control rights over land were in the hands of the *cacah* and other local elite; peasants usually worked a regular plot from which they received a portion, usually half, of the produce. This plot they might consider 'their own' in the sense that they worked it regularly and that the fruit of the land was theirs in part, but they did not own the land and could be moved off it by higher authority if this were warranted. The new pressures that were being visited on the peasantry forced modifications on peasants rights, but did not have much effect on the rights of the *cacah* or supra-village heads.

The supra-village heads were upgrading their lifestyle in the coastal areas, modeling their living arrangements on the courtly styles of the interior. This involved larger houses, expanded retinues, more non-local dress and furnishing items, and more aloof social pretensions. The *bupati* who was a sort of rustic country squire was disappearing from the landscape. The new lifestyle had to be supported either directly out of the labor of the population under their control or indirectly by trading or selling the products derived from the population. These supra-village heads involved their people in the production of coffee, indigo, and cotton which they could deliver to the VOC from whom, in turn, they could obtain import goods. Since bullion was in ever short supply, many of the transactions with the VOC were in the nature of bookkeeping arrangements in which private interests on both sides often took precedence over official requirements.

It was this sort of activity that raised concern among some European reformers at the turn of the century. Dirk van Hogendorp, H.W. Daendels, and T.S. Raffles were the most noted of these, but many others such as the ones whose reports were cited above were also concerned with the burdens being placed upon the Javanese peasant. Since there was a great deal of slack and flexibility in the Javanese production and delivery system, and since the Europeans could only with difficulty penetrate the surface of Javanese society, there was little solid and reliable information on which to develop changes. With this limited insight into the Javanese socio-economic system, the reformers thought in first instance of applying the then prevailing European economic wisdom which favored free and open markets along with individual economic advantage over the older monopolistic and mercantilistic system of the VOC. In second instance they thought in terms of responsible administration as they knew it in the Europe of their day – in Raffles' case also the reformed Indian administration as he knew it – which in practice involved either eliminating or somehow reforming the parasitic, exploitative supra-village classes so that the Javanese peasant could be freed to seek his own best economic advantage. Neither of these concepts of reform took much cognizance of the socio-economic dependency arrangements and delivery systems of Javanese society.

Efforts by Europeans to alter the structure of the Javanese socio-economic system began in 1808 with Daendels and continued throughout the entire Dutch colonial period to 1942. It is not my intention to trace this matter here, but only to focus on the initial changes which were aimed at the Javanese village. It was Raffles and his concept of Landrent which put the village at center stage in a way that it had not previously been. The Landrent System, introduced in 1813, set out to 'restore the autonomy' of the basic Javanese production unit, the village. It also made it, or rather its elected headman, the basic revenue collecting unit of the government. In 'discovering' the village and restoring it to its rightful place, Raffles had actually discovered more than there was to be found (Soetardjo 1965, p. 212). The village as residential complex had never performed the functions or filled the position which was now conceived for it. Small wonder that the remainder of the nineteenth century saw many colonial administrators and policy makers trying to fit an idealized notion of a primitive agrarian social unit to the changing reality of the village as it emerged.

It was probably because the Landrent System – the leasing of lands by the government/owner to the village, the collection of revenue (or products) by the village headman, and the elimination (or alteration) of the supra-village heads – was so far removed from the socio-economic realities of Javanese society that it could be introduced without overt resistance. The personalized control arrangement through the *cacah* system was unaffected and the Javanese continued to see relationships as personal ties, not territorial ties. The restoration of the supra-village heads to positions of salaried revenue and police officers, already in Raffles' day, may also have contributed to keeping them both satisfied and in a position from which they could exert their old influence. Finally, the designation or election of the *cacah* heads to positions within the village leadership, which occurred quite widely, kept the dependency relations as well as the land control arrangements intact. The nuclear villages, under various names by which they came to be known, were a continuation of the old *cacah* heads. Over the next couple of decades there were some realignments in this group as government interfered to meld hamlets into villages and to lay a hand to some land control arrangements, but in the main the upper elements in village life remained a continuation of the previous order. With government support, they now had more power than previously in controlling matters within their village, but they also had new responsibilities.

When the Dutch government regained control of Java in 1816, it took over the Landrent System with some modifications. This decision consciously severed ties with the old VOC system in which the Company had been both government and merchant. The expectation was that private initiative from all sides, European and native and Chinese, would now take up the role of merchant and that the government would finance itself from revenues from the land and from import and export duties. The disenchantment with this ideal during the years before 1830 has already been discussed in the first section of this paper. The expectation that the Javanese villages would now freely turn to the production of marketable export crops also came to naught. The Javanese village when left to its own devices produced mainly consumables, which incidentally were also very marketable, while the only way in which it was involved in export production was through the intervention of higher authority (either alone or in conjunction with a European or Chinese entrepreneur). This was just as it had been earlier. Within the village the nuclear villagers remained in control of most of the land with some small but independent peasants continuing to control their traditional plots. The real power in the village was clearly with the nuclear group, however.

It was upon this agrarian base that the Cultivation System was introduced in 1830. Its purpose, as stated, was to obtain commodities which would be salable on the world markets. To gain this end the System used the land and labor of the Javanese. Van den Bosch saw the need to use supra-village heads to persuade (or coerce) the villages to use their land and labor for this purpose. This was to take place within the confines of the Landrent System (Van Niel 1964b). Interestingly enough, Van den Bosch spoke still of the *cacah* – perhaps a residue of his earlier experience in Java in the first years of the century – and seemed quite conscious of the vertical ties in Javanese society. These, as already indicated, he planned to use, but actually twisted rather out of shape during the years in which his System operated. There continue to be references to *cacah* until the end of the 1830s after which the concept is abandoned in favor of dealing with individual households so that more labor could be tapped.

Recent historical research presents information about what happened in villages after 1830, when the government began to arrange for new production patterns, which puts a different interpretation on events than that presented in earlier writings. Evidence from Cirebon, Pekalongan, Jepara, and Pasuruan – all areas where government cultivations were introduced – shows that the village leaders managed to take advantage of the demands of the government in order to strengthen their hand and make personal advances within their village's power structure (Elson 1979, 1984, Fasseur 1981, Fernando 1982a, Knight 1982, 1984). By using their land rights, both personal and official, and especially by manipulating the use of forced labor under their control, they were able to make internal adjustments. In this way they gained a double advantage: satisfying the wants of the government, on the one hand, and prospering from the crop payments which flowed into the village, on the other hand. It was up to them to distribute money from the government in whatever fashion they thought best, a fashion that frequently did not coincide with what the government officials thought should be done. As the System proceeded, European civil servants were constantly attempting to regulate and control the monies which went to the village for its participation in the System. Usually these efforts had little effect in the face of the devices employed by the village leaders for keeping the major benefits in their own hands. Certain cautions are called for. Although a modification seems in order, I am not prepared to call for a total abandonment of the old views. Not all villages reacted in the same way; not all cultivation arrangements were the same; and not all changes occurred at the same time (Fernando 1982b). Yet when all this is considered, the new research affords explanations which make more comprehensible than the old view the present village household arrangements in Java. Quite simply put, present-day villages in Java manifest a definite social distinction between wealthy villagers and poor villagers. They do not exhibit either a social levelling or the social homogenization which the Cultivation System is supposed, according to earlier writings, to have induced. Villages have evolved over the past century and one-half and adjusted to various pressures and economic vicissitudes, but they have not led the way into a social dissolution of Javanese society.

If this view of social differentiation and economic staying power of the village has any merit, then two related matters must be considered. These are, the question of landholding rights within the village, and the continuance of traditions and social bonds among the villagers in the face of sharper economic differentiation. In earlier writings, as already indicated, landholding rights received a great deal of attention, though mostly within a Western rather than a Javanese context. The communalization of village lands in the sense that an increasing number of villagers gained rights to use a piece of land undoubtedly occurred both before and during the Cultivation System. Since in many, but not all, parts of Java the right to use a piece of the village lands and the obligation to perform work service in all its varieties were tied together, the broader distribution of rights to use land was a natural way for enlarging the labor pool in order to meet the growing requirements of corvée and cultivation services. Evidence indicates, however, that much obligatory labor was also imposed upon persons who had no land rights throughout the century (Schoch 1891, *Historische nota* 1905, Fokkens 1901-1902). To the Western observer, especially in the latter part of the nineteenth century, the growing communalization of landholding seemed socially destructive of the village order and also seemed to present difficulties for individual contractual arrangements for rental of land. But this matter of landholding was deceptive on both counts. Communalization arrangements oftentimes did not involve the ultimate right to the land, only its use and thereby right to the product. Village leaders were able to retain their ultimate control of a substantial portion of the village's lands. These village leaders had never, or hardly ever, worked the land under their control themselves, before, during, or after the Cultivation System. They had a wide variety of contractual arrangements at their disposal for keeping what they had, while letting others do the work both on the land and elsewhere. Small independent peasants who were not part of the village inner circle or who had crossed the village leaders might have their life made miserable. Such persons must have lost ground economically and could be forced off their land and out of the village. The households and laborers who had always been landless were not much affected by the growing power of the village head and his associates since they had always been someone's client anyway. So it came to pass that communalization, while appearing to blot out social distinctions in the village, did not do so. Nor did it present particular difficulties to private planters who wanted to rent village lands; here again the headman generally had control of the situation, and an agreement could be worked out.

This shifting in the social and economic class structure of the village did not totally alter the ties which held the village together as a social entity and as a productive unit. While villagers understood social and economic differences, the village also remained the core of the subsistence system for a large part of the population. True, persons migrated into towns and took up non-agricultural types of work while others became attached to a nearby agrarian enterprise which operated in the export sector. Most Javanese retained connections with their village, however. Even some of those who appeared to be totally apart retained ties with their village in various ways. This somewhat ambivalent arrangement was, obviously, one of the foundation stones of the kind of cheap labor arrangements which benefited the export sector of the economy. The village, which aggregated and managed this cheap labor supply, had to retain its traditional ties and bonds in order to fulfill this function. This function was not eliminated by transforming forced labor into wage labor, for the low level of the wages depended on a continued symbiosis between private-export and village economy. It was in this context that the village leaders had to build and expand their power. The realities did not require them to become independent market-oriented farmers, though in this area they did perform some intermediary functions. They could not abandon the social relationships of the village. It was the village on which they relied as their sole institutional base for the continued acquisition of power and wealth. In the context of a labor-intensive economic system, the village leaders for their own economic advancement both within the village and with the export-oriented sector, had to maintain traditional ties and social obligations.

Summation

Conceptions registered before World War II still prevail in present-day writings about nineteenth-century Java and the Cultivation System, despite publication in the past thirty years (and especially during the past fifteen) of some robust revisionary research that greatly expands our understanding of how the Cultivation System operated and impacted on Java. To illustrate how some of this recent research is changing our knowledge and insights into the Cultivation System, the preceding essay focuses on three areas which are being changed through new interpretations. These are: 1. capital formation, 2. cheap labor, and 3. village economy. These topics are central to the Cultivation System, but they are not by any means the entire System nor are they meant to tell the whole story. Nor are the new views and arguments presented in this essay meant to alter the moral perception of the System. The Cultivation System was, in the main, brutally exploitative, and was managed by greedy, power-hungry persons whose values were shaped by their respective cultural backgrounds. What should become evident in reading this essay, however, is that the System functioned somewhat differently than has formerly been thought; that the System worked its wiles in a socio-economic environment that was more sophisticated and complicated than has been conveyed by traditional writings; and that the System consequently impacted rather differently on Javanese society than earlier authors have shown.

With regard to *capital formation* (which is wholly an aspect of colonial history involving Europeans and Chinese much more than Indonesians), I follow the lead of Reinsma and Fasseur in overturning the traditional view that it was enterprise capital in Europe that forced the dismemberment of the government-controlled Cultivation System. The evidence before us today shows that the essential capital formation leading to the expansion of Javanese cultivations occurred in Java itself, and that it occurred during and as part of the Cultivation System. The government sugar contractors were undoubtedly the leaders in this capital formation, but agency houses, which had never ceased to exist in Java and actually thrived under the Cultivation System, were also able – along with retired government servants – to expand into areas that the government and its official agent, the Netherlands Trading Company (NHM), either could not make a profit in or were not interested in. In short, the Cultivation System, through a sort of government-endorsed bootstrap operation, managed to generate capital (out of the hides of the Javanese, one could say) where there had formerly been none, or too little. This capital (and there were some small private injections from Europe) ultimately came to the conclusion that it could do the job better under liberal, private enterprise arrangements, than working through the cumbersome, patronage-ridden government system, and was able to win support in the Netherlands parliament for this. Major capital inputs from Europe into Java occurred only after 1880 when the Cultivation System was already in the process of being officially phased out of existence.

So what was the impact of capital formation under the Cultivation System on the subsequent economic development of Java? There was capital in Java before 1830 (though not enough) and a great deal came into Java after 1880, so the answer to this part of the question must not be too extreme. What the Cultivation System did was to show explicitly that Java could produce certain agricultural commodities cheaply enough to compete on world markets. Once this had been shown to entrepreneurs inside and outside Java, the island became an attractive field for capital investment. It was, however, the Java-based entrepreneurs who were first aware of this and who were most intimately acquainted with the devices which the government used to make this possible. Therefore, it is not surprising that the growth of capital investment in Javanese agriculture should have its origins among the close-knit group of entrepreneurs, civil servants, and agency houses living and working in Java. The path that they opened was in the late nineteenth and early twentieth centuries expanded into a highroad for worldwide capital investment in Java and eventually the rest of the archipelago. The initial path, however, was made possible through developments in Javanese society which I discuss under the rubrics *cheap labor* and *village economy.*

Cheap labor was a feature of Javanese life long before the Cultivation System made its appearance. Part of the obligation of the lower classes to persons of higher status and authority was in the form of labor obligation. Dependency relationships, bordering on bondage in many instances, was a key determinant of social distinctions in the society. As the Dutch gained control over the north coast of Java in the eighteenth century, they found it both pleasant and profitable to make use of labor at either no cost or for very minimal cost, and to accept delivery of products without payment or far below cost. Such products, naturally, were the result of labor done by Javanese peasants for Javanese officials or patrons at very little cost, and were certainly obtained without payment of a monetary wage. The intermediate and higher levels of Javanese society knew very well how to exploit this labor and how to play the market process in gaining the most out of the products at their disposal. Since there were no rules or equity in the exaction of labor, it is not possible to estimate the number of work days provided in this manner, but it was on the increase. By the beginning of the nineteenth century there were some persons who worked half of the year on required labor for themselves and others with little or no wage payment but often with some sort of subsistence arrangement. Obligatory government service (corvée) was in place long before the Cultivation System existed, for the Europeans in authority had always assumed the sovereign right to such labor in the territories under their control. The amount of corvée seems to have increased greatly in the early nineteenth century as the government made extensive use of it for infrastructure development. The Cultivation System left this corvée in place, and added to it something called *cultivation service* which was the required work on the government cultivations. Theoretically this cultivation service was compensated in the form of crop payments, but more often than not the persons who did the actual work did not receive the payments. So far as these lower classes were concerned, work in the government cultivations seemed to them to be done for their headmen and chiefs just as all required labor had always been done. While some groups in Javanese society benefited from the Cultivation System, the lower classes became only more dependent on traditional authority, and worked without or with very little gain beyond the provision of their subsistence and security. So it came to pass that the symbiotic relationship between cheap labor and the provision of life's basic subsistence grew ever stronger, while the concept of working for a wage on which one could survive was never generated among Java's lower peasantry.

It was the *village economy* and village political structure that in the course of the nineteenth century aggregated the socio-economic realities of Javanese life, transforming the crop production and cheap labor into a functioning arrangement. The villages of Java as residential units had always contained social distinctions. They were the bedrock from which labor and produce were drawn, though only from some of the villagers. In the early nineteenth century the upper groups in the village were strengthened by the assignment of new functions and competencies which enabled the village headmen and their associates to collect in their hands control of land and labor and produce to a greater degree than ever before. Though the government, under the Cultivation System, appeared to work through the supra-village elite, in actuality the village leaders were increasingly the ones with whom government officials, Dutch and Javanese, came to deal in order to accomplish the set production goals. It is difficult to generalize. What seems to have happened in the areas of the government cultivations is that as the upper village groups gained strength and wealth, they did so at the expense of especially the middle class of villagers, whose small individual holdings were sacrificed. The lower class of villagers remained as they were, serving and dependent upon the better-situated groups. To win cooperation from all concerned and to make the system work properly, the village became closer knit and more drawn together so that the increasingly complex land arrangements and complicated work assignments could include an ever greater part of the village inhabitants. While this might have appeared egalitarian to earlier writers about the Cultivation System, the social distinctions within the village were never obliterated. Moreover, they were well known and clearly understood by the villagers. The Cultivation System continued the process, started earlier, of making the Javanese village into the lowest unit in a centralized administrative system but added to this process by making the village the basic production and subsistence unit of Java's entry into the world market economy. This function continued after the Cultivation System faded away and remained the basis of economic life in Java during the colonial period.

Finally, in responding to the original question of whether the Cultivation System made any difference in the subsequent economic development of Java, I feel that the answer should be a tentative YES. Yes, because the System impacted upon the socio-economic growth and development of all social groups in Java, but tentative, because this pattern of change was already established before the founding of the System in 1830 and continued on after the demise of the System in 1870. What I am saying here is that there was more continuity than change in the operation of the System, especially if one accepts the revisionist views that have become available in the past two or three decades. In past historical writings the System has been viewed as a radical departure from the prevailing flow of colonial policy and because of this it was thought to have impacted destructively on Javanese society, but this view of the past no longer seems tenable. The System introduced some tactical changes which made colonial exploitation more effective, but it was part and parcel of a longer historical stream involving the integration of Java into a system of market economy.

Bibliography

Alexander, Jennifer and Paul Alexander
1978   'Sugar, rice and irrigation in colonial Java,' *Ethnohistory* 25:207-23.
1979   'Labour demands and the "involution" of Javanese agriculture,' *Social Analysis* 3:22-44.

Bake, R.W.J.C.
1854   *Kunnen en moeten veranderingen gebragt worden in het kultuurstelsel op Java?* Utrecht: Dekema.

Bastin, J.
1954   *Raffles' ideas on the land rent system in Java and the work of the Mackenzie land tenure commission.* 's-Gravenhage: Nijhoff. [KITLV, Verhandelingen 14.]
1957   *The native policies of Sir Stamford Raffles in Java and Sumatra; An economic interpretation.* Oxford: Clarendon Press.

Baudet, H. and C. Fasseur
1977   'Koloniale bedrijvigheid,' in: J.H. van Stuijvenberg (ed.), *De economische geschiedenis van Nederland*, pp. 309-50. Groningen: Wolters Noordhoff.

Berg, L.W.C. van den
1891   'Het eigendomsrecht van den staat op den grond op Java en Madoera', *Bijdragen tot de Taal-, Land- en Volkenkunde* 40:1-26.

Berg, N.P. van den
1895   *The financial and economical condition of Netherlands India since 1870 and the effect of the present currency system.* Third edition. The Hague: Netherlands Economical and Statistical Society.

Bergsma, W.B.
1876-96   *Eindresumé van het bij Gouvernements besluit van 10 Juni 1867 No. 2 bevolen onderzoek naar de rechten van den Inlander op den grond op Java en Madoera.* Batavia: Ernst/Landsdrukkerij. 3 vols.
1881   *De conversie van communaal in erfelijk individueel bezit op Midden Java, getoetst aan het inlandsch grondrecht.* Leiden: Van Doesburgh.

Bleeker, P.
1863   'Statistisch-ekonomische onderzoekingen en beschouwingen op koloniaal gebied; Over de bevolkingstoename op Java', in: *Tijdschrift voor Nederlandsch Indië*, Nieuwe Serie 1, I:191-202.

Blik op het bestuur
1835   *Blik op het bestuur van Nederlandsch-Indië onder den Gouver-*
               neur-Generaal Js. van den Bosch, voor zoo ver het door denzelven
               ingevoerde stelsel van cultures op Java betreft. Kampen: De
               Oosterling.

Boeke, J.H.
1910   *Tropisch-koloniale staathuishoudkunde; Het probleem.* Am-
               sterdam: De Bussy. [Ph.D. thesis Universiteit van Amsterdam.]

Boogman, J.C.
1978   *Rondom 1848; De politieke ontwikkeling van Nederland 1840-1858.*
               Bussum: Unieboek.

Bosch, J. van den
1864   *Mijne verrigtingen in Indië; Verslag van Z. Excellentie den Com-*
               missaris-Generaal J. van den Bosch, over de jaren 1830, 1831, 1832,
               en 1833, door Z. Excell. Zelv' opgesteld en overhandigd aan zijnen
               opvolger den Gouverneur-Generaal ad interim J.C. Baud, waarin de
               grondslagen en eerste uitkomsten van het Kultuurstelsel verge-
               leken worden met de vroeger gevolgde regeringsbeginselen en de
               daaruit verkregen resultaten; en beschouwd in verband met de
               politieke en finantiële belangen van Indië en Nederland. Amster-
               dam. [Also in *Bijdragen tot de Taal-, Land- en Volkenkunde* 11:295-
               481.]

Boudewijnse, J. and G.H. van Soest (eds)
1876-1924   *De Indo-Nederlandsche wetgeving.* Haarlem/Batavia: Van Dorp.
Breman, J.
1963   'Java; Bevolkingsgroei en demografische structuur,' *Tijdschrift van*
               het Koninklijk Nederlandsch Aardrijkskundig Genootschap 80:252-
               308.
1979   'Het dorp op Java en de vroeg-koloniale staat', *Symposium* 1:187-
               215.
1980   *The village on Java and the early-colonial state.* Rotterdam: Erasmus
               University, Comparative Asian Studies Programme.

Burger, D.H.
1939   *De ontsluiting van Java's binnenland voor het wereldverkeer.*
               Wageningen: Veenman. [Ph.D. thesis Rijksuniversiteit Leiden.]
1949-50   'Structuurveranderingen in de Javaanse samenleving,' *Indonesië*
               2:381-98, 521-37, 3:1-18, 101-23, 225-50, 347-50, 381-9, 512-34.
1975   *Sociologisch-economische geschiedenis van Indonesië.* Wagenin-
               gen: Landbouwhogeschool, Afdeling Agrarische Geschiedenis, Am-
               sterdam: Koninlijk Instituut voor de Tropen, Leiden: Koninlijk
               Instituut voor Taal-, Land- en Volkenkunde. 2 Vols.

Chaudhuri, K.N. (ed.)
1971   *The economic development of India under the East India Company*
               1814-58; A selection of contemporary writings. Cambridge: Cam-
               bridge University Press.
Colenbrander H.T.
1925-26   *Koloniale geschiedenis.* 's-Gravenhage: Nijhoff. 3 Vols.

Collier, W.L.
1977   'Agricultural evolution in Java; The decline of shared poverty and involution'. Bogor: n.n. [Mimeographed.]
1979   *Declining labor absorption (1878 to 1980) in Javanese rice production.* Jakarta: Agro-Economic Survey, Bogor: Rural Dynamics Study. [Mimeographed.]
1981   'Agricultural evolution in Java,' in: G. Hansen (ed.), *Agricultural and rural development in Indonesia*, pp. 147-73. Boulder, Col.: Westview Press.

Collier, W.L., Harjadi Hadikoesworo, and Suwardi Saropie
1977   *Income, employment, and food systems in Javanese coastal villages.* Athens, Ohio: Ohio University, Center for International Studies, Southeast Asia Program.

Collier, W.L., Soentoro, Gunawan Wiradi, Effendi Pasandaran, Kabul Santoso and Joseph F. Stepanek.
1982   'Acceleration of rural development in Java,' *Bulletin of Indonesian Economic Studies* 18-3:85-101.

Coolhaas, W.Ph.
1955   'Nederlands-Indië van 1830 tot 1887,' in: *Algemene geschiedenis der Nederlanden*, vol. 10:238-52. Utrecht: De Haan.

Cornets de Groot van Kraayenburg, J.P.
1862   *Over het beheer onzer koloniën.* 's-Gravenhage: Belinfante.

Crawfurd, John
1820   *History of the Indian Archipelago.* Edinburgh: Constable. 3 Vols.

Creutzberg, P.
1975–   (ed.) *Changing economy in Indonesia; A selection of statistical source material from the early 19th century up to 1940.* The Hague: Nijhoff.
1978   'Paradoxical developments of a colonial system,' in: *Papers of the Dutch-Indonesian Historical Conference [...] 1976*, pp. 119-29. Leiden/Jakarta: Bureau of Indonesian Studies.

Daendels, H.W.
1814   *Staat der Nederlandsche Oostindische bezittingen onder het bestuur van den Gouverneur-Generaal Herman Willem Daendels [...].* 's-Gravenhage: n.n. 4 Vols.

Day, Clive
1904   *The policy and administration of the Dutch in Java.* New York: Macmillan.

Delden, H.R. van
1862   *Over de erfelijkheid der regenten op Java.* Leiden: Hazenberg. [Ph.D. thesis Rijksuniversiteit Leiden.]

Deventer, M.L. van (ed.)
1891   *Het Nederlandsch gezag over Java en onderhoorigheden sedert 1811.* 's-Gravenhage: Nijhoff.

Deventer Jsz., S. van
1865-66   *Bijdragen tot de kennis van het landelijk stelsel op Java [...]*. Zalt-
           Bommel: Noman. 3 Vols.
Domis, H.I.
1829   *De residentie Passoeroeang op het eiland Java*. 's-Gravenhage: De
           Groot.
1829   *Aanteekeningen [mijne reize op het eiland Java.]* Pasoeroean:
           Domis.
Eindresumé   *see* Bergsma, W.B.
Elson, R.E.
1978   *The Cultivation System and 'agricultural involution'*. Melbourne:
           Monash University, Centre of Southeast Asian Studies.
1979   *Sugar and peasants; The social impact of the western sugar industry
           on the peasantry of the Pasuruan area, East Java, from the Cultiva-
           tion System to the great depression*. [Ph.D. thesis Monash Univer-
           sity, Clayton, Vict.]
1982   'The transition to "free labour" in Java's sugar factories in the 19th
           century'. Paper presented to the Eighth International Congress of
           Economic Historians, Budapest. [Mimeographed.]
1984   'The Famine in Demak and Grobogan in 1849-50: its causes and
           circumstances'. Paper presented to the Asian Studies Association of
           Australia. [Mimeographed.]
1984   *Javanese peasants and the colonial sugar industry; Impact and
           change in an East Java residency, 1830-1940*. Oxford: Oxford Univer-
           sity Press.
1988   'The mobilisation and control of peasant labour in Java in the early
           Cultivation System'. Paper Asian Studies Association of Australia.
Engelhard, N.
1816   *Overzicht van den staat der Nederlandsche Oost-Indische bezitt-
           ingen onder het bestuur van den Gouverneur-Generaal Herman
           Willem Daendels [...]*. 's-Gravenhage/Amsterdam: Van Cleef.
Fasseur, C.
1975   *Kultuurstelsel en koloniale baten; De Nederlandse exploitatie van
           Java 1840-1860*. Leiden: Universitaire Pers.
1977a   *De geest van het gouvernement; Rede*. Leiden: Universitaire Pers.
1977b   'Organisatie en sociaal-economische betekenis van de gouverne-
           mentssuikerkultuur in enkele residenties op Java omstreeks 1850,'
           Bijdragen tot de Taal-, Land- en Volkenkunde 133:261-93.
1978   'Some remarks on the Cultivation System in Java,' *Acta Historiae
           Neerlandicae* 10:143-59.
1981   'The cultivation system and its impact on the Dutch colonial econ-
           omy and the indigenous society in nineteenth-century Java.' Paper
           presented to the Second Anglo-Dutch Conference on Comparative
           Colonial History, Leiden. [Mimeographed.]
Fernando, M.R.
1982a   *Peasants and plantation economy; The social impact of the
           European plantation economy in Cirebon residency from the*

Cultivation System to the end of the first decade of the twentieth century. [Ph.D. thesis Monash University, Clayton, Vict.]

1982b 'A social history of peasants in the private lands of Indramayu and Kandanghaur in the late nineteenth century.' Paper presented to the Asian Studies Association of Australia. [Mimeographed.]

Fokkens, F.

1901-03 *Eindresumé van het bij besluit van den Gouverneur-Generaal van Nederlandsch-Indië van 24 Juli 1888 No. 8 bevolen onderzoek naar de verplichte diensten der Inlandsche bevolking op Java en Madoera.* Batavia: Smits/Javaansche Boekhandel en Drukkerij.

Furnivall, J.S.

1939 *Netherlands India; A study of plural economy.* Cambridge: Cambridge University Press.

Geertz, C.

1956 *The development of the Javanese economy; A socio-cultural approach.* Cambridge, Mass.: M.I.T. Center for International Studies.

1960 *The religion of Java.* Glencoe, Ill.: The Free Press.

1963 *Agricultural involution; The process of ecological change in Indonesia.* Berkeley, Cal.: University of California Press.

1965 *The social history of an Indonesian town.* Cambridge, Mass.: The M.I.T. Press.

1980 *Negara; The theatre state in nineteenth-century Bali.* Princeton, NJ: Princeton University Press.

1984 'Culture and social change; The Indonesian case,' *Man* 19:511-32.

Gerretson, C.

1938 'Historische inleiding,' in: *De sociaal-economische invloed van Nederlandsch-Indië op Nederland,* pp. 9-24. Wageningen: Veenman.

Gerretson C. and W.Ph. Coolhaas (eds)

1960 *Particuliere briefwisseling tussen J. van den Bosch en D.J. de Eerens 1834-1840 en enige daarop betrekking hebbende andere stukken.* Groningen: Wolters.

Geschiedkundige nota

1894 *Geschiedkundige nota over de Algemeene Secretarie.* Batavia: Landsdrukkerij.

Hall, D.G.E.

1955 *A history of South-East Asia.* London: Macmillan.

Hasselman, B.R.P.

1862 *Mijne ervaring als fabriekant in de binnenlanden van Java.* 's-Gravenhage: Nijhoff.

Hasselman, C.J.

1912 'Karakter van ons koloniaal beheer inzonderheid over Java,' in: H. Colijn (ed.), *Neerlands Indië,* vol. 2, pp. 71-86. Amsterdam: Elsevier.

Heilbroner, Robert L.

1963 *The great ascent; The struggle for economic development in our time.* New York: Harper and Row.

234   Bibliography

Historische nota
1905   Historische nota over de grondbeginselen van artikel 57 van het
                   Regeeringsreglement. Batavia: Landsdrukkerij.

Hoadley, M.
1983   'Slavery, bondage and dependency in pre-colonial Java: the Cirebon-
                   Priangan region, 1700,' in: Anthony Reid (ed.), Slavery, bondage and
                   dependency in Southeast Asia, pp. 90-117. St. Lucia: University of
                   Queensland Press.

Hoëvell, W.R. van
1849   Bedenkingen tegen de mededeeling van den Minister van Koloniën
                   [...] omtrent den verkoop van landen op Java. Groningen: Van Bol-
                   huis Hoitsema.
1849-54   Reis over Java, Madura en Bali, in het midden van 1847. Amster-
                   dam: Van Kampen. 3 Vols.

Hogendorp, H. Graaf van (ed.)
1913   Willem van Hogendorp in Nederlandsch-Indië 1825-1830. 's-Gra-
                   venhage: Nijhoff.

Hüsken, Frans
1988   Een dorp op Java; Sociale differentiatie in een boerengemeenschap,
                   1850-1980. Overveen: ACASEA. [Ph.D. thesis Universiteit van
                   Amsterdam.]

Ichtisar keadaan
1973   Ichtisar keadaan politik Hindia-Belanda, tahun 1839-1848. Jakarta:
                   Indonesian National Archives.

Indonesian economics
1961   Indonesian economics; The concept of dualism in theory and policy.
                   The Hague: Van Hoeve.

s' Jacob, E.H.
1945   Landsdomein en adatrecht. pp. 65-6. Utrecht: Kemink. [Ph.D. thesis
                   Rijksuniversiteit Utrecht.]

Jonge, J.K.J. de (ed.)
1862-88   De opkomst van het Nederlandsch gezag over Java. 's-Gravenhage:
                   Nijhoff. 13 Vols.

Kanō, H.
1980   'The economic history of Javanese rural society; A reinterpretation',
                   The Developing Economies 18:3-22.

Kat Angelino, A.D.A. de
1929-30   Staatkundig beleid en bestuurszorg in Nederlandsch-Indië. 's-Gra-
                   venhage: Nijhoff. 2 Vols.

Kemp, P.H. van der
1890-1920   Between these dates Van der Kemp produced some eighty books and
                   articles which drew upon archival sources, chiefly the Ministry of
                   Colonies archive. Unfortunately these writings are almost unusable
                   since he interspersed interpretations and opinions with sections of
                   documents without clearly indicating where one began and the
                   other left off.

Klein, J.W. de
1931   *Het Preangerstelsel (1677-1871) en zijn nawerking.* Delft: Waltman.
            [Ph.D. thesis Rijksuniversiteit Leiden.]
Knight, G.R.
1980   'From plantation to padi-field: the origins of the nineteenth century
            transformation of Java's sugar industry', *Modern Asian Studies*
            14:177-204.
1982   'Capitalism and commodity production in Java,' in: Hamza Alavi et
            al., *Capitalism and colonial production*, pp. 119-58. London/
            Canberra: Croom Helm.
1984   'Rice and second crops in Pekalongan residency, North Java, 1780-
            1870.' Paper presented to the Asian Studies Association of Australia.
            [Mimeographed.]
Knops, J. and P.H. Lawick van Pabst
1812   'Java zo als het is en zo als het kan zijn.' India Office Library,
            Mackenzie Collection Private #56.
Kulke, H.
1980   'Early state formation and ritual policy in East Java.' Paper presented
            to the Eighth Conference of the International Association of His-
            torians of Asia, Kuala Lumpur. [Mimeographed.]
Logemann, J.H.A.
1934   'Over Indië's staatsorde vóór 1854', *Mededeelingen der Koninklijke
            Akademie van Wetenschappen, Afdeeling Letterkunde* 78B:131-76.
Lyon, Margo L.
1970   *Bases of conflict in rural Java.* Berkeley, Cal.: Center for South and
            Southeast Asian Studies, University of California.
Mansvelt, W.M.F.
[1925-6]   *Geschiedenis van de Nederlandsche Handel-Maatschappij.*
            Haarlem: Enschedé. 2 Vols.
Merkus, P.
1835   *Kort overzigt der financiele resultaten van het stelsel van kultures
            onder den Gouverneur-Generaal J. van den Bosch.* Kampen: De
            Oosterling.
Moertono, Soemarsaid
1968   *State and statecraft in Old Java; A study of the Later Mataram period,
            16th to 19th century.* Ithaca, NY: Cornell Modern Indonesia Project.
Money, J.W.B.
1861   *Java; or, How to manage a colony; Showing a practical solution to
            the questions now affecting British India.* London: Hurst and
            Blackett. 2 Vols.
Mulherin, B.
1970-71   'The "bekel" in Javanese History,' *Review of Indonesian and
            Malayan Affairs* 4/5:1-28.
Multatuli (E. Douwes Dekker)
1860   *Max Havelaar, of de koffijveilingen der Nederlandsche Handel-
            Maatschappij.* Amsterdam: De Ruyter.

1862   *Over vrijen arbeid in Nederlandsch Indië en de tegenwoordige koloniale agitatie.* Amsterdam: Meijer.
1870   *Nog-eens: Vrye-Arbeid in Nederlandsch-Indië.* Delft: Waltman.

Nahuijs van Burgst, H.G.
1848   *Beschouwingen over Nederlandsch-Indië.* 's-Gravenhage: Belinfante.

[Nederburgh, S.C., S.H. Frykenius, W.A. Alting Siberg]
1884   'Rapport van Commissarissen Generaal aan de Bewindhebbers, houdende voorstellen omtrent den toekomstigen staat der Compagnie in Indie,' in: J.K.J. de Jonge (ed.), *De opkomst van het Nederlandsch gezag in Oost-Indie,* vol. 12:335-58. 's-Gravenhage: Nijhoff.

Nieuwenhuys, R.
1959   *Tussen twee vaderlanden.* Amsterdam: Van Oorschot.

Nota ambtelijk landbezit
1904   *Nota over het ambtelijk landbezit van Inlandsche ambtenaren in de Gouvernementslanden op Java en Madoera.* Batavia: Landsdrukkerij.

Nota conversie
1902   *Nota over de conversie van communaal in erfelijk individueel grondbezit op Java en Madoera.* Batavia: Landsdrukkerij.

Nota verhuring
1895   *Nota over de verhuring van grond door Inlanders aan niet-Inlanders op Java en Madoera.* Batavia: Landsdrukkerij.

Onderzoek mindere welvaart
1905-14   *Onderzoek naar de mindere welvaart der Inlandsche bevolking op Java en Madoera.* Batavia: Ruygrok. 10 Vols.

Onghokham
1975   *The Residency of Madiun; Pryayi and peasant in the nineteenth century.* [Ph.D. thesis Yale University.]

Peper, Bram
1967   *Grootte en groei van Java's inheemse bevolking in de negentiende eeuw; Een andere visie, in het bijzonder op de periode 1800-1850.* Amsterdam: Afdeling Zuid- en Zuidoost-Azie, Antropologisch-Sociologisch Centrum, Universiteit van Amsterdam.

Pierson, N.G.
1868   *Het Kultuurstelsel; Zes voorlezingen.* Amsterdam: Van Kampen.
1877   *Koloniale politiek.* Amsterdam: Van Kampen.

Praetorius, C.F.E.
1842   'Gedachten omtrent de door den tijd noodzakelijk gewordene verbeteringen in het stelsel van cultuur op Java,' *De Indische Bij* 1:78-102.

Raffles, Thomas Stamford
1817   *History of Java.* London: Black, Parbury, and Allen. 2 Vols.

Ramaer, J.W.
1908   *Nota over grondverhuur op Java.* Den Haag: Algemeen Syndicaat van Suikerfabrikanten op Java.

Reinsma, R.
1955   *Het verval van het Cultuurstelsel.* 's-Gravenhage: Van Keulen. [Ph.D. thesis Vrije Universiteit, Amsterdam.]
1959   'De kultuurprocenten in de praktijk en in de ogen der tijdgenoten,' *Tijdschrift voor Geschiedenis* 72:57-83.

Residentie Kadoe
1871   *De Residentie Kadoe naar de uitkomsten der statistieke opname en andere officiële bescheiden [...].* Batavia: Lands-Drukkerij.

Ricklefs, M.C.
1978   *Modern Javanese historical tradition; A study of an original Kartasura chronicle and related materials.* London: School of Oriental and African Studies, University of London.

Roo, L.W.G. de
1909   *Documenten omtrent Herman Willem Daendels.* 's-Gravenhage: Nijhoff.

Rothenbühler, F.J.
1798   'Extracten uit eene missive van den resident van Pekalongan [...], over den staat en toestand van het comptoir Pekalongan', in: W.B. Bergsma, *Eindresumé*, Vol. II, Bijlage II.
1812   Vertoog [...] omtrent het invoeren van een ander stelsel van handel en Culture op Java. ARA, The Hague. Archief J.C. Baud, No. 1002.
1881   'Rapport van den staat en gesteldheid van het Landschap Sourabaija [1812]', *Verhandelingen van het Bataviaasch Genootschap* 41-3.

Rouffaer, G.P.
1905   'Vorstenlanden,' in: *Encyclopaedie van Nederlandsch-Indië* vol. 4: 587-653. 's-Gravenhage: Nijhoff, Leiden: Brill.
1918   'De agrarische rechtstoestand der inlandsche bevolking op Java en Madoera,' *Bijdragen tot de Taal-, Land- en Volkenkunde* 74:305-98.

Sajogyo
1976   'Kata pengantar', in: Clifford Geertz, *Involusi pertanian; Proses perubahan ekologi di Indonesia*, pp. xxi-xxxiii. Jakarta: Bhratara.

Salis, A.M.T. de
1809   *Korte aantooning van de notabelste verbeteringen en redressen [...].* Batavia: Niemandsverdriet.

Sartono Kartodirdjo
1972   'Agrarian radicalism in Java: its setting and development,' in: C. Holt (ed.), *Culture and politics in Indonesia*, pp. 71-125. Ithaca/ London: Cornell University Press.

Schama, Simon
1977   *Patriots and liberators; Revolution in the Netherlands, 1780-1813.* New York: Knopf.

Schoch, C.F.
1891   *De heerendiensten op Java en Madura volgens het Regeering-Reglement van 1854*. 's-Gravenhage: Van Stockum. [Ph.D. thesis Rijksuniversiteit Utrecht.]

Schutte, G.J.
1974   *De Nederlandse Patriotten en de koloniën; Een onderzoek naar hun denkbeelden en optreden, 1770-1800*. Groningen: Tjeenk Willink.

Selo Soemardjan
1969   'The influence of social structure on the Javanese peasant economy,' in: C.R. Wharton, Jr., *Subsistence agriculture and economic development*, pp. 41-7. Chicago: Aldine.

Setten van der Meer, N.C.
1979   *Sawah cultivation in ancient Java; Aspects of development during the Indo-Javanese period, 5th to 15th century*. Canberra: ANU Press.

Soest, G.H. van
1869-71 *Geschiedenis van het Kultuurstelsel*. Rotterdam: Nijgh. 3 Vols.

Soetardjo Kartohadikoesoemo
1965   *Desa*. Bandung: Sumur.

Sollewijn Gelpke, J.H.F.
1901   *Naar aanleiding van Staatsblad 1878, No. 110*. Batavia: Landsdrukkerij.

Staat der Generale Nederlandsche Oost-Indische Compagnie
1792   *Staat der Generale Nederlandsche Oost-Indische Compagnie [...] 14 July 1791*. Amsterdam: Allart.

Stapel, F.W. (ed.)
1938-40 *Geschiedenis van Nederlandsch-Indië*. Amsterdam: Joost van den Vondel. 5 Vols.

Steijn Parvé, D.C.
1850   *Het koloniaal monopoliestelsel getoetst aan geschiedenis en staatshuishoudkunde*. 's-Gravenhage: Belinfante.
1851   *Het koloniaal monopoliestelsel [...], nader toegelicht*. Zalt-Bommel: Noman.

Stokvis, J.E.
1922   *Van wingewest naar zelfbestuur in Nederlandsch Indië*. Amsterdam: Elsevier.

Sutherland, H.
1978   'Between conflict and accommodation: history, colonialism, politics and Southeast Asia,' *Review of Indonesia and Malayan affairs* 12-1:1-25.
1979   *The making of a bureaucratic elite; The colonial transformation of the Javanese priyayi*. Singapore: Heinemann.

Tableaux comparatifs
1846-47 'Tableaux comparatifs des principaux articles du commerce de Java et Madura, 1825 à 1844,' *Le Moniteur des Indes-Orientales et Occidentales* 1-1:116-7.

Toer, Pramoedya Ananta
1980   *Anak semua bangsa; Sebuah roman karya Pulau Buru.* Jakarta: Hasta Mitra.

Van Der Kroef, J.M.
1960   'Land tenure and social structure in rural Java,' *Rural Sociology* 25:414-30.

Van Naerssen, F.H. and R.C. De Iongh
1977   *The economic and administrative history of early Indonesia.* Leiden/Köln: Brill.

Van Niel, R.
1964a   'The Alfred A. Reed papers,' *Bijdragen tot de Taal-, Land- en Volkenkunde* 120:224-30.
1964b   'The function of landrent under the Cultivation System in Java,' *Journal of Asian Studies* 23:357-75.
1966   'Nineteenth century Java; An analysis of historical sources and method,' *Asian Studies* 4:201-12.
1967   'Proposal for training Indonesian historians', *International Educational and Cultural Exchange* 1967-Summer:35-8.
1968   'The regulation of sugar production in Java, 1830-1840', in: R. Van Niel (ed.), *Economic factors in Southeast Asian social change*, pp. 91-108. Honolulu: Asian Studies Program, University of Hawaii.
1969   'The introduction of government sugar cultivation in Pasuruan, 1830', *Journal of Oriental Studies* 7:261-76.
1970   *A survey of historical source materials in Java and Manila.* Honolulu: University of Hawaii Press.
1971   'Techniques and approaches to local history and its role in the development of Malaysian history,' *Foram sejarah pertama Universiti Sains Malaysia*, pp. 36-42. Minden: Universiti Sains Malaysia.
1972   'Measurement of change under the Cultivation System in Java, 1837-1851,' *Indonesia* 14:89-109.
1975   'Government policy and the civil administration in Java during the early years of the Cultivation System,' in: *Conference on modern Indonesia history*, pp. 61-79. Madison, Wis.: University of Wisconsin.
1981   'The effect of export cultivations in nineteenth-century Java,' *Modern Asian Studies* 15:25-58.
1982   'The labor component in the forced Cultivation System in Java, 1830-1855,' *Proceedings 30th International Congress of Human Sciences in Asia and North Africa 1976, Southeast Asia 1*, pp. 99-111. Mexico City: El Colegio de Mexico.
1982   'Landholding in Java.' Paper presented to the Eighth International Conference of Economic Historians, Budapest. [Mimeographed.]
1987   'Rights to land in Java,' in: T. Ibrahim Alfian et al. (eds), *Dari babad dan hikayat sampai sejarah kritis; Kumpulun karangan dipersembahkan kepada Prof.Dr. Sartono Kartodirdjo*, pp. 120-53. Yogyakarta: Gadjah Mada University Press.

240   Bibliography

Verslagen
1899   Verslagen van het verhandelde op de met ambtenaren en belang-
                  hebbenden bij de suiker-, indigo- en tabaksindustrie in de
                  Gouvernements-landen op Java gehouden bijeenkomsten. Batavia:
                  Landsdrukkerij.

Vitalis, L.
1851   De invoering, werking en gebreken van het stelsel van kultures op
                  Java. Zalt-Bommel: Noman.
1862   Opmerking omtrent den loop der suiker-industrie in den Neder-
                  landsch O.I. Archipel. 's-Gravenhage: Susan.

Vollenhoven, C. van
1918   'Antirouffaer,' Bijdragen tot de Taal-, Land- en Volkenkunde 74:399-
                  406.
1919   De Indonesiër en zijn grond. Leiden: Brill.
1923   Javaansch adatrecht; (Overdruk uit: Het adatrecht van Nederlandsch
                  Indië). Leiden: Brill.

Vries, E. de
1931   Landbouw en welvaart in het regentschap Pasoeroean; Bijdrage tot
                  de kennis van de sociale economie van Java. Wageningen: Veen-
                  man. [Ph.D. thesis Landbouwhoogeschool Wageningen.]

Waterloo, M.
1806   'Correspondentie Engelhard-Waterloo; De agrarische toestanden in
                  des sultans landen.' KITLV Leiden. Manuscript H696f, Stuk XIV.
1811   'Memorial relative to the actual state of Cheribon.' India Office
                  Library, Mackenzie Collection Private, #10, 2.

Wertheim, W.F.
1960   'Havelaar's tekort,' De Nieuwe Stem 15:362-79.
1978   Indonesië van vorstenrijk tot neo-kolonie. Meppel: Boom.

Westendorp Boerma, J.J.
1927   Johannes van den Bosch als sociaal hervormer; De Maatschappij
                  van Weldadigheid. Groningen: Noordhoff.
1950   Een geestdriftig Nederlander; Johannes van den Bosch. Amsterdam:
                  Querido.
1956   (ed.), Briefwisseling tussen J. van den Bosch en J.C. Baud, 1829-1832
                  en 1834-1836. Utrecht: Kemink. 2 Vols.

White, Benjamin
1973   'Demand for labor and population growth in colonial Java,' Human
                  Ecology 1:217-36.
1975   'The economic importance of children in a Javanese village,' in:
                  Moni Nag (ed.), Population and social organisation, pp. 127-46. The
                  Hague: Mouton.
1976   'Population, involution and employment in rural Java,' Devel-
                  opment and Change 7:267-90.

Widjojo Nitisastro
1970   Population trends in Indonesia. Ithaca/London: Cornell University
                  Press.

Wisseman, J.
1977   'Markets and trade in pre-Madjapahit Java,' in: Karl L. Hutterer
             (ed.), *Economic exchange and social interaction in Southeast Asia;
             Perspectives from prehistory, history, and ethnography*, pp. 197-212.
             Ann Arbor, Michigan: University of Michigan, Center for South and
             Southeast Asian Studies.

Wijck, H.C. van der
1851   *Eenige beschouwingen over Java.* Arnhem: Nijhoff.

Ysseldyk, W. H. van
1799   'Verslag over de gesteldheid van Java's Oosthoek,' in: J.K.J. de Jonge
             (ed.), *De opkomst van het Nederlandsch gezag over Java*, vol. 12,
             pp. 464-556. 's-Gravenhage: Nijhoff.

Index